Social Media Marketing for Business 2020

This book includes: The Ultimate Guide for Beginners, Make Money Online with Affiliate Programs, Growth any Business and Use Your Branding to Win on Facebook, Youtube, Instagram

By Richard Flagg

By reading this document, the reader agrees that under no circumstances is the author responsible for any losses, direct or indirect, which are incurred as a result of the use of information contained within this document, including, but not limited to, — errors, omissions, or inaccuracies.

Table of Contents

DIGITAL MARKETING FOR BEGINNERS 2020

INTENSIVE COURSE ON DIGITAL MARKETING THAT ALLOWS YOU TO LEARN HOW TO SELL YOUR PRODUCT OR PROPOSE YOURSELF TO MAJOR COMPANIES AS A SOCIAL MEDIA MANAGER

INTRODUCTION

The Digital world has changed the electronic marketing scene. Today, new powers are changing advanced marketing once more. There's more accentuation today on personalization, video, miniaturized scale content stories, human-made consciousness, visual inquiry, and voice search. We're pushing toward an existence where innovation will be indispensable in all parts of our lives, including work, family, and social communication.

Computerized advertisers already know the estimation of SEO and its capacity to help rank higher on web crawlers. The present marketing methodology is moving toward new vehicles for drawing in and assuaging clients. Computerized marketing patterns recommend clients' needs have additionally changed. They anticipate accommodation, day in and day out accessibility, an immediate discussion style, precise data, modified services, and proposals. Computerized advertisers today should remember one objective: Customer fulfillment. You have to offer your audience an exceptional encounter.

To accomplish this and measure your outcomes, you can dissect site client information. Client created substance is additional data that can give bits of knowledge into how your offering reverberates with clients. Leading advanced advertisers to include clients and make them a piece of their clan. Along these lines, clients feel like they're a piece of your brand. This passionate association is a center segment in many top computerized marketing techniques and patterns in 2019.

Given that, how about we examine the forthcoming patterns and strategies for the following two years.

Bits of knowledge Instead Of Data
Today, examination, information, reports, and dashboards are in each marketing and sales innovation product. However, comprehending what that information instructs you and precisely about it stays tricky. Going ahead, bits of knowledge will be the money of advertisers and sales activities specialists.

Those experiences, when appropriately organized, will drive the activity designs that enhance strategic execution and improve results from both marketing and sales executions. Devices like MAXG, a knowledge and proposal motor, advise advertisers what precisely to do and in what request to do it.

MAXG isn't giving current proposals but instead suggestions dependent on your organization's information, your organization's objectives, and your organization's particular procedure and strategies. It's a product that enables your organization to drive income development.

Chatbots

Utilizing human-made consciousness (AI), chatbots associate with clients using texting.

For what reason do clients love to communicate with chatbots? For what purpose do organizations incline toward chatbots over traditional strategies for correspondence? Their agreeability and productivity are two key variables.

Clients love their customized help, while businesses spare time, cash, and assets. Chatbots are the cutting edge client service partner. They hear you out, answer questions, and resolve issues inside seconds. Chatbots study you as you share more data with them. The banking and pharmaceutical enterprises depend vigorously on chatbots to take care of little undertakings and answer dull inquiries.

Human-made brainpower will push client assistance into another age. Artificial intelligence is at the core of this new chatbot wave. It breaks down buyers' activities and search examples, and pulls data from social media channels to better "train" the chatbot. This additionally helps brands in building up a more profound comprehension of how to serve their clients more readily.

The Personal Aspect Of Every Customer

How well do you know your clients?

Your next product or administration might be the consequence of your clients' input. Social media stages enable you to offer intelligent and altered brand encounters. Brands should consider bringing a customized touch over the majority of their marketing channels.

You can build sales and client unwaveringness by dealing with customized messages, substance, and encounters. This opens the entryway to have a more grounded association with your clients. Personalized words convey important news with the correct tone. They show you care about your clients. A centerpiece of your advanced marketing system ought to be tied in with offering a similar degree of regard for the majority of your clients, regardless of whether they're first-time customers or rehash buyers.

Video Content To Appeal To New Audiences

Recordings have detonated as a marketing pattern over the most recent couple of years. Take, for instance, YouTube superstars. A few makers have turned out to be overall sensations. The present computerized marketing procedures center on the video to continue drawing in your audience after some time.

Video marketing has a few center stages. YouTube isn't the main alternative. Facebook, Instagram, and other social systems are likewise intensely advancing video content. Video configuration and length are diverse for each channel, and each review audience's advantage. For instance, Instagram feed recordings are restricted to 60 seconds. However, IGTV recordings can play for as long as 60 minutes.

Live recordings are likewise winding up progressively famous. Their unedited nature makes them progressively veritable and engaging. Brands utilize live recordings to offer bits of knowledge into their workplaces, workplace, day by day schedules, and that's only the tip of the iceberg. These circumstances just better fit with an energetic video group.

Live recordings are disturbing the digital marketing industry. They offer each individual with a cell phone the chance to impart their insights with an audience continuously. Subsequently, advanced advertisers have paid attention to live recordings. Brands utilizing video messages to speak with clients are exceptionally imaginative and engaging.

At last, 360 recordings offer an alternate encounter. The original idea of these recordings keeps your audience locked in. Their vivid substance exploits giving a full-go review understanding. As 360 video is as yet a generally new substance design, they make it simpler to hang out in social media bolsters. So why not try them out?

Miniaturized scale Video, Micro-Blogs, And Micro-Moments

Computerized marketing strategies put an incentive on each minute guests spend perusing your site. Smaller-scale minutes work by conveying your message in the correct organization at the opportune time. The right blend of the substance introduced, and the time taken to pass on the message decides the result of the marketing effort. The shorter idea of the smaller-scale material works with individuals' more concise abilities to focus.

An ongoing influx of six-second recordings (which began with Vine) surprised the world. At that point came the age of five-or six-second ads on YouTube. Computerized marketing offices began to investigate the six-second region to contact their audiences. Do you see a pattern in the two ideas?

We can likewise discuss small scale blogging. We, as a whole, realize 140 characters turned into the favored method for social correspondence on Twitter. It concurred with Vine getting to be well known, which in the long run, prompted Twitter's procurement of Vine. Google's idea of small scale minutes has been a product taking shape for quite a while.

As small scale substance turns out to be progressively mainstream, we will see all the more new stages and marketing openings show up in this space.

Customer Behavior And Changing Lifestyles

Advanced marketing methodologies consider changing customer ways of life to build up their crusades. In the period of cell phones, advanced organizations can't just depend on traditional marketing channels. They have to make content that individuals can read, offer, and store on their cell phones. Computerized marketing procedures today are versatile benevolent.

Picture search and voice search are two models. They have changed the standards of web crawler marketing. Individuals are searching for a product to upload a picture and quest for comparable ones. Pinterest likewise made early inroads in the visual hunt.

Voice search is the fate of web crawler marketing and IoT (Internet of Things). Individuals use telephones and brilliant speakers (like Alexa) to look through the web. Savvy speakers are making search progressively helpful, sorted out, and intuitive. Late examinations have demonstrated that 60% of brilliant speaker proprietors use them at least four times each day. This number is probably going to increment in the coming years.

Voice-based partners, for example, Alexa, have played the job of genuine colleagues. This has made perusing and looking through progressively fun. Voice associates furnish innovation with a human touch. Accordingly, advanced marketing methodologies can be entertaining, intelligent, and astonishing on occasion.

Take, for instance, video marketing in the past imaginative groups used to design in detail to make high-production recordings. Instagram and video influencers have supplanted this with progressively credible records.

Marketing Trends - The Experimentation Spirit
Computerized marketing systems are always developing. Before you know it, another advanced pattern will be en route. We could

state video, voice, visual pursuit, and human-made consciousness are on the highest point of computerized advertisers' psyches.

There's consistently space for new expectations. The motion picture industry has seen a change in the previous decade. The presentation of Netflix and its inventive systems to reserve film undertakings has demonstrated to us how tweaking a current business model can do large new businesses.

It's protected to state video marketing still has a great deal to offer. Advanced marketing systems can bring practical development, and here and there, viral event. The idea of masculinity coordinates the soul of advertising. There's a nearby association between the two.

The development of online video marketing as of late developed with the prevalence of YouTube. The following stage demonstrates live gushing will proceed to create and turn into the essential type of excitement around the globe. We could expect live stream channels offering data about all that you anticipate that customary video should provide today. What about adding GIFs to live recordings to incorporate innovativeness and fervor?

These new methodologies work with engaging clients. Our desire to communicate has prompted the prominence of client produced recordings in any case.

The next wave could change the video maker to assume the job of revelation. What any semblance of video stars have done to improve or add another dimension to entertainment could be replicated by new entrants in the live streaming field.

Advanced marketing methodologies address the present client agony focuses. The ascent of human-made reasoning overcomes any issues among innovation and personalization. Advanced marketing patterns are relying on shared encounters to improve products, advertise them suitably, and advance the lives of clients.

The innovative part of these patterns is the thing that issues the most. Marketing systems offer a clear record of inventiveness. Which methodologies will you attempt this year and in 2020?

Reasons Brands Need to Rethink Their Social Media Strategy for 2020

Since the making of Facebook in 2004, social media has developed to over 3.25 billion clients over the globe. In any case, in the United States, this previous year points the first year since the production of social media that we've seen dormant development in client adoption. For brands that depend on social media marketing to arrive at their clients, presently might be a decent time to make a stride back and reassess your way to deal with social media.

For as far back as 15 years, brands have been culminating their social media technique and keeping in mind that a few brands as domino Nike and Coca-Cola have idealized the craft of social media marketing; different brands are as yet attempting to make sense of how Twitter functions. Regardless of whether your brand is a social media ace, social media is an essential piece of each marketing methodology.

Digital Marketing Growth Over The Years

What is the quickest developing social media stage? As per Pew Research, the development in social media clients from 2018 – 2019 is, for the most part, unaltered. Even though stages like LinkedIn and Instagram have developed in clients over the previous year, different stages like Snapchat, Twitter, and Pinterest have fallen. Leading social steps, YouTube and Facebook have generally remained a similar representing 73% and 69% of US adults who have utilized the scene in the previous year, individually.

For what reason is social media development dormant? Numerous individuals credit it to worries about phony news and security. As indicated by Malwarebytes Labs, 95% of individuals doubt social media with regards to securing their protection. As social media stages work to recover the confidence of their clients, brands should set aside this effort to reexamine how they approach social media marketing.

Five 5 Reasons to Rethink Digital Marketing

1. Social Media Platforms Attract Different Demographics

Today there are seven fundamental social media stages; Facebook, YouTube, Instagram, LinkedIn, Snapchat, Twitter, and Pinterest. Also, each draws in various socioeconomics of clients. Gone are the times of attempting to contact your audience on each stage; brands need to concentrate on the steps their intended interest groups are utilizing.

Snapchat is mostly made up of clients younger than 34 at 75%.

Pinterest has 25% a more significant number of ladies clients than men.

LinkedIn is progressively well known with individuals who have advanced education and pay, just 9% of individuals who use LinkedIn have a High School Diploma or less.

Facebook is the main stage to offer broadly to a similar measure of clients younger than 65.

Instead of attempting to arrive at buyers over each stage, center around the scenes, your intended interest group is on. This can help stretch your spending limit further and center your endeavors around the correct audience.

2. Visual Content is More Important Than Ever

With the dispatch of Instagram shopping over the whole stage prior this year, the visible substance has turned out to be more profitable than any other time in recent memory. You can genuinely put a sticker price on your photographs now. It is significant for brands to have visual substance; it's vital for you to have a top-notch visible material. Individuals can take astounding pictures and recordings on their telephones nowadays; there's no motivation behind why a brand shouldn't either.

Individuals need to like and share outwardly satisfying content, and as indicated by Animoto, recordings are the buyer's most loved kind of social media content. 54% of customers need to see more video content from brands. If your brand isn't yet incorporating video into their marketing system, you could be missing out on significant client commitment.

3. Influencer Marketing is Growing

As customer trust in social media security is diminishing, influencer marketing is expanding. Where social media ads miss the mark, influencer marketing is succeeding. The present exceptionally focused on ads remind individuals that their data isn't protected. We, as a whole, realize that dreadful inclination when you talk about a product and afterward observe an advertisement for it the following day... before you've even begun an online pursuit.

In any case, when an influencer shares a brand or product with their fans, it doesn't feel like an ad. It feels like an individual suggestion from a companion or relative. 22% of 18-multi-year-olds have made a large buy in the wake of seeing an influencer suggestion on the web. Which is the reason it shocks no one that 75%o f advertisers intend to build their spending on influencer marketing?

4. People Trust Search Engines More

Keep in mind that detail referenced before: 95% of individuals doubt social media? It turns out purchaser trust in web indexes is a lot higher. Just 34% of individuals doubt web crawlers. With highlights like Google Posts and Follow, brands could be extending their social media procedure to Google. Google's more extensive reach and expanded trust with shoppers make it the ideal spot to reach more customers, even ones who aren't looking for them.

5. Buyers Want Local Social Media

As an ever-increasing number of clients connect with brands on social media for data, it's ending up evident that national social media systems are not intended to hold nearby clients. It is difficult to remark on or advance in-store advancements for area-specific client care issues if you just have one social record for 100s of areas.

Neighborhood brand social media pages offer brands the chance to draw in with clients on an increasingly close to home level. Instagram's ongoing change to area pages makes it simpler for brands to connect with their neighborhood audience and drive more in-store traffic through on-page CTA catches like driving headings.

Social media is changing, and even though we can't anticipate the future, we do realize that advertisers should be continually adapting. The ongoing level in the quantity of social media clients means that brands ought to reevaluate their social media techniques.

CHAPTER ONE

THE BASICS OF DIGITAL MARKETING

The general public has advanced fundamentally in the course of the recent hundreds of years. We have moved from a libertarian culture to a mechanical society and now to an innovative one. The advancement into an innovation society has carried with it an astonishing number of ways one can create riches. In what way? The appropriate response is found in a single word: marketing. While the essential idea of marketing has not changed in a large number of years, the organizations where one can showcase something have been fundamentally adjusted as confirmed by the new advancement of digital marketing.

Digital marketing? This is an inquiry numerous individuals searching for methods for publicizing a product or administration are inquiring. They don't pose this inquiry out of disarray as much as expectation. Taking into account how fiercely useful numerous other new improvements in the realm of marketing have been as of late, it is protected to accept that digital marketing would convey the equivalent exceptional outcomes.

On an essential level, digital marketing alludes to utilizing the web or different types of intelligent, innovative mechanisms for particular purposes. (One case of these different structures incorporate cell phone marketing which, despite as yet being in the outset organize, has helped sell billions of dollars in products worldwide for various merchants) The coming of digital marketing is progressive since it offers significantly more than a large number of the standard methods for marketing can convey. However, many will even now stick to these more seasoned, obsolete methods of limited time publicizing. Why would that be?

One explanation is recognition. Individuals will like to stay with what they know and are OK with. Maybe their business has encountered incredible achievement in the past from print publicizing and "snail mail" direct marketing efforts. Presently, if the merchant has made progress from these strategies, they should keep on utilizing their utilization. Yet, they ought to never disregard the estimation of new improvements in the realm of marketing. If the past is any guide for the future, we as a whole understand that falling behind on progress is never a decent spot for a business to be in.

An angle energizing the notoriety of digital marketing is its incredibly minimal effort. This makes it ideal for new business and new companies since they should watch their primary concern. In any case, the advantage for setting up businesses is self-evident: why not investigate another marketing pathway if it doesn't accompany a lot of speculation or cost? Or on the other hand, in all the more premonition assessment, it might be relevant to caution organizations with beautiful pieces of the overall industry of the perils of not keeping steady over new marketing patterns and techniques. At the point when an organization falls behind, a part of the pie may decrease as progressively creative and energetic contenders exploit further particular inroads.

Digital marketing is another world that ought to be grasped by any genuine business person. It is essentially the way of things to come for all business adventures paying little mind to their size. This is something worth being thankful for also since it always opens to the entryway to trade, which keeps up a stable worldwide economy. Is that a hyperbolic articulation? The sheer billions of online trade make the appraisal resemble a modest representation of the truth.

The development of digital advancements in the most recent decades has been noteworthy. The quantity of individuals around the globe with some type of access to the Internet is developing quickly, and, in the created world specifically, shoppers have fast access through various gadgets. The measure of time spent 'on the web' is additionally developing exponentially. The digital condition permits numerous alternatives for interchanges between a business and its clients. It can suit B2C, B2B, C2B and C2C interchanges. This move from single direction correspondence among associations and clients was a significant trigger for the advancement of digital marketing as we probably are aware of it now.

Most of the customers, as of now, communicate with brands on the web, the commercialization of the Internet didn't begin until the late 1990s. From that point forward, we have watched a lot of changes and the fast development of the digital world. This development is frequently connected to the term Web 2.0; however, what does it mean? What's more, what was Web 1.0 Web 2.0 includes a scope of changes that we're acquainted with the World Wide Web in the late 1990s. Some fundamental qualities of Web locales made with the assistance of Web 2.0. incorporates the accompanying:

• These locales contain profile pages of clients, which include chosen information like age, sex, area, and so on, making the clients the most important substances in the framework.

• These destinations can make arrangements between clients, through connections, likes, companions, social systems, and so on.

• These locales can post precious substance as photographs, recordings, online journals, remarks, and so on.

• They likewise have other increasingly complex specialized highlights, including an 'open API to permit outsider upgrades,' 'blend,' the implanting of different costly substance types (for example, Streak recordings), and correspondence with various clients through personal email and so on.

Digital media reformed B2B and B2C correspondences, however, Web 2.0 gave a voice to clients. From the businesses' viewpoint, they have increased better approaches to speak with one another just as with clients, streamlining specific procedures like requesting, buying, and so on. It additionally allowed organizations a chance to set up associations with new accomplices and providers. One of the novels uses of digital media has been the development of the C2B movement. A model is a consultant enlisting site where individuals can promote their aptitudes, and organizations may 'buy' them for their ventures. Another mainstream model is when clients compose audits of their encounters with organizations.

At last, digital media has altered how individuals convey and associate with one another, offering to ascend to gigantic development in C2C action. Individuals exchange with one another on eBay, and some create a living through a full-time exchange. Others bring home the bacon playing poker on the web. Customers are never again merely the beneficiaries of what businesses bring to the table. Despite the fact that advertisers are not required to comprehend the details of the Internet, it merits increasing some essential information right now. This may demonstrate extremely valuable when taking a shot at online battles with Web architects and engineers; it will bolster comprehension of what is required and how the last crusade ought to be executed.

Digital Marketing Basic Strategies

Digital marketing alludes to the use of web-based promoting apparatuses to extend products and services to potential clients. Digital Marketing has become a vital segment of the marketing strategy of most organizations today because as much as 33% of the total populace currently invests energy on the web.

What are the advantages?

Digital marketing gives favorable circumstances that were beforehand, extraordinary. Likewise, most social stages offer their types of assistance for nothing, making them very financially savvy. Individuals also will, in general, inclined toward a web-based marketing approach due to its touch and intuitive nature. With these highlights, internet publicizing gives openings that conventional marketing barely can; and regardless of whether it might, it be able to would be a monetary and calculated lousy dream.

Since we have built up the significance of digital marketing, here are the fundamental methodologies one must apply to get the most extreme outcomes:

1. Know your crowd: Significantly, you observe precisely what your brand is, a big motivator for it, and which individuals make up your objective segment. This information will empower you to select the most proper digital stages for your brand, just as utilize accessible online instruments to target clients that will no doubt lead to sales transformations.

2. Have a far-reaching strategy: This includes you characterizing explicit objectives your brand expects to accomplish with web-based promoting. This permits you to use specific qualities of critical e-marketing stages and utilize logical instruments; for example, Google Analytics ton follow and oversee progress and objective accomplishment.

3. Have Optimized and Integrated records over every single critical stage: It isn't sufficiently only to have accounts over a few webs based marketing stages; you should likewise ensure that they are working to their fullest ability. This incorporates rich media for all your social media accounts (for example, quality photographs and recordings) and ordinary collaboration with your clients, just as a quick and stylishly satisfying site with enough backlinks and dynamic SEO (Search Engine Optimization). Most e-marketing stages additionally give offices to cross-stage joining, empowering you to synchronize your brand's online nearness consistently; furthermore, make it simpler for potential clients to find your brand across various stages.

4. Have a reliable voice: Carve out a specific specialty for yourself, which applies to your brand, and stay steady to it all through the entirety of your online movement. Saying something today and something different tomorrow could without much of a stretch confound potential clients and pursue them away.

5. Give quality substance: concerning your web marketing content, go with the abbreviation QERO, which represents Quality, Engaging, Regular, and Original. If your online material reliably has these characteristics, you can make sure of serenely prevailing upon the hearts of a few clients.

6. Utilize Smart Tools: There are plenty of web-based marketing stages, and dealing with everyone independently could be lumbering. Instead, make your work simpler and more intelligent by utilizing the assortment of savvy instruments accessible. Instruments like Buffer, Everypost, and Hootsuite empower you to handle a few social media accounts immediately, MailChimp is extraordinary for email marketing, and Adroll encourages you re-market to clients who are as of now faithful.

7. Join with Traditional Marketing: In as much as digital marketing has enormous potential, conventional marketing ought not to be discarded at this time. The best outcomes are accomplished when digital and traditional marketing procedures are joined. So by all methods have a hearty online nearness, yet additionally supplement that with TV and Radio ads, just as the ageless one-on-one client relationship.

Digital Marketing and Myths

As we as a whole know the way to progress for any organization is powerful marketing; the more the clients you have, the bigger your sales and the more your benefits. Consequently, for all, move your marketing procedures to digital marketing today. Try not to consider the dangers; there are no dangers in digital marketing. You can be sure that your cash would not go to squander as digital marketing benefits your organization extraordinarily. The advantage of digital marketing isn't fiscal, yet you can see it as increasingly more presentations for your organization and your products. Remember that as the number of individuals who think about your organization increments, so will your sales and, subsequently, your benefits.

As an ever-increasing number of firms are moving towards marketing, numerous organizations and consultancies have built up which give expert assistance in issues of successful digital marketing techniques and which strategy would be most appropriate for your business. These organizations and consultancies mainly offer guidance and provide direction and are a colossal achievement.

There are many fantasies concerning marketing and quality scores. First off, there is the legend about Google AdWords just about expanding the navigate rates (CTR), and that AdWords has a mind-boggling recipe. Presently Keyword Quality Score is fundamentally about watchword significance. It is identified with

CTR; however, a high CTR alone doesn't build your score. You catchphrases do that. The better your slogans, the more ventures your watchwords would coordinate with. Presently this would prompt a high score. Next, we have the legend about quality score resembling SEO. This is false as Google has changed its scoring technique, and now, improvement alone doesn't prompt a decent score.

Fantasy about having a multivariate point of arrival testing to improve your site page quality score isn't valid as the reason for the presentation page isn't to expand your score yet to debilitate individuals with the terrible business model and the individuals who lead to the awful client experience. Next, we have the legend about how we should utilize catchphrases that are exact matches. This is bar far the most exceedingly terrible strategy to receive to build CTR because this will limit your presentation and will be inconvenient for you. The precise match isn't allied with an excellent score. Utilizing negative watchwords is a superior choice. In conclusion, we have a fantasy about how substance arranges to lead to bring down a CTR. Again this isn't valid as substance organize CTR and search CTR is determined independently.

Who Should Learn Digital Marketing

To make it fundamental, digital marketing is just marketing of any product or organization done by methods for the web. It is a kind of "new-age" marketing methodology, which is exceptional compared to the standard or standard systems of marketing. It is particular corresponding to conventional marketing as a result of the way that digital marketing offers the upside of watching the entire edges related to your marketing strategy. Likewise, this checking can be polished in a steady reason.

Nowadays, people contribute a ton of vitality over the web. The impact of social frameworks organization locales starting late has pulled in a regularly expanding number of people to their work zones, workstations, and phones. According to late audits, it is assessed that a working Facebook customer experiences an hour on Facebook consistently on an ordinary. People nowadays put more vitality on the web appeared differently about the earlier decade. The internet has become a vital bit of the lives of many. Digital marketing likewise mishandles this condition to the best.

Digital marketing strategies are executed through various techniques. These frameworks use web crawlers like Google, Yahoo, Bing, and gets procedures like email marketing, making destinations, hails, etc.

Inclinations of Internet Marketing Over Traditional Marketing

• The best-favored situation of digital marketing is that it supports the degree of keeping an eye on the web campaigns, which is regardless of illogical because of standard marketing frameworks.

• You may examine your online fight legitimately from the earliest starting point and can choose it's empowering that too consistently. The continuous examination should be conceivable in issues related to concluding traffic to your site, acknowledging change rates, and various others.

• Creating demands, delivering visitors, showing up at your proposed premium gathering, branding related possibilities, and various points of interest are connected with digital marketing. Standard marketing is without all of these points of interest. In the end, when you have executed a campaign in the conventional marketing system, it is challenging to perform changes or other tweaking options.

• Worldwide presentation - The information that you offer can be found in a workable pace bit of the globe. Without a doubt, even you can choose or make a tendency over your goal territories.

• Compared to regular marketing, the cost of setting up a digital campaign is notably less.

• In solicitation to execute a digital marketing exertion, your essential requirements are a PC, web affiliation, and all-around data in digital marketing.

Who should go into a web marketing program?

Setting off to a web marketing planning program is a "flat out need do" for anyone should get into web marketing. Going from an association CEO to a housewife, rather anyone with a primary data on PC and web can look for after this course.

• Marketing specialists - Marketing specialists who guarantee a BBA or MBA degree, Business improvement Executives, or other experienced individuals who have been into marketing must take up this course. For marketing specialists, taking up digital marketing, getting ready framework should not be viewed as a decision to consider later. The open door has just gone back and forth that you become aware of the latest digital marketing thoughts, without which it is difficult to make due right now digital time.

• Individuals who are at present, realizing the standard marketing methodology and who should make a "switch-over" - Marketing procedures must be changed by the movements that we see and feel in our overall population. Holding fast on to the customary marketing methodologies may exhibit fatal and may negatively impact your business prospects. Those individuals who should assess digital marketing are welcome to this arrangement program. In any occasion, merging conventional marketing systems with web marketing may turn out in specific circumstances. Taking everything into account, the prerequisite to going to this course starting at now showed only the central cognizance of PC and the web.

• CEO – They can screen the marketing procedures got by his/her association and can encourage the execution techniques with the entire gathering. Having an anyway appreciation of digital marketing thoughts and subtleties makes CEO fit for giving his/her dedication and proposition to the marketing wing.

• Beneficial for homemakers - A predominant piece of homemakers have sufficient time at home in the wake of playing out their ordinary works. Those housewives who are charmed to make some extra compensation from online marketing can, without a doubt, take up the digital marketing course. For example, aesthetic manifestations, gems, careful work, dress materials, etc. can be displayed by methods for online with the least use.

• Students - Students looking for after BBA, MBA, and other marketing centered courses can take up digital marketing course as low support course near their examinations. It fills in as an extra compensation at the hour of gatherings and can bolster up your profile. Also, the individuals will be equipped for a position in IT associations as SEO examiner, Digital Marketing Executive, etc.

• Others - Web marketing isn't expected for marketing specialists or online sponsors alone. Even a layman with a comical inclination to research the horizons of digital marketing can pro this subject with smidgen duty and troublesome work.

Digital Marketing uses an assortment of digital channels like SEO (site streamlining), social media, and PPC (pay per click) to bait swarms towards an impending brand. Digital marketing uses the web as the inside component of headway, which can be found a useful pace gadget like PCs, PCs, tablets, and mobile phones.

Web marketing frameworks, for instance, web file marketing (SEM), messages structure an essential bit of digital marketing. Moreover, it also joins non-web channels like short illuminating organization (SMS) and multimedia educating organization (MMS), callbacks, etc. All these different channels structure a fused bit of digital marketing. Digital marketing is seen as a BTL Below-The-Line marketing as it centers around a more diminutive and continuously engaged assembling and works on forming unwavering customers and making changes.

SMO or (SMM), on the other hand, is a branch or subset of digital marketing that surpasses desires at progression using social media stages like Facebook, Twitter, LinkedIn, YouTube, and so on. It uses social media to promote. Social media relies strongly upon the correspondence of the customers, sharing information, and forming a system of sorts and subsequently has a 'social' segment to it. It utilizes the creation of a stunning substance that is acquainted in like way with the trap of the group towards your products or services and makes a brand following.

There are over 1.71 multi-month to month dynamic Facebook customers around the globe. This infers quantifiably Facebook is too huge to even think about disregarding and, therefore, should be an essential bit of your social media marketing systems. Online video use on such stages has been on a steady rising and is the accompanying gigantic thing to the extent of marketing techniques. SMM is also a BTL Below-The-Line marketing as it relates to detached get-togethers molded over regular premiums on social media stages.

Associations planning to address their marketing needs need to pick between a digital marketing office and a position office. If you are scanning for someone to configuration out your entire marketing strategy, by then, a digital marketing association would be a respectable choice. Regardless, on the off chance that you are looking for someone to simply manage the social media part of your strategy, by then, you are in a perfect circumstance working with an ace association.

To fulfill the growing needs of fit individuals, there are a couple of online courses in digital marketing available. A quick Google search regarding this matter will enlist a massive gathering of establishments that offer the referenced activities. The classes run for different days, where all the related subjects under the umbrella of digital marketing are tended to. Understudies increment significant bits of information into the issue that engages them to cut a claim to fame for themselves.

The digital marketing course joins a basic understanding of marketing and advancing thoughts and key data on accurate and insightful mechanical assemblies. They are moreover given broad information about email marketing, SEO/SEM, pay per click, smart marketing, online video, among others.

Social media marketing courses recall a for significance perception of the gauges of social media, massive social media districts, social media strategy, and evaluating social media. It offers an examine the characteristics and deficiencies of the social media stages like Facebook, Twitter, etc. and dives further into the most forward-thinking inclines surfacing on social media. Social media is an essential bit of digital media strategy. SM stages are used to brand a product or organization as it gives an undeniably instinctive medium open for a two-way conversation.

Digital marketing is continuously significant concerning making brand care, marketing, or reputation the officials. Regardless of the way that they have differing on the web applications, they fill the greater need for brand progress and customer change into leads and sales. Buyers have become more brand discerning with dynamic speculation and, for the most part, spoilt for choice with a lot of options available on the web. Their idea in the general marketing strategy has created a complex rendering standard strategy

Vocation Options in Digital Marketing

A vocation in Digital Marketing will leave you spoilt for decision. There are such a significant number of energizing occupations jobs in the field. While various employment jobs call for remarkable obligations, a Digital Marketer may need to wear a lot of caps every once in a while.

1. Digital Marketing Manager

Digital Marketing Managers have amazing hierarchical and relational abilities. They plan and manufacture viable digital marketing efforts, make timetables, oversee venture spending plans, allot assets for marketing efforts/ventures, etc.

2. Web optimization and SEM Specialist

Web optimization and SEM Specialists recognize imaginative ways consistently to guarantee that the organization site positions high in the SERPs (web crawler results pages). They make one of a kind methodologies to accomplish this objective.

3. Social Media Manager

Social Media Managers utilize progressed investigation devices and different measurements to see how clients cooperate with a brand on digital stages. They likewise help organizations to make drawing in social media battles and substance to catch the consideration of the intended interest group.

4. Marketing Director

Marketing Director is the leader of an organization's Marketing office. Marketing Directors distinguish and dissect the intended interest group and make marketing techniques in like manner. They additionally regulate and control the marketing group.

5. Email Marketing Specialist

Email Marketing Specialists have a fantastic composition (especially enticing composition) and altering abilities. They make and actualize appealing email crusades, dispatch offers, and curated email records for marketing through email.

CHAPTER TWO

BUILDING YOUR DIGITAL MARKETING
BRAND ON FACEBOOK

With more than 200 million dynamic clients, Facebook has turned into an individual, product, and corporate branding center. Each brand that exists on Facebook has a similar center highlights and advantages; for example, the capacity to make a page, share assets, ad multimedia, and substantially more. You have an exciting chance to use this stage for vocation achievement or as a play area for you and your dearest companions.

The typical diagram is loaded up with CEOs, VIPs, business people, and individuals simply like you who can become through

Facebook's informing framework with no limits or confinements. Facebook is additionally an ability internet searcher and part of the school admission and corporate enlisting criteria. You will be looked on Facebook by potential dates, supervisors, and instructors, so utilize the presence of mind in deciding how you need to speak to yourself. You are what you distribute, and initial introductions are everything.

1. Know your audience

Such a large number of individuals are sharing data with an inappropriate audience. Your administrator wouldn't like to know whether you just went to the washroom and, even though your folks couldn't want anything more than to spy on your association with your sweetheart or beau, you might not have any desire to share those subtleties. Since our lives are beginning to combine increasingly more consistently, you have to choose what audiences you need to interface with on Facebook.

Would you like to utilize Facebook as a correspondence stream for your family and companions? Is it correct to say that you are hoping to connect with experts that could enable you to find a new line of work? These are questions you have to begin asking yourself before you add "companions" to your Facebook profile. If you choose to open it up to the majority, at that point, you should be aware of what you offer and how that could affect individuals' impressions of you. Keep in mind; you can constrain what select clients can see on your profile, just by changing your settings, which we'll talk about additional beneath.

2. Choose your branding system

Everybody ought to have a Facebook branding technique, and it ought to be put together, not just concerning the audience you're focusing on, yet your general life objectives. Contingent upon what your identity is, the place you are in your vocation, what you're energetic about, and a specialist in, you'll need to brand yourself unexpectedly.

If you haven't pursued Facebook, at that point, you have an incredible chance to begin new and to manufacture your Facebook profile to best speak to you. If you're a current Facebook client, at that point, start breaking down how your brand is being depicted and find a way to modify it to mirror your branding methodology.

If you would prefer not to construct a branding realm, a system should, in any case, be critical to you; you're already branded, and that brand can help shape recognitions online to depict you in a positive light and help you secure decent notoriety. This implies picking what connections and media you share in your news stream to add an incentive to your brand and those you're companions with.

3. Set your security settings

Contingent upon your Facebook objectives, you may set your whole record to private or award certain people authorization to view areas of your profile. You can likewise make your full profile open for the world to see, which could be helpful to you in case you're hoping to turn out to be increasingly noticeable in your industry and will bring about your profile positioning high for your name in pursuit.

I suggest turning labeling settings off for both photographs and pictures with the goal that you can assume responsibility for your Facebook divider. You wouldn't need your companions labeling you in an image of you accomplishing something inept, OK?

4. Round out your profile totally

Facebook is an extraordinary stage where you can portray what your identity is. When rounding out the data fields, make sure to concentrate on the instruction and work segment, where you can reconnect with an individual graduated class from school or past partners that may have the option to enable you to find a new line of work.

Additionally, in the contact data field, make sure to list your blog, any sites you may claim, and connections to your profiles on other social systems. Since contracting administrators utilize Facebook's internet searcher to discover competitors, it pays to load up your profile with catchphrases that they can look against. Contingent upon your Facebook brand methodology, you'll need to advance more data in specific fields like your contact data and less in different areas.

5. Import contacts and develop your system

Every month, you ought to experience the way toward bringing in your contacts from your email accounts and your moment dispatcher screen name accounts. This will enable you to keep on becoming your Facebook arrange as you're meeting new individuals through your different channels.

6. Update your status

Refreshing your status on Facebook permits you to extend a solitary message to an enormous audience. Your situation is an impression of what your identity is and what you do. You can refresh your status with press refers to your most recent blog passage, another undertaking you're taking a shot at, or your enthusiasm for a specific activity. In light of your branding system, you'll need to refresh your status to either keep individuals educated about what you're doing, push them to your substance or both.

7. Start a gathering or a page

Facebook gatherings have less includes than Facebook pages. However, they are as yet significant. Utilize a Facebook gathering to unite individuals in your industry, become an essential supporter of that network and market your blog, your product, or yourself! Facebook gatherings let you offer connections, recordings, photographs, and start talks.

Facebook pages are for brands, extending from Coca Cola to Barack Obama and even you. These pages look like your Facebook profiles, so possibly utilize one if you have an enormous number of Facebook companions. Your brand can turn into a web sensation, holding a spot on other individuals' profiles. The additional primary advantage is that your page will rank high for your name in Google, and you can utilize it for your expert vocation while keeping your profile private.

8. Join or start an occasion in your general vicinity

Perhaps the best part of Facebook is that you can engage in your locale by joining or beginning a time in your industry. By opening up your time to everybody, you can meet new individuals and find other individuals who have shared intrigue and can bolster your profession. Incidents can likewise be listed on your Facebook page.

In case you're hoping to begin a week after week or month to month occasion and need to keep a schedule, logging it on a page is a decent technique. By starting time, you're situating yourself as a leader and a specialist, which is extraordinary for your brand.

9. Connection out to your Facebook profile

You may already have a blog and records on other social systems, including Twitter, LinkedIn, FriendFeed, Technorati, and so forth. If you do and your Facebook procedure is to advance yourself and stay open, at that point, setting a connection (and perhaps a Facebook symbol) on these different locales to your Facebook profile is a good thought.

As the head marketing official for your brand, you need to construct your companion list, with the goal that you have more individuals to market to now and later on. Think about your Facebook profile as an excellent resource and develop the value in that benefit over a fantastic remainder.

10. Feed your social systems

By utilizing Ping.fm, you can refresh your status on Facebook, just as numerous other social networks in a moment, without copying your endeavors. Additionally, you can import your blog titles on Facebook utilizing notes or by using an application called Simple RSS.

In addition to the fact that this makes you increasingly productive, however, it seems like you're adding to your locale, without you pondering it. Since Facebook is tied in with sharing, those that offer more will be recalled more, which is incredible for individual branding.

Some Power Facebook Tips to Build Your Brand and Business

If you are not utilizing your own Facebook as an instrument to manufacture mindfulness for yourself or your organization's brand, you are passing up seemingly the world's most dominant, free marketing apparatus.

Indeed, I said, "free."

Facebook is utilized by the more significant part of the world's online populace, and before the part of the arrangement had more than 1.5 billion month to month clients. Also, the average cell phone client burns through one out of at regular intervals on Facebook. AOL had a fantasy to hoard the Internet in 1985. Facebook has understood that fantasy today.

"I have a business page, and my page is for loved ones." Well, it's an excellent opportunity to begin utilizing your own Facebook to fabricate your brand, business, and mindfulness. There's Snapchat, Whatsapp, and a large group of other fun stages to collaborate with loved ones.

Your business page can now and again be compelling; however, since these pages are a noteworthy wellspring of income for Facebook, it's hard to get an excellent deal of communication on them without paying a ton. Burning through $100 in Facebook advertising to get 2000 perspectives (what worth that has is vague), 27 preferences, and six ticks aren't justified, despite any potential benefits. Facebook diminishes the natural reach of posts on these pages – they resemble playing the openings at a gambling club: you generally find out about somebody who exits ahead. However, the house wins 97 percent of the time.

Fortunately, your page can get a great deal of consideration if you use it right - and it is free. Here are 14 Facebook tips that will boost your span, preferences, and associations, which will drive attention to you and your business.

1. Be Professional

Your Facebook page should look genuine and be illustrative of your brand, business, or whatever it is you need to advance. Try not to post things you wouldn't need colleagues, clients, or providers to see. You would prefer not to estrange or mood killer potential supporters. Principle speaking, never make a post about celebrating, drinking, or anything obscene. Random putting post, and you will lose a companion or adherent - and you won't know it.

2. Keen Security

Enable your presents to be openly noticeable. Nothing your posting should be private, and you need whatever number individuals to see your posts as could reasonably be expected. Simultaneously, go to the setting: "Who can add things to my course of events?" and set to "just me." Turn on the endorsement of all labels before they show up on your timetable. You don't need other individuals' musings on your divider, and you would prefer not to be labeled at the strip club - as somebody's joke.

3. Be Friendly

Companion individuals regularly and support all companion demands from genuine individuals. Like any social-media stage, the objective is to have, however, many devotees as would be prudent, yet be careful about phony records and decrease those solicitations.

4. No Politics

Nobody ought to have the option to decide your political perspectives effectively. I generally consider what a potential client, who is inverse of my political views, would think about my posts. If you have to vent, there are many shut gatherings on Facebook where you can.

5. No Whining and Complaining

Nobody needs to catch wind of corrupt administration at the DMV, the traffic, the bubble on your toe that burst, or how bad your life is. If I wouldn't express it to a first date, I won't post it on Facebook. Face your issues, don't Facebook them.

6. Play Tag Fairly

It is a fitting and great strategy to label individuals who are in pictures or are with you at an occasion since it expands viewership and makes your post accessible to their devotees as well. In any case, don't label individuals in presents that have nothing to do with them for standing out enough to be noticed.

7. Shake The Profile Picture

This isn't LinkedIn, so you don't really must have an expert headshot, yet you do must have a fascinating picture. You need to have an image that speaks to you or your brand and makes a discussion. The objective is to get individuals to associate with you in any case you can. Here and there, when I have little to post around, an adjustment in my profile picture can produce a great deal of intrigue.

8. Like a Lot

The more you like somebody's posts, the higher amount of their jobs you will see - and they will see a higher amount of your posts. When you go by a post and don't click "like," Facebook thinks you genuinely don't care for that individual's posts and will quit indicating them to you. I like many posts ordinary (except if I genuinely don't care for it). I additionally don't act formal - regardless of whether somebody doesn't care for my stuff, I'll like his/her posts in any case. It's beneficial for me.

9. Like Comments

Like each remark on your posts. If an individual set aside the effort to remark, you ought to recognize it since it constructs association and prizes him/her for doing as such. He/she will be bound to cooperate again, and Facebook will be linked to demonstrate to them your posts. The objective is to get, however, many likes and remarks on a position as could be expected under the circumstances.

10. It's a Happy Birthday

I wish each companion "upbeat birthday." I do it as my wake-up routine. It's an opportunity to expand connections with companions and see what they are doing. Once in a while, it even advises me that I have to reach them for some business or individual reason.

11. Continuously Post with a Picture

Never make content just post. Picture posts get considerably more consideration from the watcher, and Facebook advances those posts more. Regardless of whether it's only an occasion wish to your Facebook companions, make a point to utilize an image.

12. Instagram Is a Post Booster

Whenever possible, post an image on Instagram and snap the "offer to Facebook" catch. In addition to the fact that it gives your image two opportunities to get saw, Facebook advances Instagram pictures more than pictures posted straightforwardly. Furthermore, you can alter the post on Facebook later, adding remarks and picture labels.

13. Timing Is Everything

The planning of posts is critical because Facebook elevates your post to a greater amount of your supporters if and just if it gets likes and remarks rapidly. This occasionally requires experimentation to see when your devotees respond best. Posting business-related posts late during the evening is a certain come up short. Thus, making a post that is increasingly close to home during the center of the workday won't be successful either. I have had a great deal of accomplishment with posting late evening and an early night on weekdays and mid-evening on ends of the week. Abstain from posting anything business-related in the hours before a vacation starts.

14. Be Interesting and Informative

The quality of the written substance makes all the difference. A post that says, "It's hot out" won't get indistinguishable viewership and connections from one with a cool image of an egg browning on the hood of your vehicle. Thus, a post that attempts to sell a product is a no-no. You can tell about the highlights of a product or administration without clearly selling it. Each post you make ought to be thoroughly considered cautiously on how it will assemble your brand and increment collaborations - and keep your companions needing to see more from you. Use humor when fitting since making individuals chuckle consistently attracts them to you. At last, don't be excessively narcissistic. My standard is for each self-advancing post, and I likewise attempt to have a couple of posts that ridicule myself. You need individuals to like you.

These 14 hints will get your posts more likes, remarks, and offers on the biggest social stage on earth. You will take a picture of yourself, your brand, and your organization that individuals are pulled in to. That is the thing that any great marketing effort ought to do.

CHAPTER THREE

MAXIMIZE YOUR AD ROI WITH NEWSFEEDS, VIDEO, AND BRANDED CONTENT

Instructions to Maximize Your Digital Marketing Reach

Organic reach on Facebook is at an unprecedented low of 2% to 6%, and it keeps on declining. What may amaze you is that having a huge Facebook fan base doesn't appear to be as valuable as it once seemed to be. Huge brand pages with more than 500,000 likes have the least natural reach (~2%).

Over 60 million organizations have a Facebook page, yet just 4 million are dynamic publicists. You can envision that Facebook couldn't want anything more than to tempt the 56 million non-publicists to give promotions a go.

Numerous organizations are stuck in a pre-2012 mood, trusting that if they post all the more frequently, naturally arrive voluntarily all of a sudden kick back in. In any case, that is simply not going to happen. The uplifting news is you can essentially improve your natural reach with vital paid endeavors.

#1: Starting With Optimized Content to the Generation Attention and Shares

The exceptionally shareable substance is the sacred goal of web-based life marketing, and doing your best to enhance for shares is my main substance creation tip. As individuals look over the Facebook news source, your substance needs to make individuals interruption and read. The guarantee of your substance must be thumb-halting. What you convey needs to motivate individuals to react with.

The Facebook news source calculations remunerate dynamic promoters and connecting with substance. The more responses, comments, and shares your posts get, the better their span. This goes for both natural and paid (your advertising dollars will go further).

As you build up your posting system, make sure to limit your solicit; few out of every odd bit of substance need an invitation to take action (CTA). Make a blend of substance that joins limited time posts with posts that include esteem, instruct, and engage. Furthermore, when you do incorporate a CTA, keep it straightforward.

Consider utilizing a proportion of five non-limited time presents on each one special post.

#2: Building Organic Traction

To get enough mileage from your paid reach, let the posts keep running for 1-24 hours to increase some natural footing before boosting them. While expanded natural reach is never ensured, there are approaches to give your Facebook posts a superior shot of good reach.

Here are a few hints to make your substance bound to pull in the perspectives that yield shares and reach.

Post More Native and Live Video

The video keeps on holding influence on Facebook with triple the commitment and 1200% a greater number of shares than content and picture posts consolidated. Furthermore, when contrasted with YouTube video shared on Facebook, local video transferred to Facebook has multiple times the range.

Furthermore, because Facebook's calculation factors in the time spent on a video, just as the shares it creates, you can utilize video to acquire permeability and reach on the stage.
The following is a case of an ongoing 40-minute "Ask Me Anything" Facebook Live communicate I facilitated on my business page. Keep in mind; Facebook is supporting longer recordings in the news source now.

Even though there's no complete response to what Facebook implies by "longer," go for 5-20 minutes or more if you can. Facebook is trying mid-move video advertisements in recordings of 90 seconds or more, consequently the explanation behind favoring longer recordings in the news channel. Utilize your video perspectives to make a custom group of spectators and retarget with future posts.

Make a Mix of Post Types

You can convey content on Facebook in various ways, including videos, slides, photographs, and content. While a few people may like (and in this manner share) your photographs, clients who are in a hurry may be bound to share a content post. Stir up your post types, and you're bound to draw in perspectives from an assortment of clients.

Repost Popular Posts

Distinguish content that got a great deal of consideration on the first occasion when you posted it on Facebook. At that point, repost it to catch the consideration of individuals who didn't see it the first run through and allow clients who did to return to it and offer it once more.

Utilize Organic Audience Targeting

If you have a particular substance that is bound to hold any importance with a particular sort of Facebook client, utilize Facebook's Audience Optimization device to pick an all the more benevolent group of spectators for that content.

After your post runs, allude to the Audience, Insights highlight to perceive how the post performed so you can alter the favored group of spectators and confinements for future posts.

The Audience Optimization includes additionally works with Graph API, Instant Articles (add labels to your accounts when adding to your RSS channel), and outsider distributing stages like Sprinklr.

Label Relevant Pages in Appropriate Posts

If the substance of your Facebook post makes reference to or advances another business, label the business in the portrayal/account of your post. Your post will, at that point, spring up on the other business' page, which is probably going to draw their consideration and result in an offer, expanding the potential group of spectators for your post.

Drive Traffic from Off-stage Sources

If you implant Facebook posts on your blog or connection to them using different channels, you'll help send individuals who snap on them to Facebook, improving your span. (The interesting URL for any open post on Facebook is the timestamp of the post.) Notwithstanding demonstrating your Facebook channel on your site utilizing a module, you can implant individual posts and recordings in your blog entries.

It's likewise fitting to incorporate a connection for a particular Facebook post in an email or to connect to your Facebook page by incorporating the symbol in your email footer, blog, or other site pages.

These strategies give individuals who might not have seen your Facebook content another opportunity to navigate.

Distribute From a Verified Facebook Presence

If you have a huge business, you can apply for a blue checkmark confirmation for your Facebook page. In addition to the fact that this checks imprint loan genuineness to your page or profile, yet you'll additionally get a higher need in query items, giving you greater permeability for your posts.

#3: Prioritize Audience Engagement

Accept each open the door to draw in your group of spectators since that is a piece of what keeps them returning for additional. The rules of good discussion for in-person contact apply to internet-based life as well. At the point when individuals leave a comment, perceive that they're beginning a discussion and make sure to react to any comments you get. Tell individuals they've been heard.

Likewise, recognize individuals who offer your posts. Bounce on over to the mutual post and hit one of the response catches (like or love) to tell individuals you appreciate their offer.

Keep in mind; Facebook wants to reward posts with high commitment. There's a news channel calculation signal for "recency"; posts that earn commitment rapidly are bound to get more extensive natural reach. Yet, with your progressively evergreen (as opposed to time-touchy) content, group of spectators, commitment may proceed for a more drawn out timeframe, particularly when you apply the system examined in #4 beneath.

#4: Increase Organic Reach with Paid Promotion

Here's the place you begin to pay to support the scope of your substance to improve your Facebook marketing ROI extensively. As opposed to advance everything, apply some key determination to enhance the built-up natural reach of explicit posts with Facebook promotions.

For certain posts, your goal might be to bring issues to light and expand commitment, and video sees, for instance. Be that as it may, for different posts, you'll need to advance those with a connection so you can direct people to your site. After you select your posts, choose how you need to designate your spending limit. For the best outcomes, spread out your promotion spend and abstain from blowing your whole spending plan on a solitary post with one lift or one advertisement.

Here's a model: Suppose you have a $300 spending plan to intensify a particular post. Take the first $100 and make an advertisement set to advance the post. If your post incorporates a connection to your site, pick the Traffic objective. If it's a video, you may pick Video Views as your target.

Facebook's promotion calculations will begin enhancing your natural substance and paid substance. Run your advertisement for a few days, and after that, respite it for a day or two. Next, take another $100 and make an alternate advertisement set and rehash the procedure for a similar post. At long last, rehash this procedure with the last $100.

This has demonstrated you can broaden natural reach over many numerous months, even. With a quality, evergreen post and utilizing the wave hypothesis of applying spending plan, delaying, and after that applying more spending plan, you'll discover the life of your post broadened fundamentally.

The means delineated above will help you essentially increment the natural reach of posts with paid Facebook advancement. Facebook's calculation is driven by numerous variables. Even though everybody in the Facebook people group has something to do with what they see, Facebook has different contemplations too.

For the best outcomes for your business, work with the calculation as it exists at present. Keep awake to date and make changes as the calculation shifts.

Five Proven Advertising Tips for Better ROI

There's no uncertainty that Facebook has a ton to offer to your business, and it can enable it to develop if you know the privilege of Facebook advertising tips. Yet, you can't simply present some substance on your Facebook page and anticipate incredible outcomes. You have to go past distributing incredible substance if you need to get the most astounding quantifiable profit from your marketing endeavors.

The way to discovering genuine achievement utilizing our Facebook advertising tips isn't to be reliant on natural reach in this specific informal community's news source since natural reach has been declining for a long while now (which means less commitment for brands) as Facebook keeps on offering significance to the supported substance.

Facebook has turned out to be monstrous throughout the years, so the main way your substance can transcend the rest is through focused advertisements that position you before your crowd and looking for Facebook advertising tips from other marketing specialists. By utilizing the privilege of Facebook advertising tips, you can show improvement over advertisers who are just centered around the "free" online life strategies and obsolete techniques.

As indicated by the State of Social report distributed by Buffer, it was discovered that up to 94% of organizations (of all shapes and sizes) had put resources into Facebook promotions. What's more, an incredible level of them is centered around boosting their online networking promotions spending plan in the coming years.

Do Ads Work?

The straightforward answer is true; they do. What's more, the confirmation lies in the pudding. If you check out, you'll locate each real informal organization (for example, Twitter and LinkedIn) with its very own local advertising framework set up. But then, none of them can convey the sort of results Facebook does.

This is, for the most part, because of Facebook...
• Have the heartiest highlights spread out for publicists who need to get the best value for their money?
• Has the most exceptional devices for focusing on the correct sort of clients.
• Has nitty-gritty experiences into what's working and so forth, so you can improve your battle.
• It has the greatest group of spectators, where you will undoubtedly discover your specialty crowd if you look cautiously.

This fair proceeds to demonstrate that Facebook is digging in for the long haul, and its advertising framework is the thing that your business needs — particularly when you're simply beginning. No big surprise, the number of promoters on Facebook and looking for Facebook advertising tips is developing significantly.

Presently, this doesn't imply that Facebook doesn't expect to absorb information. Despite what might be expected, Facebook advertisements may appear to be confounded from the outset. Be that as it may, don't give this a chance to threaten you. The main reason their promotion framework is modern is that it has such a great amount to offer to its sponsors. It is intended to give you better, more focused on results while helping you remain on spending plan.

Facebook is an incredible stage for brands to publicize and get an introduction, yet tragically, not every person hits the nail on the head. Without getting your work done on Facebook promotions to adapt more Facebook advertising tips, you may wind up wearing out your wallet.

This, for the most part, happens when and if you surge in, rather taking a cautious, determined approach. To put it plainly, you need a technique and utilize powerful Facebook advertising tips to show signs of improvement returns.

Given that Facebook's month to month dynamic clients continue developing, you won't have an issue arriving at your intended interest group and changing over them with a top-notch promotion crusade.

By learning a tad about how Facebook promotions work and making the correct strides (while maintaining a strategic distance from the basic mix-ups), you ought to have the option to make your advertisement crusades beneficial over and over.

How about we investigate five straightforward Facebook advertising tips to enable you to take advantage of your venture.

Five Facebook Digital Marketing Tips for Your Business

#1: Target the Appropriate Audience

One mix-up that numerous new Facebook sponsors make is they attempt to reach whatever number individuals as could be allowed with their promotion. While this isn't completely off-base, it's likewise not the correct approach. Doing so can cut down your odds of finding any observable accomplishment with Facebook promotions.

Remember that each advertisement you make and keep running on Facebook has a reason. Furthermore, this reason ought to line up with the fundamental beliefs of your intended interest group. When you target anybody and everybody, the advertisement's motivation is vanquished.

So as opposed to expanding your scope to a high number of individuals, your attention ought to be on contacting the correct group of spectators. There are three for several reasons regarding why your promotions should be super-focused towards a firmly sew gathering of individuals.

1. You need your substance to reverberate with individuals who are keen on finding your substance, but at the same time are available to impart it to other significant individuals.
2. You need to contact individuals who are inalienably inquisitive about your sort of business and need to get familiar with it.
3. You need to associate with an important group of spectators that is exceptionally open and inviting to your message.

At first, it might feel wrong to focus on a little gathering of individuals; however, over the long haul, which is how you get more transformations. That is how you develop.

Focusing on the correct group of spectators and offering a custom-made message to them is tied in with understanding your clients and their decisions. Which implies, you should...

• Know what stages appeal to them and utilized them for the most part.

• Know how they converse with one another and what language/tone they like.

• Know what sort of substance appeals to them the most and how they connect with it.

• Know their general inclinations, likes, dislikes, and so forth.

You can use Facebook's Audience Insights highlight to get a more grounded, clearer comprehension of who you are focusing on and why you ought to do as such. It'll give you an elevated perspective on your crowd and simultaneously enable you to jump into the littlest of subtleties.

#2: Get the Landing Page Right

Each individual that navigates to your advertisement needs to see a pertinent offer that includes esteem. What's more, you just have a couple of moments to demonstrate to them that you're the correct arrangement. How would you do that?

With the assistance of an appropriate, well-built point of arrival that encourages you to arrive at your objective. Alongside the other Facebook advertising tips, this one about concentrating on the presentation page ought not to be disregarded in case you're not kidding about getting results.

The thing is, snaps to your Facebook advertisements can end up costly in case you're not changing over them reliably. Which is the reason you have to get your guest's consideration with a focused on the point of arrival and convert them into a lead or client?

When you get the presentation page right, your odds of accomplishing superior ROI increments, regardless of whether it is getting individuals to enroll for your online class or have them download a free eBook or purchase your new programming device, everything relies upon where they land and how you treat them.

The more effective the duplicate and the plan of your point of arrival is, the better transformations you will see with your advertisement.

This is how you can make your Facebook promotions point of arrival progressively effective as far as changing over guests:

Instructions to Create an Effective Facebook Ads Landing Page

• Know Your Goal

With regard to the duplicate of your point of arrival, you may experience considerable difficulties picking between a long or short form. However, this shouldn't be that troublesome if you are clear about what you need to accomplish with your Facebook advertisement crusade. Your change objectives quite often decide the length of your point of arrival duplicate.

In case you're just watching out to create a lead or catch your guest's email address, at that point having short duplicate bodes well. However, when you have a lot greater objective to accomplish, for example, making trust with your group of spectators or selling them an item or administration, at that point, your duplicate ought to be longer with all the more persuading subtleties alongside social evidence.

At last, you have to concentrate on the bob pace of your page as much as the transformation. As it were, you should make your duplicate intriguing and significant enough with the goal that individuals invest some energy in it. The time they spend on your page is certainly a metric that you ought to consider, particularly when you need to see better long haul results with your promotions.

• **Improve the Visuals**
Utilizing legitimate visual components on your point of arrival goes far with regards to getting genuine outcomes. Likewise, great, pertinent visual components add to the general progression of the presentation page and make the substance

simple to check and devour. Which means lower bob rates and better change rates.

Last, however, not the least, visuals can be incredibly amazing when appealing to the feelings of your guests and making them make a move without adding to your duplicate. For example, the decision of shading your suggestion to take action catch can affect the changing pace of your page.

• **Say No to Distractions**

Your presentation page ought to streamline things for your Facebook promotion guests, not entangle them. Which means you ought to abstain from utilizing any diverting components that messiness your page, for example, superfluous route connections or social symbols that drive individuals from the page. If something isn't adding to the general objective of your presentation page, it ought to be dodged no matter what. Fewer diversions for the guest means better outcomes from your greeting page.

In any case, this doesn't imply that you shouldn't include components that help fabricate trust and validity. While your greeting page ought not to have route joins, it can have connections to your protection arrangement, which enables your guests to settle on the choice.

You additionally need to ensure that your greeting page is completely responsive. You can't expect that all clients will touch base to your point of arrival through the work area. Try not to trust that somebody will get to your presentation page utilizing his cell phone just to be disappointed with the page not rendering appropriately. That would be a misfortune in your part. Along these lines, make certain to test the page first on all gadgets.

#3: Make the Image Count

Facebook promotions are unique about the advertisements you find on the Internet, or other web-based life locales. When you're running a Facebook promotion, you have to utilize the correct duplicate, yet also, a picture that enables your advertisement to stand apart from the rest. Utilizing an off-base picture can mood killer your potential group of spectators or more terrible; it may not, in any case, get a note.

To make your Facebook advertisement battle fruitful, it's urgent that you have all components set up, particularly the picture related to your promotion. All the testing and tweaking you do to your advertisement duplicate won't have any kind of effect if your promotion is imperceptible basically because of an awful picture.

So how would you guarantee that your picture has any kind of effect on your battle? How would you make the most of it?

Use Text Creatively

While the facts demonstrate that Facebook never again rejects advertisements dependent on the measure of content the picture contains, message still issues. Contingent upon the content you're adding to the picture, Facebook gives you a rating of low, medium, or high.

Despite everything, you have to recollect that Facebook adores or rather favors promotion pictures that contain practically no content. So if you are going to utilize the message in your advertisement pictures, at that point, you have to do it inventively. As such, you should rehearse curtness and ensure you're not including any content only for its hell.

The ideal approach to decide how much content ought to go into your advertisement picture is to test a couple of various variants of it. This will give you a vastly improved thought on what's working and so forth.

Abstain from Choosing a Random Stock Image

No, there's no mischief in utilizing stock pictures in your Facebook advertisements. Yet, if you are going to utilize one, guarantee it is exceptionally pertinent to your promotion's message. You can't simply pick something that just looks appealing; however, it has zero association with the advertisement duplicate. The stock picture needs to stick out and yet, and it must be interesting to your image. Despite what you select, test a couple of stock pictures to figure out which one brings you the most changes.

If you have the opportunity and the cash, you might need to go out there and snap your pictures. These will be much superior to the stock picture alternatives Facebook offers you from its library. By and by, test any picture before you go full throttle.

Be Consistent

Ensure the picture you decide for the advertisement is reliable over your promotion duplicate and the presentation page. The picture needs to line up with the general message that you're sending to your prospect. It should enable them to associate with your promotion on an enthusiastic level. This can happen when you center on consistency. All other Facebook advertising tips won't give you the sort of results you need in case you're not reliable.

For instance, in case you're running a Facebook Newsfeed advertisement about your web-based business store, utilize a picture that mirrors the experience that your guest will feel once they are on your site. Additionally, the duplicate and the pictures you use on the point of arrival should coordinate your advertisement inventive with the goal that the guest doesn't encounter any subjective disharmony.

Keep Testing

Regardless of how great you get with Facebook advertisements, you have to continue testing a distinctive variant of your promotions to locate the most noteworthy change over one. There is the wrong spot for a mystery with regards to running a beneficial Facebook advertisement crusade. Everything comes down to the numbers.

Try not to tragically base your battle on the suggestion of other Facebook publicists. What worked for them may not work for you and the other way around.

You have to test alone to discover what works for your very own business. Significantly, you complete broad testing (by putting aside a test spending plan) with the goal that you can contrast numerous advertisement varieties with discovering which ones are working the best for you. Simply after you are certain, a crusade is giving you positive outcomes should you contribute further. Up to that point, continue testing.

#4: Leverage Video Ads

Facebook is giving tremendous significance to video advertisements and will keep on doing as such. So if you are not utilizing video "newsfeed" promotions, you are leaving cash on the table.

Even though Facebook's natural reach is declining, recordings have a unique spot in its newsfeed. Which implies, by grasping video, you can experience the better natural reach and a higher commission rate when contrasted with different kinds of substance.

The motivation behind why Facebook is offering weight to video substance is basic: its clients are observing more recordings than any time in recent memory. As much as 100 million hours every day!

With regard to social advertising, Facebook recordings are spending cordial as well as have a superior reach. Facebook knows this, which is for what reason they're urging sponsors to utilize video advertisements. Of all the Facebook advertising tips that we have talked about over, this one has picked up the most noticeable quality in the online advertising world.

With regards to making recordings advertisements that get an ideal rate of return, you can't pursue the instances of recordings you find on YouTube or Vimeo. Video promotions on Facebook must be organized, remembering the crowd you're focusing on and what they would discover appealing in this specific social condition.

How about we see what you can do to guarantee your Facebook video promotion crusades are organized the correct way.

1. Your video promotion on Facebook should intrigue. It needs to catch the eye of the watcher in the initial 3-4 seconds to affect. Why? Since the Facebook newsfeed is packed, and clients have numerous different alternatives to take a gander at. So you need your video promotion to intrigue enough for them not to proceed onward.

2. While adding sound to your video promotion is suggested, it's not the most basic center territory. Rather, centers around making recordings where you intrigue the client with zero sound. It's hard to believe, but it's true, your recordings should be compelling when quiet. The greater part of the Facebook clients, of course, watch recordings in quiet mode and tend to up the volume if the video is fascinating enough.

3. Test various varieties of your video advertisement to discover which one lures your group of spectators the most. Testing every variety will give you the space to change your advertisement and refine it for better outcomes.

Facebook video advertisements have the monstrous potential for organizations all things considered. They can enable you to improve your ROI while making a more grounded association with your intended interest group.

#5: Build a Proper Sales Funnel

Selling on Facebook isn't saved for the tip-top few or brands that have profound pockets. Your business can sell on Facebook with the assistance of natural substance, paid promotions, and a couple of our Facebook advertising tips. Selling on Facebook is significantly increasingly viable when you make a business channel that causes you to accomplish your motivation.

The reason for a Facebook deals pipe is to heat your intended interest group or support them before pitching them an item or administration. This strategy works since utilizing significant messages for various clients (at various stages) can make it simple for you to persuade them to change over.

Facebook promotions work incredibly well for this reason, as you can target forthcoming purchasers at all phases of the business pipe. Even though Facebook is utilized for drawing in clients, it can likewise be utilized to create an enormous number of offers with the assistance of a solid pipe.

Deals pipes will, in general, fill a hole and instruct clients to make a move by making request additional time. It gives clients their very own reasonable thought agony focuses and how your item/administration can address them. To put it plainly, a Facebook deals pipe will enable you to take an alternate way. It's one of those Facebook advertising tips that will stand the trial of time.

The best part about structure a business pipe is the way that you can make various kinds of promotions focused on a wide range of clients. Here are two essential advances that you have to take to begin making a business channel on Facebook.

• Create mindfulness about your image with the assistance of natural posting, applicable Facebook advertisements, and referral challenges. This is the first and the most unpretentious advance to getting the client into your business pipe.
• Once your objective clients are made mindful of your item/administration, they arrive at the thought stage, where you have to reveal to them why they have to put resources into your image. This is where you give enough evidence to enable clients to move to the following stage. Make a point to address agony focuses and a similar time deal with any protests they may have. For instance, noting comments on your Facebook advertisements is an incredible method to do this.

We've given you our five best Facebook advertising tips, so you can use this recently discovered information to develop your business. If you need to pick our cerebrums somewhat more, at that point, get in touch with us to plan an opportunity to talk or peruse through our administrations to figure out how our web-based life marketing organization can enable you to expand reach with your advertising endeavors.

CHAPTER FOUR

THE SECRET TO HAVING SO MANY FOLLOWERS IS TO BECOME AN INFLUENCER

Social media influencers are extremely popular at present. Brands need to work together with them to extend their span and drive changes. The adherents of influencers, then again, anticipate master advice and suggestion from them.

With the prevalence of influencer marketing, it is just regular that individuals are ending up progressively curious about how to turn into an influencer.

Notwithstanding, constructing and holding a network of gave devotees isn't as simple as it has all the earmarks of being. It requires steady exertion on an influencer's part. Before we talk about some helpful hints on the most proficient method to turn into an influencer, how about we investigate the idea of social media influencers.

Translating the Enigma of Influencers

In basic terms, influencers are social media characters with an enormous number of faithful and drew in adherents. Most influencers share neighborly compatibility with their fans.

The fans, thus, frequently view these influencers as good examples and pursue their proposals. Influencers are frequently seen as power figures or specialists in their separate specialties. Attributable to the openness of social media stages, influencers can build up close to home associations with their adherents. In contrast to traditional big names, their lives aren't covered in quality of secret.

Instead, influencers regularly uncover a look at their own lives to their devotees. This is decisively what causes them to build up inviting bonds with their fan base. Influencers are the social media superstars who have a specific measure of influence with their fan networks.

The most noteworthy factor that recognizes influencers from prominent famous people is that the previous add their special and bona fide voices to their substance. This encourages them to gain the trust and dependability of their adherents. 70% of twenty to thirty-year-olds guarantee to be more affected by bloggers than big names.

The Perks of Being an Influencer

Advanced advertisers and brands have understood the significance of teaming up with influencers. The greatest advantage of influencer marketing is that it gives advertisers direct access to an influencer's dependable fan base. It additionally spares advertisers the issue of distinguishing and focusing on the correct audiences. That meticulous errand has already been finished by the influencer. That is the reason that 86% of advertisers' utilized influencer marketing in 2017.

What's more, who hates having the option to affect other individuals' lives and impact their choices? Truth be told, as per gen.video, the best and believed wellspring of driving transformations are social media influencers. This unmistakably shows influencers have the ability to persuade their adherents.

The Challenges Faced by Influencers

Today, numerous individuals try to progress toward becoming influencers. It seems like a worthwhile vocation choice and life decision for some individuals. Be that as it may, behind the majority of the glamour and excitement of an influencer's social media profile, their untruths a truckload of diligent work and tolerance.

Building and holding a steadfast fan following on social media isn't a cakewalk. This is ending up progressively troublesome as more individuals are attempting to move toward becoming influencers.

Along these lines, gaining the trust of your devotees is a careful undertaking. It requires tenacious exertion on your part to make your substance bonafide and catch the eye of your audience. Also, as an influencer, you must be incredibly mindful when teaming up with brands. Your adherents become faithful because of the individual and fair touch you add to your substance. Assaulting them with a supported substance can hurt your notoriety for being an influencer and withdraw your adherents.

If you are still enticed to carry on with the life of an influencer, read on to figure out how to turn into an influencer.

Instructions to Become an Influencer

The life of an influencer is envied by many. What we frequently neglect to perceive is the tireless exertion they need to take care of to carry on with the existence of extravagance and fabulousness.

A simple method to choose your specialty is to assess your qualities and shortcomings. Pick a specialty that enables you to grandstand your qualities and sharpen your abilities further. Choosing a specific specialty will enable you to streamline your audience and tailor your substance to suit their inclinations. Normally, when settling on the most proficient method to turn into an influencer, you can pick one of the accompanying classifications:

• Travel
• Lifestyle
• Fashion
• Food
• Beauty
• Sports
• Gaming
• Entertainment
• Tech
• Health and Fitness

You don't need to restrict yourself to only one of these classes. You can join at least two of these specialties. Ensure the individual specialties line up with each other. For example, you can consolidate travel and way of life or excellence and style when you settle on your specialty.

It isn't required for you to adhere to these built up and understood specialties. The way to turning into an influencer is by adding your one of a kind voice to all that you do. Along these lines, don't stop for a second to try and cut your specialty that enables you to show your qualities just as your characteristics.

Pick Your Platform

As an influencer, you need an incredible nearness on the web. Notwithstanding, that doesn't imply that you should utilize each social media stage and circulation channel out there. Contingent upon your specialty, specific steps may be more qualified for your substance than others.

For example, if you are a design blogger, Instagram would work preferable for your visual substance over different stages, for example, Twitter and LinkedIn. 93% of social media influencers lean toward Instagram as it conveys the best outcomes. Nonetheless, that doesn't imply that you should concentrate the majority of your exertion on Instagram if your specialty doesn't line up with the stage.

You ought to likewise consider the stage that your audience is well on the way to utilize. For example, if your intended interest group incorporates twenty to thirty-year-olds, you should concentrate your exertion on Snapchat and Instagram. If you use numerous social media stages, ensure that you tailor your substance for each channel.

For example, advanced marketing master, Neil Patel, effectively uses Twitter to advance his blog entries and other substance. This is evident thinking about a large portion of his intended interest group (business people, computerized advertisers, content makers, and so forth.) is probably going to visit this stage for important substances.

While it is prescribed that you select the stage that is most appropriate for your substance and target audience, you shouldn't overlook other conveyance channels. Instead, you ought to endeavor to obtain a fundamental working learning of different channels so you can use them later on if the need emerges.

Organize Your Content

Excellent substance is maybe the most robust response to the subject of how to turn into an influencer. It is critical to distribute remarkable and bona fide material that resounds with your audience.

This is the best way to keep your audience snared to your substance. Notwithstanding the kind of content you make, it should be significant and profitable.

Contingent upon your specialty and circulation channels, you can pick various kinds of substances, for example, blog entries, photographs, recordings, digital broadcasts, and so forth. It is essential to add your mark voice to each bit of substance you make. That is the thing that will recognize you from other individuals who are likewise attempting to make sense of how to be an influencer.

It is critical that you locate the novel eccentricity or quality that recognizes you from different influencers in your specialty. When you have distinguished this particular selling recommendation (USP), consolidate it into your substance, however much as could reasonably be expected. In addition to bailing your substance stick out, this will likewise build up your picture as an influencer. It is advisable that you coordinate this USP into your supported substance too.

Tune in to Your Audience

A powerful method to guarantee that your substance collects footing is to make content that your audience needs. To get significant substance thoughts, you can run a speedy Google scan for your specialty. Look down to the base of query items to locate the long-tail catchphrases that are being utilized by your intended interest group. You can likewise look through stages, for example, Quora and Reddit, to get a thought of what your intended interest group is discussing.

If you need your substance to hit home for your audience, you should have a profound comprehension of your adherent network. Most social media stages have an investigation segment that can give you significant experiences about your intended interest group. You gain admittance to audience socioeconomics information, for example, sexual orientation, geographic area, occupation, online conduct, and so on.

Also, you should give close consideration to the remarks area of your social media and blog entries. It tends to be a goldmine of new content thoughts that your audience needs to read/watch. You can likewise gather information and request that your adherents reveal to all of you about their inclinations and agony focuses.

Up Your Hashtag Game

If you are thinking about how to turn into an influencer and exceed expectations at it, the appropriate response is to utilize the privilege hashtags. Your substance possibly ends up important and significant when it contacts the correct audience. A compelling method for giving expanded permeability to your substance is by adding suitable hashtags to your social media posts. This is particularly helpful for individuals who are simply beginning as influencers and need to develop their audience.

Recognize the most important and slanting hashtags in your specialty. At that point, those in your presents on getting your substance seen by a completely new audience may have been uninformed of your reality. When utilizing hashtags, you ought to be mindful so as not to flood your posts with extra ones. Just use hashtags that line up with your picture as an influencer.

In addition to utilizing famous hashtags, you can likewise make your extraordinary hashtag to broaden your range considerably further. Urge your adherents to upload content without anyone else profiles utilizing your branded hashtags. This promotes your hashtag and assembles mindfulness about you in your supporters' social systems.

Look after Consistency

Distributing fantastic substance all the time is one of the best approaches to hold your audience's consideration. When you convey great substance all the time, it makes a feeling of expectation among your audience.

That, like this, supports audience commitment and builds your scope. It is advisable that you make a timetable for the majority of the substance you plan on distributing in the following couple of months. You can likewise make a week by week or month to month arrangement to keep your audience snared.

In addition to utilizing well-known hashtags, you can likewise make your one of a kind hashtag augment your compass significantly further. Urge your devotees to upload content without anyone else profiles utilizing your branded hashtags. This promotes your hashtag and manufactures mindfulness about you in your supporters' social systems.

Look after Consistency

Distributing great substances all the time is one of the best approaches to hold your audience's consideration. When you convey great substance all the time, it makes a feeling of expectation among your audience.

That, like this, supports audience commitment and builds your range. It is advisable that you take a course of events for the majority of the substance you plan on distributing in the following couple of months. You can likewise make a week by week or month to month arrangement to keep your audience snared.

Work together with Other Influencers

When you are beginning, and as yet considering how to turn into an influencer, banding together with somebody knew in your specialty can be of incredible assistance.

You should have the option to offer something of utilization to the next influencer to entice them to team up with you. If the greater influencers appear to be distant, you can considerably join forces with smaller-scale influencers who have little yet profoundly connected with fan bases.

Manufacture a Website

If you ask somebody how to turn into an influencer, they are probably going to offer you a ton of guidance on substance systems and social media stages.

Not many individuals will disclose to you the effect a site can have on your notoriety for being an influencer. Any individual who is remotely acquainted with marketing and branding knows how significant a site can be. As your fan base develops, numerous individuals will be enticed to run a speedy Google look for your name. Having a well-structured and completely useful site adds believability to your picture and causes you to win the trust of your intended interest group.

Additionally, having a well-planned blog area on your site further builds up your position in your specialty. It additionally improves natural hunt traffic to your site, in this manner growing your span considerably further.

Host AMAs, Contests, and Giveaways

If you are considering how to turn into an influencer with a committed adherent network, the appropriate response is to keep them locked in.

One of the best approaches to help audience commitment is to have an AMA (ask me anything) session on the foundation of your decision. In addition to keeping your audience connected with, it will likewise help build up your ability in specific subjects in your specialty.

Another shrewd method to improve commitment is to declare a giveaway. Regularly, you offer your devotees a reward in return for preferences, remarks, and offers on your posts. You can likewise request that they label their companions on the giveaway declaration. A challenge is like a giveaway, and then again, the members are required to upload explicit substance or utilize your branded hashtag to be qualified to win.

Challenges and giveaways likewise help you connect with a wide audience and develop your adherents. You can work together with different influencers or brands in your specialty to make them increasingly successful. Ensure you determine the guidelines, deadline, rewards, and so on and report the victor at the guaranteed time. Probably the best response to the subject of how to turn into an influencer is to has giveaways and challenges to keep your audience locked in.

Go Live

The most straightforward response to the subject of how to turn into an influencer is to keep up an individual association with your audience.

Most stages, for example, Facebook, Instagram, and YouTube enable clients to go live and share constant updates with their devotees. You can utilize this to your advantage and give your audience a look at the off-camera activity at an occasion or a gathering. It makes your devotees feel nearer to you and strengthens their dedication.

You can likewise have a live AMA session to speak with your supporters continuously. This is a very successful methodology to support commitment. Simultaneously, it additionally enables you to get a reasonable thought of what your audience likes/despises and anticipates from you. Ensure you advise your supporters about the session in advance.

React to Your Fans

As your audience develops and more individuals start valuing your substance, they are probably going to leave their criticism in DMs and remarks.

Reacting to every single remark may be a massive undertaking. It is advisable that you answer to whatever number as could reasonably be expected. A reaction from your side approves the trust that your fans put in you and makes them feel progressively associated with you.

Also, you can likewise do a whoop for an astoundingly positive input you get. It makes the sender feel compensated and reinforces their confidence in you. If you need to realize how to turn into an influencer, the key is to esteem your audience individuals as much as they esteem you.

The response to the topic of how to turn into an influencer is not a straightforward one. It might take you long stretches of diligent work and tolerance before the outcomes begin to appear. The key is to locate your novel voice and use it to make a one of a kind picture for yourself as an influencer. Distinguish a particular specialty and circulation channel that is most appropriate for you.

Also, any individual who has the scariest thought of how to turn into an influencer will disclose to you the significance of making a certified substance that interests your audience. You additionally need to endeavor to keep up an individual association with your supporters. At exactly that point, you will have the option to fabricate a dependable and drew in the fan base that won't flutter an eyelid before confiding in your suggestions.

CHAPTER FIVE

BUILDING YOUR DIGITAL MARKETING BRAND ON INSTAGRAM

Maybe more than some other social media stage, Instagram offers you the chance to make a buzz truly. Associating with similar individuals who offer intrigue and need to see business as usual data permits you an uncommon chance to pick up devotees that will love you. Despite everything, it takes some expertise and thought to stand apart from the conceivably many other accounts they are following.

Get Strategic on Instagram

Like any of your other marketing endeavors, you need to get innovative on your Instagram account. Framework an arrangement and system by thinking about the accompanying elements:

• Goals and Objectives: As with any marketing system, you need to choose what you need to accomplish with your record. Is it getting some email addresses, web visits, brand mindfulness, sales, or something different through and through? Deciding your objectives will enable you to think of your substance.

• Your Target: You will likewise need to think about your optimal objective, as this will likewise enable you to build up your substance plan just as demonstrate to you what sorts of Instagram account you ought to pursue.

• Finding Your Niche: Choosing a specialty will enable you to concentrate on the most proficient method to turn into the go-to for whatever you are selling. Take a gander at your opposition to see where they see themselves. Specialty it up, and you will end up being an idea leader individuals need to tune in to.

• Planned Content: Set out a timetable so you can stay steady with ordinary posts. You additionally need to have the arrangement to figure out what you will post, how regularly, and when. Your program ought to likewise incorporate the hashtags you will use for each post.

• Assessment: Make sure you are setting aside the effort to follow your outcomes, including remarks, likes, supporters, traffic, transformations, and any adjustments in sales.

Brand It Well

The better you know your brand, the simpler this progression gets. You have to comprehend what your identity is and where you are coming from to think of the ideal approach to draw individuals into your reality. Play-Doh has branding under control.

They know who their audience and clients are and keep them interested in their posts each day. You have to demonstrate supporters esteem, with your products and services, however, with the substance that they will take a gander at. You need them to state, "Hello, I like this! Show me more." However, you would prefer not to become involved with attempting to be excessively one of a kind, so individuals can't make sense of you.

Remember that your branding ought to stay steady over the entirety of your marketing endeavors, so your tone and way ought not to vary from any of the other marketing you have done or are doing. Be predictable with your branding hues, textual styles, and logos. Consider what individuals will see and if they will be interested enough to tail you.

You have to keep things alluring to your audience and ensure your present customers don't get killed because you are not remaining consistent with the brand they adore. You need a strong subject that is clear and brief, so your brand reverberates with your clients.

Remember to Hashtag

Brands get found utilizing hashtags. They are the breadcrumbs that lead to your entryway, site, or administration. Figuring out how to hashtag well will enable you to get a greater commitment. Try not to be reluctant to get motivated by the challenge and see what they are utilizing. Hashtags address your specialty. You can likewise take a gander at a portion of the most loved records you may pursue and perceive how they are utilizing hashtags. That furnishes you with certain approaches to get imaginative with your hashtagging.

Clear decisions incorporate your products and services. If you are not yet a hashtag master, here are a few plans to get roused:

• Images you are utilizing
• Your specialty and industry
• Your ability

• Your people group or where you may be at an occasion

Use in any event two words in your hashtags when conceivable, and don't be hesitant to focus in on those industry trendy expressions.

Making all things equal

The most prevalent Instagram records will, in general, be individuals who are conspicuous in the network who are doing some after of their own.

Influencers in your industry and network are a decent spot to begin as this permits others in the network to see you drawing in with them. It's a universe of you like me, and I'll like you, so sharing is fundamental.

Strikingly, Instagram is the main Instagram account. How would they do it? They influence the absolute best records and offer their posts over and again. You would prefer not to be seen as they stood up the record with no time for other people. You need to fashion connections by supporting others in the network.

You can do that by enjoying and remarking in a constructive way, which gives individuals a chance to see you and says, "See, I'm cool as well." It gives you that truly necessary road cred and afterward gets individuals interested to perceive what you are about. When they get the opportunity to see you, they will need to tail you as well and before long discover your worth.

Be mindful so as not to escape with sharing. Continuously ensure it is pertinent to your brand with the goal that you keep your supporters occupied with the story you are attempting to tell. If you adore pups so be it, however, if young doggies have nothing to do with the pants you are selling, remain quiet about the little dogs.

Keep It Up, Keep It Engaging

Social media can be a test and requires some serious energy. You must be on Instagram always, so you can be reliable and dynamic for individuals to see you. It requires exertion. Post at any rate once a day was utilizing significant and intriguing posts. Furthermore, referenced, it's a two-way road, so you likewise need to stay aware of the preferences and remarks for the records you are following and that are tailing you.

Instagram is a prominent stage where permeability and cooperation are everything. Stay reliable and stay aware of your presenting all together on stay top of the brain. Chanel is one of the tops of the line Instagram accounts.

They utilize recorded references to Coco, the originator of the brand, yet design flashbacks that keep fashionistas locked in.

Keep things energizing and ensure your presents have everything required on the draw in your supporters including:

• Images: Excellent quality symbolism is an unquestionable requirement to keep individuals intrigued. Pictures should coordinate your brand and interest and allure interest.

• Location: Tag your business area or an occasion your organization is holding to help commitment.

• Captions and Text: Remember the eight-second rule for consideration, so compose clear inscriptions that are drawing in and indisputable in their informing.

• Call-to-activity: Get those snaps and offers.

• Hashtags: An unquestionable requirement to keep you pulling in new fans.

• Engage: Do unto others as you would have them do unto you, and keep those remarks coming to urge others to do likewise to you.

Call for Engagement

This part of Instagram is significant. You need to add some type of an inquiry that will get individuals occupied with your posts. It shouldn't be accomplished for each post, yet you ought to do it regularly.

Here are a few thoughts:
• Do you incline toward downpour or day off?
• List a couple of things or pictures and ask: Which do you like best 1, 2, or 3?
• Ask them to utilize a particular emoticon to indicate they loved your post or discovered your post supportively.
• Ask a yes or no inquiry.
• Give them a size of 1 to 10 about another product.

Get them to label a companion they think should see your post.

Be Neighborly

Instagram is very 'nichey' and network-based. It is great as it encourages you to cultivate associations with different records that have similar styles and interests.

You can make connections to use different devotees and check whether you can think of innovative approaches to keep your associations. A few people will begin a story that is proceeded on another record. Doing this urges individuals to tail you and energizes others in your locale to consider you to be a cooperative person. You should place some exertion into these cross-promotions and contact the records that you need to work with, yet it can demonstrate to be justified, despite all the trouble at last.

If your financial limit permits, consider utilizing influencer marketing. These small scale influencers have a huge number of adherents and give solid network presentation. Since you need to pay to get to an influencer's audience, give it a shot first to check whether it expands commitment and improves your range.

You can likewise search for clear increments in traffic and changes, also sales.

Last contemplations

Instagram is the best social media stage to give an inside look into what your business is about. You can share posts about occasions you have held, particularly if they have solid connections to the network.

Nike is an ideal case of how to draw in adherents. They utilize inspirational ads to move execution that works both on and off the court. Philanthropy occasions focus on the news, and even an anecdote about a staff part all add a human touch to your business. Despite everything, you need to keep up your brand tone and way yet recount stories that help individuals privately see your incentive.

Utilize these tips, and soon you become Instafamous.

The Correct Use of Instagram Ads

So you're running paid hunt and show ads through Google, you're advertising on Facebook, LinkedIn, Twitter, and even some specialty industry-related social locales. Maybe you're notwithstanding running some guerilla advertising efforts, or ads through NPR. In any case, oddly enough, you expelled Instagram, uncertain if it would yield ROI.

I'm here to educate you that today isn't the day to disregard Instagram! While Instagram might be more youthful, with fewer clients, than its parent organization Facebook, Instagram is the breakout star of the family that everybody needs to sit by at the Thanksgiving table. Instagram gives a stage to recount to visual stories through different ad designs, and numerous advertisers have seen this divert yielding higher ROI in contrast with their other advertising efforts.

Today Instagram has 800 million dynamic clients, as per Statista, and the pace of quick development it has seen since 2013 is really surprising. Be that as it may, with such a large number of dynamic people looking through their feeds at extremely inconvenient times of the day, how on the planet can a little business like yours stick out?

This is the place of Instagram advertising becomes possibly the most important factor. Like Facebook, with fame comes mess, and getting through that messiness naturally to have a genuine effect can feel about outlandish. To concentrate on the perfect individuals, at the opportune time, with the correct message and symbolism, Instagram ads are your ground-breaking vehicle to do only that...

What Is Instagram Advertising?

Instagram advertising is a strategy for paying to post supported substance on the Instagram stage to arrive at a bigger and more focused on the audience. Instagram is a visual stage; content ads are not a thing here. Or maybe you need a picture, set of pictures, or video (which can be joined by content) to contact your audience with Instagram ads.

The energizing part? Instagram advertising works! In March 2017, more than 120 million Instagrammers visited a site, got headings, called, messaged, or direct informed to find out about a business dependent on an Instagram ad. As indicated by Instagram, 60% of individuals state they find new products on the stage, and 75% of Instagrammers make a move in the wake of being propelled by a post.

Like Facebook ads, tossing some cash behind a post will lead to more introduction for your brand, just as more authority over who can see your post.

The amount of Instagram Ads Cost?

This is a precarious inquiry to reply, as expenses depend on an assortment of elements, and as you may have suspected, these components are not all uncovered to us by the stage. The model depends on CPC (cost-per-snap) and CPM's (cost per impressions), and costs are resolved by Instagram's ad closeout.

"The expense of Instagram ads are affected by numerous components — everything from your audience to your ad criticism," says Andrew Tate from AdEspresso. "A ton goes into seeing how to advertise on Instagram."

AdEspresso as of late dove into $100 million worth of Instagram ad spent in 2017 and found that the normal expense per click (CPC) for Instagram ads in Q3 extended somewhere in the range of $0.70 and $0.80. While this is a useful benchmark, it will differ contingent on the closeout, audience, rivalry, time of day, day of the week, and so on.

A few advertisers find that Instagram ads regularly have a higher commitment. However, this can cost them. As indicated by Keith Baumwald, author of Leverage Consulting, Instagram ads expenses are marginally higher in expense than Facebook. On the splendid side, advertisers do have command over how their financial limits are distributed. For example, you can pick between a day by day spending plan to restrict the sum spend every day or a lifetime spending where you would set up your ads to keep running for a timeframe until the financial backing is drained.

Different approaches to control your Instagram ad spend incorporate setting your ad plan (for example, you can determine certain hours of the day you need your ads to run), setting your ad conveyance technique (there are three alternatives: interface snaps, impressions, and every day one of a kind reach), just as setting your offer sum (manual versus programmed).

Easy Steps to Start Advertising on Instagram

Learning the intricate details of another advertising stage may appear to be overpowering from the start. The uplifting news here is that in case you're advertising on Facebook, there isn't a lot to learn. Instagram ads can be arranged directly through the Facebook Ad Manager. In case you're not advertising on Facebook, don't fuss. We'll walk you through the procedure underneath, and there is additionally the choice to make some basic ads legitimately inside the Instagram application.

Advertisers who are further developed or running a generally huge ad set can likewise design their ads through Power Editor or Facebook's Marketing API. Instagram Partners is additionally accessible for businesses that need to purchase and deal with different ads, deal with a huge network, and convey content at scale. We'll center on making ads through Facebook Ad Manager, which is the most widely recognized strategy because of its usability and the capacity to redo these ads to a higher degree than what is conceivable inside the application itself. While arranging Instagram ads isn't excessively unpredictable, there are many strides to know about. Beginning with...

1. Explore to Facebook's Ad Manager

To explore to ad administrator inside Facebook, essentially pursue this connection, accepting that you're signed in to the proper Facebook account.

Note: There is no particular Ad Manager for Instagram; Instagram ads are overseen through the Facebook Ads UI.

2. Set Your Marketing Objective

Presently for the fun part, picking your crusade objective. Fortunately, the objectives are named in an obvious way. Need more traffic? Select the traffic objective. Hoping to build brand mindfulness? Pick the brand mindfulness objective. You get the essence.

One thing to know about is that Instagram ads just work with the accompanying objectives:

- Brand mindfulness
- Reach
- Traffic (for snaps to your site or the application store for your application)
- App introduces
- Engagement (for post commitment as it were)
- Video sees
- Conversions (for transformations on your site or application)

While these objectives are natural, some join a couple of additional design steps, which I'll go through for you.

Brand care: Take an extra-long lunch. No extra methods here! This is the most standard target that will endeavor to exhibit your ads to progressively potential people at risk to be charmed. How does Instagram choose this? It's a puzzle, anyway, this target will presumably reveal some new and notable individuals to your brand.

Reach: If reach is what you're scanning for (as in enhancing what number of people see your ads) by then, you'll just make a point to pick your Instagram account when making the promotion itself. It's moreover critical that if you want to run an Instagram

Story promotion, "reach" is by and by the fundamental objective you can pick. The sweet thing is that you can misuse Facebook's part trying component, which empowers you to part test two ads to see which one yields more presents. NOTE: Split testing is also open for Traffic, App Installs, Video Views, Lead Generation, and Conversion targets.

Traffic: If you want to send more people to your website or application store to download your application, this is the fitting goal for you. The extra fundamental methods you'll need to take is picking between those two other options, by then enter the URL of choice, and let the traffic jam in!

Duty: Who needn't bother with more likes, offers, and overall responsibility? If your goal is a responsibility, one thing to note is that you, by and by, can simply pay to play for "post duty" on Instagram. Facebook will empower you to pay for "page responsibility" and "event responses," yet this isn't right now open to Instagram.

Application Installs: If your primary objective is application introduces, you've gone to the ideal spot. To design this, you'll have to pick your application from the application store during set-up.

Video Views: Videos are regularly a venture of time and cash, so not advancing your video on Instagram would resemble purchasing a plane ticket to Hawaii, and leaving it in your work area. Fortunately, this objective is clear and doesn't require additional arrangement steps.

Lead Generation: Who doesn't need more leads? If that is your principal objective, this goal is for you. Simply note that lead age ads don't give the majority of the equivalent pre-filled fields as Facebook. Instagram, as of now, just supports email, complete name, telephone number, and sex. These ads additionally have, to a greater degree, a boundary than Facebook lead age ads, since when leads snap to open the ad, they'll have to navigate to round out their data. On Facebook, leads can round out their data without all the additional clicking. The other set-up piece is that you'll have to make a lead structure when making your ad.

Transformations: Last, however, surely not least, we have changed. This objective enables you to drive your leads to make a move and convert on your site or inside your application. The additional set-up here expects you to design either a Facebook pixel or application occasion dependent on the site or application you're hoping to advance; this will enable you to follow changes.

3. Arrange Your Target Audience

Since you've chosen your goal, you have to focus on the fitting audience to get your ads before the perfect individuals. This is the genuine excellence of Instagram ads since you'll be utilizing Facebook's profundity of statistic learning to contact the ideal individuals. In case you're new to this procedure, here's a once-over of your focusing on choices, which you can layer to get an exactly focused on the audience. (For example, if you need to target ladies, in New York, between the ages of 19 and 65, who are keen on yoga and wellbeing sustenance, you can do only that!)

Area: If you need to be focused on a nation, district, state, city, postal division, reject or incorporate certain spots, area focusing on will enable you to do the majority of this, and that's just the beginning.

Age: This helps you to target ranges from age 13 to 60+

Sexual orientation: Selecting between all, men, or women

Dialects: Facebook prescribes, leaving this clear except if the language you're focusing on isn't basic to the area you're focusing on.

Interests: Interests are likewise under "Itemized Targeting" with different sub-classifications to dive into. If you are searching for individuals intrigued by refined refreshments, sci-fi motion pictures, and flying, those choices are accessible for you!

Practices: And one more "Itemized Targeting" choice with different sub-classifications to investigate. Regardless of whether it be buying practices, work jobs, commemorations, or different practices, the alternatives appear to be perpetual.

Associations: Here, you'll have the option to target individuals associated with your page, application, or occasion.

Custom Audience: It let you upload your rundown of contacts enabling you to target leads already in your pipeline or clients who you're looking to upsell.

Clone Audience: If your custom audience is tapped to their potential, make a carbon copy audience. This will permit Instagram to discover individuals who have comparative qualities to your different audiences.

When you've arranged your audience, Facebook will likewise give you a manual for how explicit or broad your audience is.

This is a significant instrument to focus on because you need to find some kind of harmony of your audience not being excessively tremendous (since it's imaginable, not focused on enough), yet additionally not being excessively explicit (in the red zone), since there may not be numerous individuals (assuming any) to reach with such huge numbers of layered targets.

4. Pick Your Placements

Since you're focusing on your optimal statistic, it's an ideal opportunity to pick your positions! This is basic if your objective for a crusade is to just demonstrate ads on Instagram. If you disregard this progression, Facebook will enable your ads to show up on the two stages.

This isn't a negative thing; however, if you have content that you've made explicitly for Instagram, you should choose "Alter Placements" here.

From here, you can determine Instagram as a position, just as if you'd like these ads to show up in the feed or potentially the narratives segment of the stage.

5. Set Your Budget and Ad Schedule

If you know about how spending plans work through Facebook, AdWords, and other computerized advertising stages, this progression ought not to be excessively trying for you. If not, at that point, take a full breath; while you probably won't know precisely where to set your every day or lifetime spending when running your first Instagram ad crusade, this accompanies experimentation, just as experience. What's more, the beneficial thing is you have the control to interruption or stop your crusade whenever if you feel your spending limit isn't as a rule appropriately designated. While I normally lean towards day by day spending plans since it ensures your financial limit won't be spent too rapidly, lifetime spending plans enable you to plan your ad conveyance, so there are pluses and minuses to the two alternatives. I would likewise advise investigating the advanced alternatives presented underneath. For example, if you offer physically, you'll have the control to choose how much each lead is worth to you.

You can likewise run an ad timetable to target explicit occasions of day and days of the week when you realize your audience is most dynamic on the stage. This is a too profitable approach to streamline your financial limit. As an update, this is accessible for those utilizing a lifetime spending plan.

6. Make Your Instagram Ad

Presently the time has come to make your Instagram ad!

Ideally, in the wake of making the strides above, you already have some substance at the top of the priority list for the ad you are hoping to advance. This piece of the set-up may appear to be unique, relying on your battle objective. However, you'll generally have a couple of ad design choices to browse. So as a subsequent stage, how about we talk about the different ad organizes accessible.

Instagram Ad Formats

If you are a bad chief, you might need to prepare yourself. Instagram has six ad organizations to browse. Two are for Instagram stories that show up at the highest point of the channel in a way like Snapchats. The other four are configurations intended for the Instagram feed, which are all the more ordinarily utilized by advertisers.

#1. Picture Feed Ads

This is your most standard ad design, and likely the one you see regularly looking through your feed. These ads are single pictures that will show up as a local encounter as your objective lead is looking through their feed. The beautiful thing about these ads is that they don't feel like ads, particularly when progressed admirably.

Here are some additional subtleties to know about:

Specialized Requirements
• File type: jpg or png
• Maximum document size: 30MB
• Minimum Image Width: 600 pixels
• Image Ratio: 4:5 least, 16:9 most extreme

• Text length: 2,200 most extreme (*although Instagram prescribes remaining underneath 90 for ideal conveyance)

• Hashtag Number: 30 greatest (*you can add additional in the remarks)

Bolstered Objectives

• Reach
• Traffic
• Conversions
• App Installs
• Lead Generation
• Brand Awareness
• Post Engagement
• Product Catalog Sales
• Store Visits

Bolstered Call-to-Action Buttons

• Apply Now
• Book Now
• Call Now
• Contact Us
• Get Directions
• Learn More
• Get Showtimes
• Download

#2. Picture Story Ads

Same idea as above; however, these are for Instagram stories! Subtleties beneath:

Specialized Requirements

• Image Ratio: 9:16 prescribed
• Minimum Image Width: 600 pixels

Bolstered Objectives

• Reach
• Traffic
• Conversions
• App Installs
• Lead Generation

Bolstered Call-to-Action Buttons

• Apply Now
• Book Now
• Contact Us
• Download

3. Video Feed Ads

Breathe life into your ad with a video! If you've placed the time in to make a quality video, at that point, you ought to completely be advancing it through your Instagram feed.

While most video records are upheld by Instagram, they suggest utilizing H.264 pressure, square pixels, fixed edge rate, dynamic sweep, and stereo AAC sound pressure at 128kbps+ (PRO TIP: if your video isn't meeting this necessity you can generally run it through the video transcoder, Handbrake, to make these adjustments).

Specialized Requirements
• Video Resolution: 1080 x 1080 pixels (at any rate)
• Maximum record size: 4GB
• Video Ratio: 4:5 minimum, 16:9 greatest
• Video Duration: 60 seconds greatest
• Video Captions: discretionary
• Image Ratio: 4:5 least, 16:9 most extreme
• Text length: 125 characters most extreme prescribed
• Hashtag Number: 30 most extreme (*you can add additional in the remarks)

Upheld Objectives
• Reach
• Traffic
• Conversions
• Lead Generation
• Brand Awareness
• Post Engagement
• Store Visits

Upheld Call-to-Action Buttons

• Apply Now

• Book Now

• Call Now

• Contact Us

• Download

#4. Video Story Ads

This is another incredible spot to run video ads since stories are the place clients frequently hope to see recordings, so the "selling" some portion of advertising doesn't feel as constrained. The suggested video specs for uploading are equivalent to a record above, and here are some additional subtleties to remember!

Specialized Requirements

• Video Resolution: 1080 x 1920 pixels (at any rate)

• Maximum record size: 4GB

• Video Ratio: 9:16 greatest

• Video Duration: 15 seconds greatest

• Video Captions: not accessible

Bolstered Objectives

• Reach

• Traffic

- Conversions
- Lead Generation
- App Installs

Upheld Call-to-Action Buttons
- Apply Now
- Book Now
- Call Now
- Contact Us
- Download

#5. Merry go round Feed Ads

Next, we have merry go round feed ads. How fun are these! This arrangement enables you to demonstrate a progression of scrollable pictures as opposed to only one single picture.

This ad type extraordinary for extremely visual brands, similar to those in the nourishment business, furniture vendors, dress alternatives, get-away goals, vehicle vendors, and so on. Yet, they're not just for "attractive" businesses; they can likewise work to adapt your brand or hotshot your way of life by demonstrating the individuals behind your product or money related organization.

The carousel configuration enables you to browse up to 10 pictures inside a solitary ad, each with its very own connection. Video is likewise a possibility for these ads.

Specialized Requirements
• File type: jpg or png
• Maximum record size: 30MB
• Minimum Image Width: 600 pixels
• Image Ratio: 4:5 least, 16:9 greatest
• Text length: 2,200 greatest (*although Instagram prescribes remaining underneath 90 for ideal conveyance)
• Video Duration: 60 seconds most extreme
• Hashtag Number: 30 most extreme (*you can add additional in the remarks)

Bolstered Objectives
• Reach
• Traffic
• Conversions
• Brand Awareness
• Lead Generation
• Product Catalog Sales

Bolstered Call-to-Action Buttons
• Apply Now
• Book Now

- Contact Us
- Call Now
- Download

#6. Canvas Story Ads

What's more, last, however, certainly not least, we have the most up to date addition to the ad design family, Canvas ads. Their ads are genuinely vivid, enabling advertising to make a 360 VR experience inside their story. They're just upheld using cell phones, and very adaptable for the advertiser, yet you will require some specialized cleaves. These ads work with the picture, video, and merry go round. Look at this manual to get familiar with Canvas ads.

Specialized Requirements
- Minimum Image Width: 400 pixels
- Minimum Image Height: 150 pixels

Bolstered Objectives
- Reach
- Brand Awareness
- Traffic
- Conversions
- Lead Generation
- Post Engagement
- Video Views

• Store Visits

Bolstered Call-to-Action Buttons
• Apply Now
• Book Now
• Contact Us

5 Instagram Advertising Best Practices

Since you have the essential standards of Instagram advertising down, the time has come to get the most elevated ROI conceivable by following these prescribed procedures to make extraordinary Instagram ads.

#1. Impart Each Ad with Personality

Regardless of whether it be an entertaining goof, an enthusiastic video, or only a captivating picture is flaunting your way of life; if your Instagram post doesn't feel refined, at that point, you won't arrive at your commitment potential.

Individuals use Instagram to be engaged, diverted, or astonished. Regardless of whether it's while you're on the train to work or when you are loosening up in the wake of a monotonous day of work, nobody is hoping to bounce on Instagram to see an exhausting corporate advertisement. This is the reason engaging feelings are consistently the best approach. Look at this fun post from Shape Magazine as an ideal model.

#2. Ensure Your Ad Is Contextually Relevant

What works with one social media stage won't work with another. For example, your business likely wouldn't advance a similar substance through LinkedIn as they would through Twitter, as the audience is ordinarily in an alternate perspective.

The equivalent goes for Instagram. Put yourself in your objective purchaser's shoes and know about where they are. Do you think your lead is probably going to download and read your 40-page digital book? Likely not. Guarantee your ads don't feel excessively sales-driven because this isn't normally what Instagram is utilized for.

#3. Use Hashtags...

In any case, don't simply hashtag #food or #love. Get progressively innovative, and do some client research to see which hashtags are bound to be scanned for by your audience. Likewise, don't try too hard with hashtags. This can make your post look somewhat messy and edgy.

The perfect number? TrackMaven investigated 65,000 posts and found that nine hashtags are the perfect number for the most elevated post commitment. They likewise found that more drawn out hashtags regularly perform better.

#4. Run a Contest

Advancing a challenge or giveaway is by a long shot, one of the best approaches to arrive at your objectives quicker with Instagram advertising. Why? Since individuals love rivalry and free stuff! What better approach to get your audience excited for your brand?

#5. Post at Optimal Hours

I talked somewhat about this during the planning venture of Instagram ad-set up; however, utilizing the ad-plan include (which is just accessible with lifetime planning) is an extraordinary method to get individuals at the opportune time.

If you realize your audience well, this shouldn't be too difficult even to consider determining, however, experimentation can likewise work here. Consider your vertical. In case you're an online retailer, when do individuals regularly search for attire on the web? Or on the other hand, in case you're a vehicle vendor, what days of the week do you see the most astounding spike in site traffic? Posing these inquiries is a decent spot to begin.

Right away, put forward, and advertise on Instagram! This is one stage you ought not to disregard, and this guide ought to give you enough assets to move toward becoming insta-popular.

CHAPTER SIX

THE POTENTIAL OF YOUTUBE ADVERTISING - MORE FOLLOWERS AND HOW TO MONETIZE THE VIEWS

Around the world, five billion YouTube recordings are observed each day. YouTube is as prevalent as ever, with clients spending a normal of 40 minutes a solitary YouTube session. Following this computerized move, the following thing to learn is the way to profit on YouTube. All you need is video altering programming and exactly a PC, and you can begin on YouTube.

The most effective method to MAKE MONEY ON YOUTUBE

While it is conceivable to make noteworthy pay from YouTube as a substance maker, it isn't the simplest either. Four hundred hours of video upload to YouTube every moment over the world. Numbers don't lie. In this way, the challenge is truly extraordinary, and profiting on the web turns out to be all the more testing. Here are some ground-breaking systems you can utilize to kick off your gaining potential from YouTube.

1. BEING A YOUTUBE PARTNER AND THEN EARN FROM ADS

For some YouTubers, ads structure the basic income stream. This is resulting in turning into a YouTube Partner. As a YouTube accomplice, you profit in various ways. You can profit from ads on your recordings, channel enrollments, in addition to Super Chat highlights. These talks give watchers on a live visit expanded perceivability from the streamer by boosting their remarks.

Be that as it may, there are some guidelines to see before turning into a confirmed YouTube Partner just as certain essentials expected to begin. Beside religiously adhering to YouTube's ad manages, you more likely than not had the option to gather at least 4,000 video watch hours on your channel and 1,000 supporters inside the most recent a year.

There is no solid course of events or configuration to get these essential hours. You can have about100 hours each on 40 recordings, and there you are. At that point, if you are the viral maestro, you can get the 4,000 hours or 24,000 full sees on one video. For instance, the well-known global hit Gangnam Style took a suffering five months to accomplish 1 billion perspectives. Be that as it may, Despacito was less patient racing to 1 billion perspectives in scarcely 97 days.

In this manner, it tends to be that unconstrained – or lethargic, contingent upon the charm of your substance and your system. Presently, after effectively accomplishing the 4,000 hour-limit and winning your place as a YouTube accomplice, we would now be able to discuss the cash.

In your Video Manager, a green "$" by your recordings demonstrates that you would now be able to take advantage of YouTube adaptation. Nonetheless, you may not generally have the option to put together your income age concerning YouTube from advertising alone. There are different roads by which you can merge your gaining potential on YouTube.

Our next adaptation outlet is utilizing member joins.

2. YOUTUBE MONETIZATION: USE AFFILIATE LINKS ON YOUTUBE

Advancing member connections can be a huge acquiring open door for direct that idea top to bottom instructional exercises just as sagacious product surveys. For instance, if you suggest a product and a client visits your connection to purchase, you'll start procuring commissions. You can put these connections in an initial couple of lines of your portrayal and talk about your connection in your video content.

Posting subsidiary connections on YouTube shares a run of the mill similarity to advancing member interfaces on your blog. Hence, you shouldn't pour partner connects all over your YouTube content only for the money related advantage. Remember that watchers will possibly pursue these connections when they trust you are a confided in an asset.

To construct trust with your audience, help your partners take care of solid issues. Make recordings that offer arrangements that you have recently achieved yourself. There are a lot of partner programs for you to join. You can join a wide range of projects in a single spot on a prominent offshoot system like Shareasale, CJ, or Impact.

3. Profit ON YOUTUBE WITH FUNDING FROM YOUR FANS

If you've fabricated an after of steadfast fans, urging them to crowdfund your channel can enable you to subsidize your new recordings and benefit. A stage like Patreon acquaints more consistency with the way toward getting paid for your substance. For as meager as a dollar, your fans can make memberships to their preferred channels, notwithstanding returning home with some selective prizes from their preferred substance makers. Tipi is another administration that enables you to appreciate a combo of repeating and one-time gifts.

For-benefit and charitable channels the same are utilizing this fan-subsidizing with their audience to keep their video tasks running easily. As long your substance is intriguing, engaging, or offering some incentive, you would be stunned at how your watchers open the conduits of liberality.

4. Ace YOUR YOUTUBE SEO

For YouTubers who have not constructed a noteworthy after yet, you need to step up your game and augment YouTube SEO in 2019.

To do that, perform watchword research like you typically would – in any case, think somewhat better dependent on what individuals are scanning for on YouTube. Next, ensure you are utilizing high-esteem catchphrases in your video title, portrayal, and video labels.

Once propelled, you can check your YouTube "Traffic Source: YouTube search" report to get a thought of what individuals are scanning for when they discover your recordings. When all is said in done, Google gives video results to watchwords on the most proficient method to, surveys, instructional exercises, and amusing video terms.

There are additionally five key YouTube SEO positioning variables to consider:
• Number of remarks
• Subscribes in the wake of viewing a video
• Thumbs up/disapproval proportion
• Video length
• Click-through-rate on the YouTube list items

5. Benefit as much as possible from YOUR YOUTUBE MARKETING FUNNEL

Advance your YouTube channel for sales. Pick your specialty, become a YouTube accomplice, and start arranging your marketing pipe.

YouTube is one approach to spread your message. However, you can make more cash by utilizing YouTube as one with a blog. That way, you're gathering more email addresses and, in the long run, offering products to your fan base.

For instance, if you compose a blog entry about an offshoot product, you're prescribing, repurpose that content, and make a YouTube video installed in the post. At that point, send clients from YouTube back to your blog, and the offshoot connects to both win commissions and fabricate blog readers.

6. BECOME AN AMAZON INFLUENCER

The Amazon influencer program is winding up progressively well known. This influencer program enables you to boost your YouTube (social media, when all is said in done) nearness to profit through Amazon proposals.

In the wake of joining the program, you can audit and prescribe products and direct your watchers to Amazon to buy using associate connections. At the point when your watchers navigate and make Amazon buy, you get your cut of the commissions – ordinarily 8-10%.

Be that as it may, this program isn't available to everybody: social media supporter check and different measurements direct endorsement chances.

7. Investigate EXTRA GAINS FROM YOUTUBE RED SUBSCRIBERS

Youtube Red enables clients to pay $9.99 for without ad YouTube sees. Indeed, even without ads, content makers can, in any case, create cash and make 55% of income, in light of view time. There are blended audits on whether YouTube Red increments or diminishes CPM rates.

With YouTube Red, your watch time matters, so check your YouTube Analytics to see your measurements like watch time and video commitment.

The amount MONEY CAN YOU MAKE ON YOUTUBE?

The short answer: it depends.

By utilizing ad adaptation, partner connections, and selling supported positions in your recordings, you can augment your income potential. On YouTube, you can profit from ads on a CPM, CPV, and CPC premise. With expense per impression (CPM), a commonplace YouTuber makes $7.60 per 1,000 perspectives. In any case, by Google's approach, makers get 55% of income accumulated from advertisements while Google keeps 45%.

Presently if you are utilizing associate marketing as a channel proprietor, advertisers dispense installment with various models

– ordinarily cost per deal or cost per lead. Here, your profit legitimately connects with the number of transformations and deal commissions you get from advertisers.

You can likewise sell supported product positions in your recordings. Here YouTubers make cash by undercutting either notices or increasingly expanded product suggestions on brands searching for presentation. If you have had the option to fabricate a quantifiable after on your channel, brands will pay you. This cost may run from $20 to $50 for every thousand perspectives they jump on your channel. So if, for instance, their video on your channel hits a million perspectives, you can be moving to manage an account with somewhere in the range of $20,000 to $50,000. This technique is a superior method to adopt when you aren't creating a huge number of perspectives.

The amount MONEY DO YOUTUBERS MAKE?
For a huge number of YouTubers, this answer might be nothing, or scarcely anything. For mainstream YouTubers, this could be millions every year. It's getting harder to profit, as ad income can go from $0.35 to $5 per see, with the sheltered supposition that being $1 per 1,000 perspectives. The gainfulness of your channel is attached to both your perspectives and your specialty.

YouTubers in exceptionally saw specialties like bullet point articles, news, big name tattle, cosmetics and excellence, and mainstream bombs rapidly pull in income with a large number of perspectives. There are additionally YouTube income number crunchers to enable you to see the amount you can make dependent on video perspectives and commitment.

What sum do YouTubers procure for every 1000 perspectives?

By our past stipulation, YouTube content makers can, by and large, gain from $0.30 to $5 for every 1,000 perspectives their recordings accomplish. In certain situations, this can be higher, while it's sheltered to expect this number is a $1 CPM.

What number of perspectives do you have to money out on YouTube?

When you accomplish an equalization of $100, YouTube pays you.

Would you be able to gain from YouTube pay per supporter?

YouTubers channel proprietors don't get installment from YouTube per supporter.

Profiting on YouTube is conceivable. However, it's difficult to profit with just YouTube alone. It's imperative to have a stage that you possess like a blog and use YouTube as an auxiliary traffic stream. One advantage is that YouTube SEO isn't yet as aggressive as natural SEO. If you can get in now and start creating traffic, you'll be a superior spot by 2020 when the challenge is progressively furious.

CHAPTER SEVEN

USING TWITTER BY EXPLOITING ITS DIGITAL ADVERTISING AND LEARNING TO HAVE MANY FOLLOWERS

The immense number of Twitter adherents have gradually and steadily assumed control over the social media space. Twitter's month to month clients was brought to 330 Million up in 2017, giving basic, sans spam and advantageous highlights. Private ventures to enormous undertakings use Twitter to share data about their products and services routinely. Nonetheless, Twitter use for marketing and particularly for brand building, remains immensely under-misused. The absence of brisk outcomes doesn't give individuals a chance to see its full esteem.

Adapt rapidly to quit concentrating on inappropriate things. It is critical this is the prime purpose behind not getting results. In this manner, don't treat your business handle as another individual profile on any social media channel. More nearness on the stage doesn't ensure overwhelming traffic. A lethargic record brings no outcomes.

Continuously make a powerful association with the present and imminent clients, by following a very much considered system. This procedure brings about the brand presentation, just as brand building. Even though there are a few proposals accessible in open space, the accompanying systems demonstrate to be the best ones.

Technique #1: Engage your audience and start with structure traffic

Start with sending this technique. It works if you are taking this course just because or have been getting restricted traffic. Moreover, utilize this methodology if you have been investing energy remarking on each post with no achievement yet. Albeit the following posts is a notable system, we will examine this later.

Make an expert looking profile to pull in more Twitter devotees

This must be your initial step. Consequently, it causes it to discuss your business targets succinctly. From that point, add data about your business. Also, add a depiction to tell individuals what your identity is and what your motivation is. Regardless, don't leave the profile or foundation picture clear. With your profile portrayal, make a short, compelling outline of your business. Incorporate pertinent catchphrases (for Twitter search) and a backlink to your site. Keep in mind that an easygoing site guest's ability to focus is constrained, and they may be pulled in if the primary look is snappy.

Then again, inexactly done profile is a non-starter. The guest's advantage is murdered on the principal look itself. Consider social media advertising like informal advertising. As a result, it makes or demolishes traffic independent from anyone else.

Keep your profile refreshed consistently

An obsolete profile considers your demonstrable skill badly. A refreshed profile mirrors that you are alive in your business. Make a solid first stay of commitment. An expert looking profile does all that.

Concentrate on posts which have a huge followership

A portion of the perspectives in social media marketing can be drawn legitimately from the financial exchange. The securities exchange rides on notions. Individuals in securities exchanges purchase or sell stocks according to the market notion. Utilize this central perspective in social media marketing. Ride on the intensity of the post, which has a huge followership. The overwhelming stream will take you miles downstream. Improve your perceivability in a split second. You are significantly more liable to prevail by utilizing it. Some of the accessible instruments like BuzzSumo help in accomplishing this. Concentrate vigorously on posts that have already circulated the web. Successively, this is the subsequent stage. It has been distinguished as perhaps the simplest tip for expanding traffic. Pursue the same number of individuals in your industry as you can. Accordingly, this will empower you to interface with applicable individuals constructing a positive circle.

Do an online survey

There are different methods for improving traffic. Other than a few different ways exists for drawing in the present and planned clients. One of them is making on the web surveys. Planning a straightforward survey is a basic assignment. Like this, it very well may be administered on a wide assortment of subjects. Also, administering an online survey is, likewise, a simple assignment.

It doesn't take more than a tick for the clients to take an interest in a survey mirroring its comfort to take an interest. Decisively improve your traffic calculation by administering on the web surveys. Moreover, guarantee far superior commitment via consequently sending the consequences of such online surveys.

Paying others to tweet about you

Indeed, it is anything but a mystery. Paying another person to tweet about you is some other reliable technique. This could be a key move to draw in a more extensive client base, yet there are a couple of things you have to look at before having another person tweeting about you.

Use video

Pictures express more intense than words. Besides, recordings score better over pictures in imparting thoughts. This is valid on social media too. The traffic levels are higher in picture posts while it is significantly higher in posts containing recordings. Have a go at presenting pictures and recordings on upgrade traffic.

Use Call to Action

A Call to Action (CTA) is an absolute necessity need to move your audience from aloofness. It urges your audience to go about according to your objective. Normally, it resembles tossing a goad and trusting that the fish will swim to it. Include your audience by incorporating CTAs in your tweet. Subsequently, you will get more traffic. When a decent traffic level is accomplished, transform them into sales leads. Start posting social messages, which address your clients. Your audience should discover these messages enlightening, accommodating, and notwithstanding energizing.

As per Twitter, one of the best calls to activities is to request a download. Advanced Tweets in timetables that unequivocally request that individuals download joined by a connection increment URL clicks by a normal of 13%.

Technique #2: Automate your posts

How great it would be if an instrument existed to computerize our posts. An enormously prevalent stunt with Bloggers used to time their posts for most extreme perceivability. One of the top Blog-ace proposes distributing posts explicitly on Thursday evenings. This uses the accessibility of guests at the end of the week. This idea normally spills out of the universe of motion pictures. Motion pictures are discharged on a particular day of the week. Time your posts, much the same as a timing securities exchange, for greatest increases. There are instruments accessible on the Internet that can do this for you.

Additionally, you can naturally reuse your prominent posts. Use calculations from Web-Tools like Post organizer. The web robotization liberates you from boring work. Use this time in different exercises, notwithstanding when your business is getting permeability even while you rest.

Request retweets in your posts. While it might appear to be frantic for certain, individuals would be glad to retweet if you ask them if your substance is important. Essentially, you will acquire traffic by intensifying. Truth be told, as indicated by HubSpot's "Study of Social Media" investigation, utilizing the words "Please ReTweet" in your tweets will create 4x more retweets.

Finding steadfast clients is robotization in itself. Improve your client base by finding faithful clients. A returning client turns into your advertising operator and brings forth more traffic. The power which faithful clients can bring is tremendous. They are motors for creating traffic independent from anyone else.

Technique #3: Listen to your clients ALWAYS

Keep in mind that the essential target of a key marketing effort is to interface with your clients. Nowadays, clients anticipate that you should be on social media. They are taking this course more regularly for client assistance. A quick all day, everyday backing is the need of great importance. Twitter gives a stage to ongoing correspondence the two different ways. You are told when a client leaves a message. Therefore, the client gets a speedier answer. Endeavor to accumulate important data for settling on the best business choices. Attract from what your clients are stating. All client questions must be reacted rapidly. The client support fulfillment is intensely influenced by your reaction time.

Correspondence is a two-way process. Maintain your essential duty of shutting the correspondence circle. Believe yourself to be the prime supporter. Don't simply continue posting. Care for your client's input. Then again, don't trust that individuals will come search for you. Continuously give arriving at a shot to your audience. Ask updates to get lost. Make roads to keep your clients locked in. Businesses are putting resources into time to connect and get individuals with their clients normally have greater achievement.

While dealing with your adherents, make a point to examine the contender's supporters. You can see insights regarding how now and again they post. Pursue a portion of the individuals with the goal that they tail you back. Request an answer to your posts. This is one of the CTAs referenced before. The dominant part of your audience would be glad to answer, expanding your traffic.

A viable battle sets up you as an Industry Leader and Influencer.

Technique #4: Focus on Quality

Continuously do appropriate schoolwork before bouncing the temporary fad. In correlation, the outcomes between solid and steady and not readied is very apparent. A social media marketing

Mission Statement must be set up before wandering out in this zone. The Mission Statement gives the heading of a way to deal with a business. Consistently, this is the premise of value content on the social media stage.

Compose a Mission Statement referencing clear rules. Therefore, your unaware followings must end. Particularly applicable, don't permit the further posting of bearing less substance.

Another significant perspective is to pursue the most recent patterns. Convincingly, slanting up is on well-known themes. Both have a nearby connection with one another. Sensibly, ride with the stream to ride the prevalence surf. High inclining gives knowledge into your market needs. It provides you with guidance for your best course of action. Twitter Analytics gives you a chance to break down what number of perspectives and how much commitment your tweets are getting. When you take a gander at your investigation, you can perceive what your audience reacts to best (picture posts, Hashtags, Videos, Links, and so forth.). You have to always deal with structure your commitment levels. Examining and taking a shot at your Twitter account examination will enable you to do this.

The greater part of all isolates different client fragments. Plan your reactions coordinated at various client fragments. Accordingly, give each section a feeling of consideration.

Realizing your client requires steady exertion. You have to contribute your opportunity to comprehend their preferred. The venture made in realizing your client returns overwhelming benefits over time.

Despite any of the methodology recommendations above, it works just if you have a very much spread out the site as a back-up. You can't depend on 100 percent on the posts alone. Your handle must lead to your business site. Regardless of whether the site is of one page. This site must reflect what you should offer to your audience.

Social media marketing isn't a choice in this day and age. In any case, it should be a Mission explicit exertion by an association to best use the full intensity of the current stages. The amazing ascent in the quantity of Twitter adherents has made it significant. Indeed, even in this space, a portion of the standard procedures of client commitment continues as before as in others on the web or disconnected stages. The reason for a decent battle is a very much spread out site, regardless of whether a short one. Likely working up traffic doesn't naturally mean lead age even though improving your traffic is an initial step.

The clients will draw in if they are continually taken care of. You have to go to them with an administration mindset. A social media client care is all-day, everyday support. Adhere to this to be fruitful in this battle. Notwithstanding, it is the quality that makes you a Leader and Influencer. Quality is required in choosing your present on the isolation of your client reactions. I trust that the above rules will prove to be useful to dispatch and adequately work your social media marketing efforts.

Five Creative Ways to Use Multimedia to Engage More Twitter Followers

Social media speaks to the focal point of current marketing, yet that is old news already. Today, advertisers are delving further and more profound into social system examination to make the more successful strategy to approach target clients. The reason is straightforward – you can't draw in more Twitter supporters utilizing outdated marketing models.

Twitter is one of the quickest changing correspondence directs in that regard. This system is loaded with leads with enormous sales potential, yet you need to keep awake to date with marketing patterns to profit by such potential. In this article, we will demonstrate to you the main five multimedia strategies to connect more Twitter adherents.

Why Twitter?

A ton of brands considers Twitter the most significant channel for social media marketing. Various examinations uncover its impact, so we chose to show you a couple of details to demonstrate this point:

• Statista reports Twitter has 330 million month to month dynamic clients.

• And clients send 5.500 million tweets once a day, which makes 8,150 posts each second.

• Hootsuite says that 90% of individuals who pursue small and medium-sized businesses on Twitter intend to buy from that equivalent organization.

• Around 80% of Twitter use originates from cell phones.

• 30% of Americans who gain $75k or more use Twitter.

There is considerably more information that uncovers the significance of Twitter in contemporary marketing, even though that is sufficient to give you the early introduction. Continue reading and figure out how to get more Twitter adherents by utilizing multimedia content.

Using Multimedia Content for More Twitter Followers

The essential standard of Twitter correspondence is fairly basic: you get 280 characters to express a thought or offer intriguing news. Be that as it may, this kind of short correspondence can't acquire you enough adherents any longer. You need to go path past 280-character tweets to amplify the system's potential. Here are five multimedia strategies you should endeavor to accomplish your objective.

• Add pictures

As per the research done by Louise's Visual Social Media, tweets with photographs get 150% more re-tweets than Twitter posts without pictures. In this way, you have to keep your Twitter exercises picture wealthy to make them additionally engaging and to appeal to a normal buyer.

Photographs don't just "talk a thousand words" yet, also serve to acquaint devotees with ongoing impetuses. For example, you could utilize pictures to report the present rebate advancement or dispatch a challenge with honors for the most inventive supporters. The model underneath shows how even advanced posts with pictures get more commitment than advanced posts without pictures.

Other than that, pictures can drive a considerable measure of traffic to your point of arrival, in this manner expanding the number of leads and supporters too. You should not be dismayed with too much content alongside photographs. However, you do require great hashtags to pursue the visual substance.

Another fascinating choice to acquire Twitter supporters is to plan infographics. Scripted reports that scan for infographics has expanded by over 800% in only two years, recommending that it has tremendous potential on Twitter also. Such multimedia substance is moderately simple to make, yet it is stuffed with a wide range of valuable information. Simply keep it significant to the intended interest group, and you'll get yourself more Twitter supporters than previously.

• Audio digital broadcasts

You may have heard that "video executed the radio star." Sound shows truly looked like a vanishing sort of substance a couple of years back. However, things changed with the ascent of the Internet. Today, over 40% of individuals in the US tune in to web recordings, as indicated by Convince and Convert.

It's an ideal alternative for many suburbanites and office laborers who can tune in to the sound substance out of sight. The best thing about it is that you can distribute webcasts on Twitter. You simply need a strong bit of hardware and a decent specialty related theme to make this sort of multimedia content.

Concerning, you should purchase an amplifier, PC with a sound card, and an advanced sound recorder. Other than that, you likewise need sound altering programming (which you can discover online for nothing). Attempt to record a few scenes before you start posting on Twitter because your audience needs to tune in to digital broadcasts all the time.

Remember that digital recordings take after a genuine exchange, so you needn't bother with an exacting arrangement. All you need is a fascinating point, and a couple of industry specialists and the discussion will take a characteristic stream effectively.

• Videos are required

Twitter clients don't care for reading excessively, thus the 280-character limit. They need to concentrate just on the subject fundamentals, so there is no better method to give them what they need and add more Twitter devotees than posting a short video. This sort of substance is multiple times bound to get shared by clients contrasted with the standard content kind of tweet. These are the three essential motivations to make video content:

• Product instructional exercises:

Hubspot reports that 4x the same number of buyers would want to watch a video about a product than to read about it. Instructional exercises are the most straightforward approach to clarify thing details and advance your business.

• Entertain: People don't need you to tweet 100% special substance constantly. As the obvious actuality, they generally request amusement, and your responsibility is to give it as video cuts.

• **Tell a story:** Storytelling video is a helpful strategy to get Twitter supporters familiar with the qualities that your brand or association speaks to.

Much the same as digital recordings, video content additionally requires great gear, yet you should devote more opportunity to composing a screenplay. If you go live, you can extemporize a little yet at the same time remain interesting or offer breaking news. In any case, if you tweet pre-recorded video, you need to keep it profoundly expert and quality.

Luckily, the video offers you a lot of structures to engage the current supporters and pull in new ones. You can shoot video webcasts, video blogs, go live or off-camera of your organization, and so forth. It doesn't make a difference if your video is for instructive or educational purposes, including these media on your tweets is a surefire approach to reel in new devotees. Also, if you don't have time or information on how to do it, procure the group of experts to do it for you, and you'll see the devotee check is expanding.

• **Add a Twitter offer catch to your blog**
As much as sound and video substance is flooding the Internet over the most recent couple of years, there are as yet a large number of clients who lean toward reading a decent blog entry. If

you join content with different sorts of substances, your blog will bring you numerous new adherents.

For example, an Impact study uncovered that blog articles with pictures get 94% more perspectives. You should utilize this reality and compose top-notch posts upheld by photographs, infographics, or YouTube recordings. Adding a Twitter catch to the presents permits readers to offer your substance with an online network, expanding the general brand mindfulness.

Since, by far, most of the sites are fueled by WordPress, we prescribe you download the Social Share Buttons module. It's an apparatus that empowers you to add the Twitter catch to your blog without wasting time with programming and code changes. See above for a model or simply take a gander at the top and base of this blog entry.

• **Mind the substance quality**
The last tip we have for increasing more Twitter supporters is coherent, however vital, so we need to give it more space here. You need to focus on substance quality, which means you need to proofread everything to ensure your duplicate is impeccable.

Cunning advertisers realize that it's ideal for giving experts and online collaborators a chance to help you in that regard, so we present you a few arrangements:

LYFE Marketing: The office offers substance marketing services that will drive more clients to your site from your primary rivals just as increment your change rate in record time.

Superior Papers: Expert essayists and editors at Superior Papers can proofread your substance as well as make it for you if you come up short on thoughts or would prefer not to do it without anyone's help.

Hemingway App: This apparatus expels blunders from your content, yet its basic role is to distinguish complex expressions and thickly pressed sentences and recommend substitutions.

Grammarly: Grammarly is the most prevalent proofreading application. The essential variant is for nothing out of pocket, and it will assist you with finding and take out all errors. If you want to improve your style of composing, pay for the exceptional form, and you'll have the option to think of a vastly improved substance.

In light of research, half of unfollows happen when a record distributes an excessive number of tweets inside a brief timeframe range. Regardless of how intriguing your tweets might be for you, if you flood your supporters' courses of events, at that point, they will hit that "unfollow" catch.

Twitter is one of the biggest and most productive social media systems marketing-wise. Most organizations use it to develop the number of adherents and produce significant leads for their brands. Notwithstanding, you can't do it just by posting 280-character tweets.

CHAPTER EIGHT

MAKING THE MOST OF LINKEDIN POTENTIAL TO MANAGE YOUR PROFESSIONAL IDENTITY

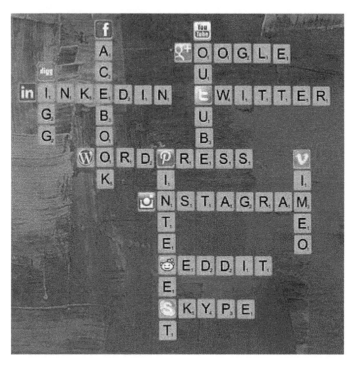

LinkedIn is the world's biggest expert systems administration stage. It's likewise one of the most compelling social media systems, with more than 575 million individuals in 2018. That is a lot of potential contacts!

Individuals utilize the site to stay in contact with business partners, customers, and collaborators. Be that as it may, it can accomplish such a great deal more – support your profile, assemble familiarity with your brand, and help you to enroll the perfect individuals, for instance.

We will take a gander at nine different ways to utilize your LinkedIn to represent individual, proficient, and hierarchical achievement.

Ways to Get the Best From LinkedIn

1. Complete Your LinkedIn Profile

Your profile can be ground-breaking some portion of your brand. All enlisted LinkedIn clients will have the option to see it (except if you set it to private mode). You can likewise have an open profile that can be found by outer web crawlers so that even individuals who are not enlisted with LinkedIn can see it.

LinkedIn's inside inquiry calculation just discovers profiles that position as "complete," and these can get over 20 fold the number of perspectives as inadequate profiles. It's significant, subsequently, to finish yours. Here are the fundamental things to recollect:

• Add a decent quality photograph of yourself, ideally one taken by an expert picture taker. Look brilliant, grin, and don't have any diversions in the shot.

• Make your profile shimmer by adding a foundation picture (in some cases called a "standard" or "spread" picture) that mirrors your character and your calling.

• Mention your industry and area in your headline.

• Include a compact rundown of what your identity is, your main thing, and what you bring to the table. You have about 1,800 characters to play with. However, you don't need to utilize them all. You can likewise connect to, or upload, six instances of your work to make your profile shimmer.

• Add your present position and portray what it includes. Be explicit. Try not to say, for instance, that you're an "incredible communicator" – regardless of whether you are one! Instead, give subtleties of your relational abilities, and instances of how you've utilized them. Once more, you have 2,000 characters.

• Add your past work history, training subtleties, and at any rate, four aptitudes or subject matters.

As you add more subtleties to your profile, you can keep tabs on your development from "Novice" to "Intermediate" to "Elite player" utilizing the Profile Strength bar.

2. Contact and Connect With Other LinkedIn Users

LinkedIn empowers you to coordinate with individuals and expert associations in your industry. This is an extraordinary method to keep awake to date with the most recent advancements and to impart data to others in your field.

You can welcome anybody to the interface (and acknowledge their solicitations to associate with you). However, they should have their LinkedIn record to utilize the site.

LinkedIn spares the associations that you make to a rundown called My Network. When you make another association, you get entrance not exclusively to that individual's profile, however to their freely accessible associations, as well. These become your "second-degree associations." This opens up significantly all the more systems administration openings, as you would then be able to welcome them to interface straightforwardly with you.

You can likewise present any two LinkedIn associations who haven't yet associated with each other, however, who may profit by doing as such.

The number of associations that you have influenced your inquiry positioning on LinkedIn. It's a smart thought to go for in any event 50 "first-degree" associations.

3. Start Talking!

When you've made your associations on LinkedIn, the Messaging office enables you to have ongoing discussions with them. The Active Status highlight reveals to you which of your associations are on the web – pay special mind to the green speck alongside their profile pictures.

Also, the Smart Replies work – short, naturally created, logical reactions (for example, "What time?" and "Incredible, much appreciated!") – can keep your discussions snappy and productive.

If you have a Premium record, you can likewise utilize InMail. This enables you to send private messages to any LinkedIn part with no earlier presentation or additional contact data.

4. Give and Receive Recommendations and Endorsements

Your associations can state "suggestions" for your profile, and offer "supports" of your abilities, and you can do likewise consequently.

Suggestions are close to home tributes that stress your expert capacities. Expect to gather a bunch of these (somewhere in the range of five and 10 is a decent "dependable guideline") by asking individuals you've worked with to think of one for you.

Request that they feature the specific properties or accomplishments that have intrigued them, as opposed to making general remarks, for example, "Bella was amusing to work with."

Supports are basic warnings affirming that you have specific expertise. They may come up short on the effect of custom-composed suggestions. Yet, if an association underwrites you for your leadership abilities, for instance, it can assist you with standing out from the group.

5. Use LinkedIn Groups

All LinkedIn individuals can set up or join gatherings to examine thoughts and offer industry news. This can be an incredible method to build up your expert system.

You can utilize the pursuit bar at the highest point of your profile page to search for intriguing gatherings to join, or you can discover new bunches using the ones you've already joined. When you're a gathering part, you're ready to join bunch discussions, pose inquiries, and send messages to different individuals.

LinkedIn gatherings can be a profitable wellspring of data, thoughts, and backing. Offer your insight with individuals in your gatherings, and they'll likely react in kind.

LinkedIn cautions against self-advancement in gatherings. Demonstrating your skill is great; unwarranted stopping of your organization's products isn't. You can be blocked or expelled from a gathering if you defy its norms or code of etiquette.

6. Make Engaging Content Especially for LinkedIn

Similarly, likewise, with other social systems, you can post straightforward content updates, pictures, and connections to different locales, and you can share posts from different clients. In any case, ensure that your post is valuable, instructive, and pertinent to your expert associations. Furthermore, you might need to catch up on your composition abilities!

You can likewise record or upload videos legitimately to LinkedIn from your gadget. This enables you to share your bits of knowledge and encounters or to help your association's brand character. Utilize the implicit channels and "stickers" to light up your video, and add inscriptions for individuals who watch with the sound off.

LinkedIn additionally enables you to distribute full articles, using its Publishing Platform. The articles that you compose show up on your profile. They can be shared by different clients, and may likewise show up in web search tool results. However, you hold the rights to any unique substance that you distribute. This is an extraordinary method to grandstand your industry mastery.

SlideShare is another alternative for conveying brilliant substance. It's implanted into LinkedIn and enables you to post introductions and infographics.

Adding hashtags to your posts can assist your substance in reaching more clients. Type a hashtag into the pursuit bar to discover what number of individuals tail it, and to see the sort of substance that interests them.

7. Discover New Hires – and New Opportunities

As indicated by LinkedIn's figures, 20,000 businesses in the U.S. are utilizing the site to select new staff. The administration enables you to look for individuals who have the particular aptitudes and experience that you need in your group. It can even supplant traditional enlistment advertising altogether, contingent upon your industry and the position that you have to fill.

The Advanced Search office empowers you to look by a wide range of criteria: area, organization, previous organizations, industry, language, philanthropic interests, schools, and degrees of association.

LinkedIn's paid Recruiter plans give you many more alternatives and can assist you with sourcing, organize, contact, and deal with your rundown of competitors. Pipeline Builder enables you to contact potential enrolls naturally when they visit LinkedIn, and the Find Nearby office targets neighborhood contacts.

You can utilize LinkedIn to search for employment, as well. Just as perusing the activity advertisements, numerous individuals use it as an examination instrument. Assume that you have two employment bids on the table, for instance. You can utilize LinkedIn to become familiar with your potential new managers and collaborators and to figure out the associations' corporate societies.

A Premium Career record enables you to scan significantly more effectively for openings for work that match your inclinations and range of abilities and to discover who has taken a gander at your profile over the most recent 90 days.

8. Lift Your Organization's Profile

LinkedIn can build the perceivability of your business or network. Do it right, and you can make significant enthusiastic associations with your potential clients and representatives.

Consider setting up an organization's LinkedIn page, so buyers, customers, providers, and new contracts can explore your organization. Your page administrator can likewise utilize LinkedIn examination to get an image of the individuals who visit the page. This can assist you in targeting your substance all the more adequately.

LinkedIn can profit your association in different ways, as well. You can utilize the site to investigate your opposition, potential accomplices, and new providers, for instance. Furthermore, the paid record, Sales Navigator, additionally enables you to contact likely prospects and to monitor key staff changes in your industry.

You can incorporate LinkedIn with different stages and services – your LinkedIn updates can be naturally presented on Twitter, for example. Along these lines, think about how your association's utilization of LinkedIn lines up with its general social media technique.

9. Watch Professional Etiquette on LinkedIn

Accomplishment on LinkedIn relies upon creating and keeping up a decent notoriety. This implies it's essential to seem proficient consistently. In this way, abstain from posting the sort of close to home material that you may put on Facebook. What's more, abstain from spreading bits of gossip or tattle – you never know who'll read them.

Be cautious when you request, or make, a presentation, and do so just if you accept that the two gatherings can profit. Continuously be aware of what you state about your association.

Lastly, recollect that trustworthiness is simply the best approach – abstain from overselling and don't weave the realities when you examine your accomplishments!

Key Points

LinkedIn is the world's biggest expert systems administration site. You can utilize it to assemble associations in your industry and to keep in contact with partners, over a significant period. It's a priceless instrument for quests for new employment and enrollment, and an extraordinary method to keep awake to date with industry news, upgrade your expert notoriety, and increment the perceivability of your brand.

To get the best from LinkedIn, utilize the accompanying procedures:
1. Complete your profile.
2. Contact and interface.
3. Start talking.
4. Give and get suggestions and supports.
5. Use LinkedIn Groups.
6. Produce connecting with substance.
7. Find new enlist – and new chances.

8. Boost your association's profile.

9. Observe expert manners.

Instructions to Use LinkedIn Effectively

LinkedIn is the top online webpage for expert, social, and professional organizing. The website capacities as an online catalog of individual experts and associations, and encourages the procedure of expert systems administration without leaving your office.

Starting in late 2018, LinkedIn had the greater part a billion individuals over 200 nations, including officials from the majority of the Fortune 500 organizations.

While people use LinkedIn for expert systems administration, associating, and occupation looking, organizations use it for enrolling and for sharing organization data with forthcoming workers. It's a fabulous site for occupation looking, too. You can figure out how to utilize LinkedIn viably and comprehend the ideal approach to utilize LinkedIn's assets for occupation chasing and assembling your profession.

Beneath you will locate some speedy tips on the best way to utilize LinkedIn successfully, alongside connections to the additional top to bottom articles on every theme to enable you to capitalize on every one of the assets and apparatuses LinkedIn brings to the table.

Beginning

You'll see it snappy and simple to begin utilizing LinkedIn. Start by pursuing a record, make your online profile, and add a profile photograph. The site offers two fundamental levels of participation: Basic and Premium. The Premium level has four subcategories: Premium Career, Sales Navigator, Recruiter Lite, Premium Business, and LinkedIn Learning, each with its own expense.

The Basic record offers highlights, for example, informing, profile creation, and approaches to apply to work postings. In contrast, the Premium records have added highlights and assets to grow your online nearness and let you get increasingly out of the administration.

When you sign in, you can begin utilizing LinkedIn to associate, system, and the quest for employment.

Why Use LinkedIn?

LinkedIn extends to helpful assets for employment opportunity searchers, giving data, going about as an announcement to feature your one of a kind incentive, and making your data open for selection representatives who might search for what you bring to the table.

Sign-Up on LinkedIn

Ready to begin? It's straightforward. Explore to LinkedIn.com, enter your first and last name and email address in the demonstrated region, and make a secret phrase.

Pick a Professional Photo

You'll need to establish a decent first connection on any individual who perspectives your profile, and a major piece of that is the image you pick. You ought to settle on an expert looking photograph as opposed to an easygoing shot. You don't need to dish out boatloads of money for a `headshot, yet care ought to be taken when picking the correct garments, foundation, lighting, and so on. For your LinkedIn profile picture.

Compose a Good Profile Summary

Your LinkedIn profile outline is an opportunity to put your best foot forward, particularly if you are keen on new position openings. LinkedIn has a 2,000-character limit for this area, and you need to capitalize on it. The organization prescribes composing three to five short sections and leaving a lot of blank areas, so readers' eyes don't coat over when they arrive on your page. The organization additionally proposes utilizing short, tight sentences, maintaining a strategic distance from language, writing in the primary individual, and utilizing watchwords.

Try not to be hesitant to infuse a portion of your character into your profile rundown to make it significant, yet avoid whatever appears to be excessively amateurish or could be disputable. At last, ensure you proofread this area cautiously, as you would an introductory letter for an employment form. Grammatical errors and messy composition will send an inappropriate sign.

Improve and Tweak Your Profile
In addition to a rundown, your LinkedIn profile can contain your work involvement, training, aptitudes, and supports and proposals from others in your system. Your profile causes you to get found on LinkedIn because it contains accessible watchwords in the data you post about yourself.

Your profile profits by including important catchphrases that web crawlers and contracting directors search for. Counting these trendy expressions in your synopsis, interests, previous occupation titles, and aptitudes can enable you to stick out.

Solicitation LinkedIn Recommendations
Proposals are another extraordinary method to make your LinkedIn profile stick out. Positive suggestions composed by past bosses, customers, or partners can demonstrate a procuring

supervisor what sort of worker you are and what your qualities are. You can demand suggestions from your LinkedIn associations.

Use LinkedIn Endorsements

Supports are a speedy and simple route for your expert contacts to help show different clients where your skill lies.

Incorporate Your LinkedIn Profile Address on Your Resume

Counting your LinkedIn URL on your resume makes it simple for planned bosses to visit LinkedIn to get familiar with you and your abilities and capabilities. LinkedIn will allow you a URL, except if you make a custom one. To make a custom URL, click the "Me" symbol at the highest point of your LinkedIn landing page and select "View profile" starting from the drop menu. Then, click "Alter open profile and URL at the right-hand side of the page." Try utilizing your first and last name. If that is taken, attempt a center introductory or your full center name.

Simply ensure that your profile is state-of-the-art before including a connection to it on your resume.

Sending Messages and Invitations

When you pursue LinkedIn and make a profile, you can begin to construct a system of contacts, incorporating individuals with whom you interface on an expert premise, an instructive premise, or dependent on another regular intrigue. Send contact solicitations to individuals who meet at least one of these goals. When you message individuals inside or outside of your system, keep it proficient. You'll expand your reaction rate if you keep your messages on point.

How Big Should Your Network Be?

What number of individuals do you need in your LinkedIn system to make it a successful apparatus for employment looking and professional organizing? The short answer is, it depends. The correct associations could easily compare to the genuine number of associations you have. In a perfect world, you need associations that are applicable to your profession, which can conceivably lead you to an opening for work or can give significant advice.

Going after Positions on LinkedIn

Occupation searchers can scan and go after positions straightforwardly on LinkedIn. You can view and also contact your LinkedIn associations, which might have the option to allude you for work. Directed quests, for example, the advanced individuals or organization discoverers can hone your extension and help you find precisely what you are searching for. You can channel the advanced pursuit by area, industry, graduated class status, or the number of representatives to get increasingly succinct, explicit list items.

Looking through Company Profiles

LinkedIn organization profiles are a decent method to discover more data on organizations where you have an intrigue. You'll have the option to check whether you have any associations at the organization, new procures, advancements, employments posted, related organizations, and friends measurements.

More Tips for Using LinkedIn

Subsequent to reading this article and the related connections, ideally, you have a strong handle on the best way to utilize LinkedIn viably. The following are a couple of more tips for utilizing the site.

Stay up with the latest

The more complete your LinkedIn profile is, the better your odds to be found and reached. Utilize your LinkedIn profile like a resume and give planned bosses point by point data on your aptitudes and experience. Also, make sure to modify your profile's novel URL to make it simpler to discover and expand its perceivability.

Procedures to Update Your LinkedIn Profile When You're Unemployed

Refreshing your LinkedIn profile to mirror that you're jobless can make an issue. Despite the fact that you may be jobless, you should, in any case, present yourself in a positive light to forthcoming bosses and to systems administration contacts.

Utilizing the LinkedIn Mobile App

The LinkedIn Mobile App highlights incorporate looking and survey profiles, welcoming new associations, getting to LinkedIn answers, and significant system refreshes. You can send and get messages, look into client or organization profiles, and even upload your resume to employment opportunities all in the palm of your hand. Utilize the application to keep your pursuit of employment pushing ahead when you're on the road.

Abstain from Being Scammed

LinkedIn has indistinguishable difficulties from different destinations, so watch out for tricksters.

CONCLUSION

Digital marketing is the utilization of media stages and sites to advance a product or administration. Despite the fact that the terms e-marketing and advanced marketing are as yet overwhelming in academia, social media marketing is ending up progressively prevalent for the two experts and specialists. Most social media stages have worked in information examination instruments, which empower organizations to follow the advancement, achievement, and commitment of ad battles. Organizations address a scope of partners through Digital marketing, including present and potential clients, current and potential workers, writers, bloggers, and the overall population. On a key level, social media marketing incorporates the administration of a marketing effort, administration, setting the degree (for example, increasingly dynamic or inactive use), and the foundation of a company's ideal Digital marketing "culture" and "tone."

When utilizing digital marketing, firms can enable clients and Internet clients to post client created content (e.g., online remarks, product audits, and so forth.), otherwise called "earned media," as opposed to utilizing advertiser arranged advertising duplicate. Truth be told, there's currently an expected 2.62 billion dynamic clients of social stages, and rising each day. Hell, even hounds presently have their very own social media accounts.

In any case, it's implied that social media has altogether more potential than only filling in as a gathering for sharing selfies and images. That potential is something that has been perceived by almost every organization as a chance to help develop their business - numerous brands even feel 'undetectable' without some kind of social media nearness. Here and there, this is valid - social media can be utilized as a ground-breaking marketing instrument by businesses in almost every sort of industry. In any case, while social is a significant marketing instrument, the greatest misstep that most businesses try with their social media endeavors is that they center a lot on vanity measurements.

What number of supporters do you have? What number of preferences or offers do you get?

Most importantly, these sorts of measurements don't really make a difference past the shallow allure, all things considered, as a business, what is important is your real main concern. It doesn't make a difference if you have 100k supporters if that audience never changes over into clients in any capacity. So how might you adapt your social media records to support transformations? Here are three different ways to begin.

1. Direct Sales

The primary model is maybe the most self-evident, yet additionally, a frequently ignored chance.

There are different approaches to make direct sales to your social media audience - anyway; numerous businesses appear to overlook this is even a choice in light of the fact that there's so much social media advice out there which cautions against a lot of self-advancement.

100% - this is valid - few out of every odd post can be about your next 'enormous deal,' or extravagant schmancy new product include - else you won't have an audience to attempt to offer to by any means.

That being stated, there is a period and spot where making a direct CTA is proper. This is especially viable when you have the correct harmony between intriguing substance and an engaging product.

I'll admit, a few businesses are more qualified to coordinate sales on social media. Inside the structure, furniture, design, land, and other outwardly engaging businesses, for the most part, improve, essentially on the grounds that the visual idea of their products is all the more engaging in the social substance condition.

2. Video Marketing

2018 is the time of the video, and it's evaluated that up to 80% of all web traffic will be video by 2019.

It's likewise no mystery that YouTube and Facebook can pay profits with the appropriate measure of traffic, while there's additionally the enormous potential for procuring as an influencer or associate advertiser that produces top quality substance.

So disregard leads for a minute (I know - difficult to do) and how about we center on adapting social media by utilizing better video content.

There are a couple of approaches to profit with video content:

- Ad income from racking up perspectives
- Influencer advancement
- Affiliate marketing

Unpack Therapy takes advantage of each of the three open doors effectively. Their substance is all high caliber and very product-driven, which loans well to influencer and partner marketing.

The quality and consistency of their substance drives incredible commitment and viewership, which has helped them fabricate a tremendous audience, making their engaging record brands.

The vast majority of their recordings get a huge number of perspectives, which implies that off the bat, they're ready to increase uninvolved income from as.

Their tremendous audience is likewise what makes them so speaking to brands hoping to get before a draw in an audience, which opens up huge amounts of chances as an influencer or associate.

Numerous organizations will pay gobs of cash to get included on a channel like Unbox Therapy, essentially in light of the fact that it can mean considerably greater bucks for their sales.

3. Lead Generation

This is an excessively significant strategy for adaptation that each business ought to be centered around when attempting to get increasingly out of their social media accounts.

Each client that joins your audience on social media is a potential client - it just takes a smidgen of the procedure to begin changing over them.

There are many ways to create leads from social media that it can once in a while be overpowering; anyway, the greatest misstep that most businesses make is working their social media with the presumption that leads will simply seem dependent on the unimportant presence of their records. Shockingly, this is infrequently the situation.

It's totally important to utilize additional marketing procedures so as to catch leads. While there is traverse, constructing a connection with the audience and changing over them into leads are two altogether different practices. The reason they're so fruitful with lead age on social media is on the grounds that their sales pipes consistently lead with worth.

Here are a couple of ways that they pull this off:

- They make unfathomable substances for their blog, which is superbly shareable and effectively motivates traffic to their website.
- They normally have online classes with persuasive and quick idea leaders, which makes an immediate call for email catch that is effectively advanced on social media.

- They make free assets like their free CRM or free receipt generator, which are too shareable on social media.

The quality and incentive behind their substance cause them to keep constructing their audience and catch leads dependent on a reasonable worth trade - individuals are significantly more eager to surrender their email or offer some data if they realize that they are receiving something consequently.

SOCIAL MEDIA MARKETING FOR BEGINNERS 2020

INTENSIVE COURSE ON SOCIAL MEDIA THAT ALLOWS YOU TO LEARN HOW TO SELL YOUR PRODUCT OR PROPOSE YOURSELF TO SIGNIFICANT COMPANIES AS A SOCIAL MEDIA MANAGER

INTRODUCTION

Marketing has been advancing as far back as the beginning of production. Prior, the organizations used to be situated towards the production of merchandise and used to be centered on the greatest production with a little center around quality. Gradually, the assembling organizations are beginning getting worried about the nature of their products, and later with increment in rivalry, they woke up to the need to set off to the client legitimately for selling. In this manner, marketing was conceived, and different marketing systems developed.

Various Approaches towards marketing: After the 1980s, associations began advancing their products with the various clients with the assistance of publicizing and direct correspondence with the client. Social marketing advanced during the 1990s in which different strategies were utilized to achieve some objective planned for structure a superior society.

The contrast between Social Marketing and Commercial Marketing: Commercial marketing is centered exclusively on benefits, while social marketing is based completely on society. Presently, with the advancement of web and different stages, for example, websites, social systems administration destinations, for example, Facebook, YouTube, and so on, different associations have begun utilizing these stages for marketing themselves with the utilization of social media marketing.

It encourages them to fabricate affinity with the clients by blending different parts of marketing like an advertisement, direct marketing, and attention. Expectedly, marketing used to be finished with the assistance of outside marketing specialist co-ops, for example, advertisement organizations. These organizations used to sort out each part of the advertisement. This circumstance has changed significantly after the ascent of social media marketing as it encourages them to connect with the clients straightforwardly.

The job of the Internet: This sort of marketing has a ton of help from the web. This is because the organizations can connect with various potential clients online who can get to enormous data about the products and services of the organization on its site.

Further, with the fast extension of the web, social media can be gotten to by anyone who has a web association. Therefore, the requirement for exceptionally valued advertisements was finished by this technique helping these organizations to spare cost, increment viability, and increment buyer fulfillment.

Various organizations around the globe have utilized this type of marketing to receive overwhelming rewards. Purchasers can contact such organizations on their discourse discussions where they can list their issues, proposals, protests, and so forth. The social media battles of organizations like Dell Computers and Starbucks have been very fruitful in connecting with their clients. Starbucks has a nearness on different social systems administration destinations like Facebook, Twitter, and YouTube and has its very own blog foundation, which is Starbucks Idea. Such organizations take buyer criticism effectively and are known to have expanded consumer loyalty to incredible levels.

There have been sure ineffective crusades also, for example, those by Nestle, Volkswagen, and Wal-Mart. These organizations had enrolled nearness on such sites and even had their web journals also, yet they couldn't associate with their clients. This is because these organizations didn't pay any significance to the input given by their particular purchasers.

CHAPTER ONE

THE SOCIAL MEDIA

Social Media is all over the place. There is no getting away it.

Twenty years back, there was a rise in nuclear families buying PCs. This engaged a consistently expanding number of people to bounce on the Internet. By then, there were PCs for each individual inside the nuclear family. By and by, there is a constant creation of people obtaining Smartphones, which almost complete most of the components of your standard PC. This is making it more straightforward for everyone to be on the Internet in a rush. It is as of now subtle a point during the day where you can't find a good pace.

What do people look at while on the Internet? - Social Media.

Everyone is constantly electronic bantering with their associates, sharing what they're doing, and finding what others are up also. It's going on for the day, reliably. Social Media never rests.

What is Social Media?

The best way to deal with describing Social Media is to isolate it. Media is an instrument on correspondence, like paper, radio, or TV. Like this, Social Media will be a social instrument on correspondence.

This would be a webpage that doesn't just give you information, anyway it will associate with you as you get the information. These participations can be as fundamental as mentioning your comments or allowing you to settle on an article. It can even be as many-sided as Flixster endorsing films to you subject to the assessments of others with practically identical interests to you.

Endeavor and consider standard media as a solitary heading street where you can scrutinize a paper or check out a report on TV, any way you have particularly confined ability to give your thoughts on the issue. Social Media, of course, is a two-way street that empowers you to bestow too. This empowers you to communicate your suppositions and examinations on any issue and have them open for exchange with others.

Is Social Media and Social News the proportionate?

It is not hard to confuse Social Media with Social News since we now and again insinuate people from news bunches as

"The Media." To intensify the circumstance, we moreover get confused with the way that a Social News site is also a Social Media site as it falls into that progressively broad class.

Saying that Social News is proportional to Social Media looks like stating that Cars are Transport. A Car is a kind of vehicle, obviously so are Bikes, Boats, and Planes. While Social News is a sort of Social Media, so are Social Networking and Wikis.

Here are a couple of examples of Social Media Websites:

Social Bookmarking: Delicious, Blinklist, and Simpy. You work together by marking locales and search through destinations bookmarked by others.

Social News: Digg, Propeller, and Reddit. You partner by ruling for articles and comment on them.

Social Networking: Facebook, Twitter, Hi5, and Last.FM. You partner by including mates, following people, commenting on profiles, joining social affairs, and having talks.

Social Video and Photo Shares: Flickr and YouTube. You team up by sharing photos or accounts and commenting on customer passages.

Wikis: Wikipedia and Wikia. You team up by including articles and changing existing articles.

Social Networking relies upon a particular structure that empowers people to both express their peculiarity, evaluations, emotions, and contemplations while meeting people with equivalent interests. The structure will, when in doubt, fuse having profiles, associates or lovers, blog passages, devices, and as often as possible, something novel to the site itself. For example, on Facebook, no uncertainty about it "Punch" someone, on Twitter, you can "Re-Tweet" someone, and on "Bebo," you can share love once every day.

Profile: This is the spot you balance an online portfolio for major information about yourself. It permits you to move a photo of yourself, notices where you live, how old you are, your inclinations, and some character questions. The requests are typically something standard, for instance, "What is your favored Film/Book/Color?"

Partners: We've all got allies, and there is no vulnerability that your associates are currently on these districts. Buddies on your Social Networking regions are trusted in people of the site that are allowed to post comments on your profile or send you private messages. You can similarly observe how your friends are using Social Networking, for instance, when they post another picture or update their profile. This is the way by which we remain related.

Buddies are the bread and butter of Social Networking. I should point out that not all Social Networking goals will insinuate your sidekicks as "colleagues." For example, on Twitter, they are known as "aficionados," and on LinkedIn, they are known as "affiliations."

Get-togethers: Most Social Networking goals will use get-togethers to empower you to find people with similar interests to you. It can be used for to partake in trades on explicit focuses, for instance, Global Warming or The Lost Series.

A social occasion can be named anything from "Reepham High School '08" to "Little felines" to "One Direction Fans." They are both a way to deal with express your inclinations and partner with comparable people. I should moreover point out that not all Social Networking areas name them "Get-togethers." For example, on Facebook, they are known as "Frameworks," and on Google+, they are known as "Circles."

Talks: One of the fundamental spotlights of social events is to make collaboration between customers as an exchange. Most Social Networking districts reinforce all trades, giving they're appropriate. You will find that by far, most of them empower you to post included substance, for instance, Photos, Videos, or Songs which are related to the subject.

Locales: Blogs are a part that some Social Networking goals will have. These won't be as expansive as a Wordpress or Blogger, anyway, they are still there for you to keep people invigorated. Consider it an increasingly drawn-out Status or Tweet. Sometimes there are minutes when you'd prefer to share something reasonably long anyway; just would favor not to start up a full-time blog. This is the spot the blog feature ends up being valuable.

Contraptions: Another strategy for mentioning to people what you're excited about is through Widgets. Some Social Networking goals have what we call a 'Device Gallery.' From here, you can pick which Widgets suit you and post them on your profile. This empowers people to take reviews, for example, or experience another piece of music. Surely, even balance a survey that you've defined.

Why Start Social Networking?

Social Networking, as I've expressed, is everywhere. There are huge numbers of people starting now on Social Networking regions, and a regularly expanding number of people join every day. Other than informing and calls, it is the most excellent and fundamental way to deal with a partner with your friends and family. It's glorious and not just for singular use. A colossal number of businesses have flourished because of Social Networking. It's a free ad and engages you to make a reputation for yourself. You're prepared to propel yourself, explain cutting-edge offers, game plans, and general news.

A huge part of us has leisure activities or things that we are extraordinarily enlivened by, for instance, Films, Books, Games,

Sports, and Music. Social Networking empowers us to associate with others who offer comparable interests. It's an inconceivable technique for finding new things. You will find that people will near interests may like something other than what's expected furthermore, which subsequently, will get your favorable position. For example, if you and someone else share comparable energy for the band 'Enter Shikari,' you may find that they, in like manner, acknowledge various gatherings of a similar kind that you have not thought about.

Am I too old to even think about evening consider beginning Social Networking? No.

You're never too old even to consider evening consider beginning Social Networking. When you're worried over it being unreasonably irksome or particular for you to use, by then don't be. Social Networking regions are planned to be clear and easy to use with the objective that they can expand their gathering of onlookers to everyone. There isn't an age most remote point to Social Networking. It fits not to let kids on without parental supervision yet other than that approval and sign up!

You will find that there are definite social affairs focused on people of explicit ages. There will be others of a near age if not more prepared than you, who can help you with explicit issues or issues you may have with Social Networking. If you have children or grandchildren, approach them for help. Social Networking has ended up being normal for kids these days accordingly; consequently, they should have the choice to control you through everything that you need to know.

How might I start with Social Networking?

Much equivalent to taking off to a get-together, going outside, or joining a book club, Social Networking can be a huge amount of fun.

It will, in general, be profitable for your business or possibly calling, many equivalents to going to business workshops or a conference. Social Networking infers different things for different people. Everyone has their increments from it, yet you'll never grasp what you can achieve or experience through Social Networking until you give it a shot for yourself.

The most notable Social Network, Facebook, has come to more than One Billion customers. This consolidates well-known individuals, for instance, Actors, Comedians, Musicians, Bands, Sc.

In case you're hoping to increase notoriety or attempting to self-advance your business, then Social Networks, for example, Facebook, Twitter, and MySpace, are incredible for publicizing yourself. Social Networks, for example, LinkedIn and Google+ are better for increasing great business contacts and associations.

It joins the possibility of a customized radio station with Social Networking, which hence enables you to make your playlists and will recommend music to you dependent on your preferences and interests. It additionally enables you to tune in to playlists that have been made by your companions; this is especially useful for when you're at a gathering and need brisk access to a decent determination of tunes!

Lamentably while there are a lot of various Social Networking locales that take into account most interests and needs, there isn't one explicitly provided food for everything. This is the place the client made gatherings on destinations; for example, Facebook proves to be useful. Facebook accompanies an inquiry box; this empowers you to look into whatever is on Facebook. In case you're attempting to discover a gathering to talk about the contamination in the ocean, I ensure that there will be a Group or Page devoted to such discussions.

Tips To Grow Sales Using Social Media

Social media has turned into a selling power for the marketing scene, and advertisers are exploiting it. The ongoing study demonstrates that about 75% of sales and buy choices are done through social media assessments in a single manner or the other. Indeed, even how we work together and keep up client relationships has changed definitely inside the most recent couple of years, all as a result of social media. The customary method for selling both disconnected and online has changed from email marketing, organizing, telephone calls, and eye to eye discourses to practically finish social media selling. That been said, it doesn't mean our customary methods for selling are never again great or being used in any case; we rather utilize them joining social media offering data and analyses to develop sales utilizing social media.

Developing sales utilizing social media

Social media selling is straightforward; however, a strategic method for contacting your group of spectators' dependent on their socioeconomics and at the perfect time through the correct source contingent upon the most well-known social media channel your neighborhood or worldwide crowd are utilizing at a specific time. Using your systems on Google+, Twitter, LinkedIn, and other social systems, you will have the option to effectively recognize potential prospects, at that point gain insight on your group of spectators' needs and difficulties, and afterward, influence this information. This important data will clear a path for you to connect with them in the discussion that will offer you the chance to email, call or even meet them face to face and present your ideas to them. It is no news that the possibilities of social media have help advertisers reveal new selling chances and build up the current business connections that lead them to develop sales utilizing social media.

To prevail on social media, you need to design appropriately, set out a reasonable methodology, dedicate some time, and buckle down work before you can even consider prevailing on social media selling. The following are probably the best tips each selling rep ought to follow in other to be fruitful on social media.

1. Characterize your Brand or Products/Services

Before you even start anything on social media, you, as an individual or gathering need to characterize your brand, products, and services initially. Is it that you have the best quality products with the most reduced expense, or do you offer the quickest and effective services inside your specialty? Do you need your crowd to consider you to be the best group or gathering of specialists in a specific field? Everything must be first characterized. You will then decide how you need to be seen according to your crowd and know the correct wellspring of the social system you should utilize.

2. Make and complete your social media profiles

In the wake of characterizing your brand and having full learning of how you need to be seen on the media among your group of spectators and potential customers, the following thing you have to will be to make pulled in records on all the social media stages inside your compass. Regardless of whether is Facebook, Twitter, Pinterest, Instagram, and make and update your LinkedIn profile. Combine your site with the previously mentioned social media destinations, not the LinkedIn organization page. Ensure you don't have past data on those pages that will hurt your brand and make debate among your guests and potential clients. These social media pages speak to your brand, products, and services to an extraordinary degree, and they should be kept perfect and loaded up with data engaging clients as it were.

3. Distinguish your focused group of spectators and follow them

There are such a significant number of methods for scanning for your focus on a group of spectators on the social system nowadays. You know them effectively by what they like, their memberships, what they offer and view on everyday bases. Another approach to scan for your crowd is through LinkedIn. LinkedIn is an incredible apparatus for this since they enable you to look for individuals as per their socioeconomics, for example, by their titles, areas, explicit offices, organizations, businesses, and that's just the beginning. The same thing should be possible with Twitter and now with Facebook presenting refreshed on an explicit objective group of spectators to expand commitment. You could likewise locate your potential clients through your rivals' fan pages and make endeavors to steel them in manners I won't examine here. If you need more data about this, email or contact the administrator of this post.

4. Manufacture your social Network with your focused group of spectators

In the wake of becoming more acquainted with who you're focused on, the crowd on those social systems is, Start assembling your system with the individuals you know by welcoming them to like and share your pages. There is a lot of chances that those individuals may know who you need to offer to and ensure you include every one of the individuals from your over significant period employment puts, your family and companions, and urge them to share your data among their companions. This, without a doubt, will prompt your pages pulling in new individuals; thus, the development will proceed. Utilize Facebook, Twitter, LinkedIn, and Google+ to begin this procedure.

5. Recognize stages your group of spectators are utilizing

Knowing the social system stages you're focused on a group of spectators are on routinely will help you a great deal in focusing on them and expediting them to your pages the same social systems channels. You need to comprehend where you focused on a group of spectators, invest the greater part of their energy, talk about their difficulties, and offer data about subjects intriguing to them. When you recognize those stages, join the gatherings, and buy into those stages. There are chances you would meet a great deal of your focus on a group of spectators there and convert them to turning into your fans and endorsers. You would improve you invest more energy in those social stages where your group of spectators invests a large portion of their time. These will prompt more endorsers and potential clients you would keep for eternity.

6. Develop sales utilizing social media

Learn and screen your Potential customers on those social media stages

A few apparatuses like Tweetdeck, Hootsuite, and Google Alerts are simply incredible tranquillity of programming that can enable you to screen progressively what your potential clients are discussing on the web, which will enable you to react to them conveniently rapidly. Your intended interest group is persistently sharing data on social system locales like Facebook, LinkedIn, Twitter, Google+, and more, which send messages to what their needs and needs are. Here and there, even their profile update may survey what their needs are at once. Realizing all these will give you incredible knowledge on what to make and how to target them dependent on their conduct on social media.

7. Offer Target and important substance that will dazzle and draw in your group of spectators

Since you have characterized your brand, make and improved your social media profiles, recognize your intended interest group and where they invest the vast majority of their energy in the social media stages, began building your social system, and started becoming familiar with your intended interest group, the following test will be to begin offering extraordinary data about your products, services, and brand. This will help build trust and set up yourself as a specialist inside a specific field. Nowadays, you have to share focused on significant experiences with your forthcoming clients as quality substance utilizing the distinctive social media stages they use and ensure these substances are sent to them on the correct occasions and through the correct source.

Social Media Advantage For Brands

Social media has progressed toward becoming standard, and as somebody stated: each medium getting to be social. I generally think of a few brands and their dispositions to social media, content marketing, and the board. It is obvious from each edge, aside from the view that most brands are neglecting the "social" before social media. This is the thing that separates social media from different sorts of media. To exceed expectations in social media, you start with developing a social media attitude. Most have not comprehended what this stage offers.

All that we are right now doing is significantly titled toward social media misuse, which depends on publicizing and indecent inner self-advancement. This influences corporate brands all the more, however.

Most have focused essentially on standard conventional media. They have dismissed, or would we be able to state they are unconscious that the best way to get by in this time is a two-way correspondence media that grasps the conventional as well as online media stage. As we probably are aware, the present pattern today is for brands to find out about their ladies clients initially, stand out enough to be noticed using social media stages like blogging, Youtube, Xing, Facebook, Bookmarking, RSS, Podcasting, videocasting, Wikis among numerous other accessible online media.

The development of these new media has opened up a chance to look for feeling, associate, court, date, and offers overwhelming recommendation that will snare the lady of the hour. Today clients are never again getting one mode fits all ideas by the conventional media. Some corporate brands here appear to pivot non-interest in online network expanding on such pardons that we are not yet on the web, nor are there perceived customer fora that have a real union of shoppers on the web. Additionally, no administrative expert here focuses on or gives any thoughtfulness regarding whatever they need to state can. They additionally guarantee that online discussions here have no effects on corporate execution. Some additionally guarantee that social media is strange to us. My answer is that social media isn't an outsider. The reality remains that numerous things had been a piece of us just that we don't precisely mark them until the westerners help us out.

The possibility of social media, content marketing is established in social ceremonies where two or three get connected before they could begin dating. The procedure necessitates that the suitor's goal must be built up through family contacts, honesty checked, and a relevant guaranteed is made that he is keen on a serious relationship and not flings. Without these individual verifications, nobody formally permits the proposing couple to begin dating. If this is disregarded, at that point, the lady of the hour to be would be trained.

Attracting a parallel this old-fashioned custom, the clients need the brand today to demonstrate that what is important is her, not cash making. The clients need to make sure that out of varieties of suitors-products, a services-your brand can step up to the plate of beginning a discussion, the client needs to make sure your brand isn't simply being a tease, paying special mind to short throws yet a genuine relationship that will upgrade her way of life. Brand through social media, substance, and social marketing set up a bate by stacking the correct words in their substance to persuade, instruct, engage the lady of the hour that they are out to improve her life even before selling anything.

The client needs to perceive the amount of your licensed innovation will be made accessible without charges. The client needs to discover you are a provider. One of their main avenues for affection is blessing sharing. A supplier without string joined consistently takes the show. Social media, content marketing requires a great deal of responsibility. It requires some investment before social media and substance marketing have an enormous effect. Any brand that can indicate an abnormal state of responsibility in social media will consistently convey the day.

Run of the mill contextual investigations of brands with effective utilization of social media incorporate Tony Hseih. Tony supporters on Twitter today is more than one forty million. Hseih is the overseeing Director of Zappos.com. Tony, through his 'tweet,' has a course to meet with clients at a bar while numerous in his position will rather cover up under the pretense of occupied timetable. Tony uses Twitter to construct communication with clients; he uses twitter to take care of issues for customers. The quality of Tony Hseih and Zappos people group has been utilized to fortify associations with Zappo's brand disconnected. Zappos customer uninhibitedly gives their thoughts on what they need. This guide leads to the co-formation of brands, products, services.

As occupied as Richard Branson of Virgin gathering maybe, he additionally keeps up a twitter account. He has utilized his twitter record to respond to inquiries from furious clients just as virgin possibilities. The virgin gathering likewise has a coordinated site that permits news updates, blogs, among others. Southwest Airlines has utilized social media to fabricate solid association that effects on the brand's disconnected cooperation

A genuine case of the utilization of social media to spread messages and associations was as of late exhibited by Michael Jackson's PCP. As we are, for the most part, mindful, it was once intimated that he executed Michael Jackson through medication overdose. About seven days prior, he utilized YouTube videos to spread his piece of the case. This video spread over the web just as a prevailing press. The notoriety of virtual network has been taking off high with more individuals focusing on scholastics and marketing interchanges professional examining it ahead of time nations. Yet, Nigeria brands have expected 'I couldn't care less frame of mind.' Countries and brands are not viewed as in reverse due to their area yet dependent on frames of mind, mien to the utilization of innovation that will help progress. Building passionate association, unwavering ness with the brand is turning into a simple thing through social media.

Social media has turned into an incredible stage to relate to, associate, impart brand components. This frequently begins in online gathering and led to a disconnected, helpful relationship. Today, almost three billion of the seven billion possibilities are presently associated with social media stages. Concurred, the proportion is still delayed here; however, the number is expanding every day. Through social media, brands can light trust in the hearts of the lady of the hour, fabricate thought administration. Your brand rivals may have a better product; services, however, will miss out to you if you can assemble a solid association with them before you request that they purchase through enormous advertisements.

If your brand can give away enough data, answers to concerns, and demonstrate that you are nearly genuinely dismissing your own best enthusiasm, of tight plans, to serve these voracious, penniless ladies that craving your brands become increasingly open, legitimate with them which is the embodiment of social media. Social media don't permit smoke screens, pointless insurance of corporate brand's disappointments. I am of the sentiment that if our financial industry's Managing Directors have been dynamic in social media, there is the probability of increasing open compassion rather than this annoyance, fit of rage they are currently accepting from different points. Their devotees would have had the option to guard them and take the proper position that may have given them delicate arriving in this difficult period.

Since our brands have focused on one type of media, standard, disclose to me for what reason should their ladies not shut out their futile gloating through publicizing? Reveal to me for what reason is it hard for brands n our condition to see penmanship on the divider that their ladies presently want their real voices that are not shaded with languages of self-serving moneybags? The brands' ladies are currently likewise apprehensive, wary of marketing. For what reason should the ladies be faithful when the component of trust is shaking?

They are having set up that given us now a chance to analyze a legitimate method for taking an interest in social media, which is currently being traded for web.2.0. For brands to effectively take an interest in social media, brands need to watch, tune in, locate customers' sleeping medium. In doing this, the brand should initially characterize its social media technique through cautious assessment of the brand's assets, dissect the intended interest group, and distinguish targets. Having done this, the brand should cautiously pick or access stages that fit their objectives. This will illuminate the choice to run a blog or just to take part in different gatherings like Twitter, Facebook, discourse board, social media bookmarking, StumbleUpon, among others. Make certain you realize that such stages are utilized by your specialty group of spectators. Distinguish the top influencers of your industry online through acknowledgments given to their assessments, remarks, grants, and so forth.

To do this successfully, the brand may consider making the situation of network or social media/learning the board supervisor or contract expert who has track records in abilities like network the board, online notoriety the executives, observing, following, webcast, videocast, web joins and so forth. These aptitudes don't require a software engineer's information, and in undeniable reality, they are utilized by client relations, brand, and Public relations specialists. The main prerequisite is the energy that is upheld with demonstrated outcomes. The said trough or specialist should likewise comprehend gathering rules, notoriety programming, realize how to convey substance without making offense as this might be counter-productive. Extraordinary capacity to make subjective substance for websites, make profiles, and guarantee such writes in online catalogs is additionally fundamental. Social media, content marketing, the board is viewed as gathering of publicly released; an intuitive and client-controlled online application used to grow the encounters, learning and market intensity of the clients as members in business and social procedures, the social media scene is essentially about discussion before any marketing effort.

Brands should along these lines consider a recommendation that it must show that your brand cares is interested in discovering what the worry of the clients is, contribute, ensure the substance merits their consideration, explain issues, assemble discussion that will prompt solid relationship, acquire a great deal of innovativeness, exhibit the brand's character and qualities appreciated, form network, clan, bring change, ingrain mental fortitude and be exceptionally pledge to a reason it has faith in.

Give me a chance to finish up this piece by featuring how a brand can begin to take an interest in social media and substance marketing. Substance marketing is a craft of understanding what your clients need, need to know, and the study of conveying it to them helpfully and convincingly. The substance must take part in helpfully and convincingly. To begin with, the brand needs to manufacture trust and believability. This is gigantic work. This turns out to be simple if your brand can set aside an effort to tune in to clients first. By that brand finds their issues, and the substance is in this manner custom fitted to give the arrangement.

Abstain from blabbering about your brand or your skill as much as I do know the way that your brand needs to set up the line that your brand merits their considerations. This can endeavor your brand's endeavors to become suspect. Your clients need instructive substance without introductory marketing turn. The substance additionally must constrain, engaging to gain the scarcest element on the marry time/persistence. The incredible substance must aides, explains, illuminated, and associates. The language of the substance must be tuned in to your industry. A substance that takes care of issues drives traffic and expands the deal rate.

Social media and substance marketing make your customers consider you're to be a special asset, confided in a consultant, and a brand that makes them look great. This will make them to happily trade their cash and loyalties for your promise to the relationship. When you have such a great amount to give, they won't hold on to inform others regarding your brand. Some different elements become an integral factor here; however, let us close the present piece by saying that the brand has a few open doors when it attaches the two-path correspondence of standard and advancement of new media.

Points of interest Of Using Social Media

Greater destinations are proceeding to utilize the intensity of Social "mindfulness" on these Social Sites.

I have had the option to draw in most of the traffic so distant from social media, and it has been an extraordinary beginning stage to do as such. Each new blog should initially draw in and activate the upsides of social media destinations.

One of the points of interest being the utilization of its traffic as of now on the locales. The capacity to include associations with each site. Lastly utilizing it whenever you need any two of the past focuses.

With one notice of a social site, everybody knows the development of it ordinary. Pinterest. It is currently authoritatively the "third" biggest social media site, outperforming even LinkedIn. It has been named, "50 Best Websites of 2011" as per Time.com and its rundown.

Each social site's pattern right currently must be the representation of the interface. The pattern has been developing with Pinterest's model as the prime interface. It has grown a pattern to incorporate that style on the Internet Dreams.

Social media, when all is said in done, has been an immense point of convergence of progress on the web since the "human" appears to discover association with one another an absolute necessity need part of life.

Below are the best 8 points of interest social destinations offer. You, as well, exploit the social site's offers. Discover beneath, and get the "Points of interest" recognized! If you don't mind, share it!

1. Get Instant Traffic

With Facebook having over 845 multi-month to month dynamic customers as showed by jeffbullas.com and Pinterest with 10 million, it shows to exhibit that social media is one of the most found a workable pace the web.

Why not misuse the traffic a bit of the social media districts get? It is significant to your site to get that traffic and get your brand dynamically "careful."

Not most of that traffic is what you will require. Only a smidgen of the numbers. The little package that is high-centerd around and what you genuinely want to pull in to your site. There are a few subtleties that justify seeing on the web. Of all of them, it is genuinely obvious Facebook is the "Ruler" and worth investing energy into. It could be unmistakable for you since you could be all the more charming on Twitter.

It is about what time you put assets into a social site and reliant on that is the yielding return.

2. Talk And Connect With Your Peers

Your companions could be site owners or bloggers that have their substance, and they're scattering it to the social masses. Social media has made it a likelihood and a "flat out need" to shape the relationship with your companions.

Partner and speak with them. That is one of the most noteworthy assignments for a youngster. Essentially saying, "Hi, how are you" is a stunning opening to an affiliation. In like manner, offer to fill them in about whether you could share any substance they may have.

Having the right top WordPress modules accessible to you is the slightest bit closer to misusing social media. Ask them really to guarantee they understand you shared their substance as they are progressively proficient at responding with a comparable action.

3. Catch A Following!

Getting traffic from social media is a sure something anyway to get them to like or tail you is another since social media traffic is known for traffic that movements all over, it makes colossal spikes by then winds down the next day.

A small amount of the time you are planning to get traffic from a social visitor, endeavor the other to get them to tail you. Asking is a start, and giving momentous substance is moreover a start in getting them to join.

4. Get More Help To Share Your Content

Since social media is about affiliations and sharing what best points of interest them, posting your article, there may interest them as well. They will look at it, and what they see may empower you in any case sharing.

One way to deal with getting more offers to structure a touch of substance is to remember your allies for it to a great extent and mention that they share it. The other is to contact your "veritable" perusers or disciples you are in an incredible relationship with and ask them a comparative course as well.

5. It Is Free To Use

There is no cost included and use them as much as you can. Set up a profile that looks tackled and has most of your current "information." Begin following and become a close acquaintance with the best number of as you can, and bit by bit refine your request.

It is permitted to share and use the features of the social site, for instance, get-togethers or get-togethers. Think about the likelihood of partner with other "near" people and sharing what you bring to the table. Keep this philosophy at an anticipated reason. You'll see the prizes.

6. A Huge Database Of Ideas

On the social goals, in specific locales of it, there are many looking for answers to their issues. People are scanning for courses of action, and one of the spots they are glancing is in social media where they may tail one of their instructors, for instance, a blogger or mentor.

Issues = Ideas. You can, in like manner, get contemplations by observing what is the example out there and getting a bit of that vibe. Look at other substances and examine for yourself what is getting hits on it. It isn't hard to understand that. Look at the social signs, for instance, comments or enjoys, retweets, etc...

You are watching out for your resistance on a very basic level.

7. Social Media = Social Networking

Absolutely the focal piece of tolerating achievement on Social Media. That could be possible as its other name. If you are not sorting out with others on these goals, and just siphoning just your substance and believing it gets apparent.

Most likely not. It isn't. The principle way it would be is if your fans or close ones offer and assist you with progressing further. That is something I expected to learn and didn't think of it as that way. Right now, your close by affiliations and help each other out with sharing. That way, you will have the choice to show up further down the channels of social media.

8. Increment Your Brand "Name"

Indeed "huge" name organizations that have existed before social media frenzy have hopped on this medium to develop their business significantly more. As indicated by eMarketer.com, 88% percent of advertisers concur that social media has developed their brand "mindfulness."

Regardless of whether you haven't had your site exist before social media, this is the ideal opportunity to develop that name of your site into the brand that can be known by a more extensive mas, when developed. An intelligent system is to investigate the enormous canines and catch "a few" of those stunts they use because they have more involvement in the field.

Recap Of The 8 Social Media Advantages

There you have it. The eight gigantic focal points recorded here you can't miss of social media commitment. It could likewise be the best ten favorable circumstances of utilizing social media for your site.

No more reasons not to utilize social media as is it, and if you are utilizing it, I am certain you are not utilizing its full focal points. I was doing likewise till I rediscovered, myself, on what the genuine significance of social media is.

Work on every one of these eight points, each in turn. These are intended to work and venturing stones the following degree of your social media commitment.

Out of every one of these focuses, the genuine key to progress on any social site is commitment and time—the time you spend on showing signs of improvement on that particular social media site.

CHAPTER TWO

HISTORY OF SOCIAL MEDIA

The story and history of Social Media

The historical backdrop of social media is a significant achievement for businesses and sites. Social systems administration may appear to be a genuinely new wonder on the Internet with Twitter and Facebook being the two most famous, however as a general rule, social isn't and never was simply conceived of these two stages. Facebook and Twitter were taken off about thirty years after social began the Internet. The facts confirm that it was not until 2004 and 2006 when Facebook and

Twitter commenced that social media began to change the world and how that individual convey on the web, however in all actuality, social media began with email, Usenet, the internet, websites, and AOL moment envoy. The historical backdrop of the Internet is the historical backdrop of social systems administration.

Social Media History

The wonders of social systems administration bloomed in 1994 with the making of Geocities, which enabled its clients to arrangement sites demonstrated after certain urban regions. Around then, more than 1,500 web servers were online in 1994, and individuals were alluding to the Internet as the Information Superhighway.

• In 1971, an administration association called ARPA (Advanced Research Projects Agency) sent the primary email.
• In 1980, the Usenet worldwide appropriated Internet dialogue framework was propelled, and with it, thousands rushed to the message sheets to talk about music, science, writing, and sports.

These two occasions signal the beginning of social systems administration.

What do individuals do with social media?
• Posting and sharing

- Reading and survey
- Linking and remarking
- Interacting with brands
- Interacting with fan pages
- Playing games
- Chatting and informing

What is social?

- It's colossal. Facebook would be the third most populated on the planet if it were a nation, behind just China and India.
- The measure of video transferred to YouTube consistently is over 24 hours (twofold from the year-earlier).
- The number of YouTube recordings saw every day is more than 2 billion (twofold from the year-earlier).
- The number of pictures facilitated on Flickr is more than 4 billion (that is multiple times more than the Library of Congress).
- The number of organizations utilizing LinkedIn to discover and draw in workers is 95%.
- The number of relationships a year ago between individuals who met through social media is 1 out of 6, which is twice the same number of individuals who met in bars, clubs, and other social occasions.
- The normal number of tweets every day on Twitter is more than 27 million (that is eight times more than the year-earlier).

Who is social?

The greater part of humankind is younger than 30. So if you need a feeling of where the world's media propensities are going, it bodes well to watch what children are doing.

Arriving at clients

Social media is the ideal approach to arrive at your most compelling clients, and the best way to arrive at your most skeptical ones. Social media is the rocks of the Internet. We need it, we need it, and we experience to pull back when we don't have it.

The eventual fate of business and social

Social media is a perspective. It's not about sales or ads or navigates rates. It's tied in with seeking after connections and cultivating networks of purchasers. Businesses that desire to develop a need to reevaluate their whole business marketing process. Social expects businesses to make arrangements because, with social, clients are in the middle, and they are in charge.

Even the odds

Social media is significantly making everything fair and associating us more than ever. Along these lines, overlook your brand. You don't possess it. You can invest a wide range of energy and cash attempting to make a popular assessment, at the end of the day, it's up to the general population.

Social media is reclassifying everything.

- How we work
- How we play
- How we learn
- How we share
- How we find
- How we make
- How we gripe
- How we celebrate
- How we grieve
- How we worship
- How we impact
- How we team up
- How we research
- How we assess

The principles of social media are fundamentally equivalent to media.

1. Listen
2. Engage
3. Be genuine
4. Be conscious
5. Have fun

Social media is the progressing discussion of the planet. It's the wellspring of news, and all the more regularly than not, social is the home on the Internet. It's the landing page and where the vast majority invest energy on the Internet. Social media is the standard. It moves the media mouthpiece and continually circulates to the hands of people in general.

Social Media Condensed History

Social Media has starting late transformed into a principal bit of our normal presence, anyway it's been around for a long time before Twitter and Facebook. Social media has changed comprehensively available while it used to be obliged to those with an all-around understanding of the development and underground software engineer circles.

Social media has reliably been around two things: socializing and information gathering. Setting up the two together and then you have an arrangement of information sharing. Some segment of the draw of social media has to do with "finding stuff out," especially if the information being alluded to is something you're less expected to consider (in this way things like Facebook stalking). It looks good, by then, that social media started with the telephone in the 1950s. Different "phone phreak" packs created, fascinated with the telephone system, and how to attack it. Some segment of what started the phreak advancement was the amazing cost of making a call. The people who had the creative abilities to do so did whatever they could to find a course around it, hacking into lines they didn't have to pay for. They, in like manner, caused every day to practice concerning enlisting phone association test lines and meeting circuits so they could hold virtual social affairs.

In the 1970s, another type of social media rose. It was known as the BBS, or the "release board framework." At the point when BBSes previously showed up on the scene, they were little servers fueled from a PC appended to a phone modem. BBSes worked much on how numerous gatherings and websites do today; individuals could take part in network discourses, internet games, transfer and download documents, and so on. The principle issue was that the PC was not a standard family unit item. They were huge, costly, slow, and wasteful, therefore seriously constraining the number of individuals the effectively took an interest in BBSes.

In the 1980s, social media was especially an underground marvel. There were some genuine BBSes. However, the vast lion's share of them was, in one way or another, associated with the grown-up substance, privateer programming, hacking hypotheses, revolutionary developments, and infection codes. As a result of the idea of a great part of the online association, genuine names and characters were carefully monitored, and the web was not a spot for individual data sharing.

Social media turned out to be increasingly "social" in the mid-1990's the point at which the internet ended up accessible to the majority. Some sites were the principal endeavors to draw in social media with more standard culture, yet their initial cycles were moderate and costly. As the Internet turned out to be all the more promptly accessible and administration turned out to be quicker, talk frameworks, for example, the AOL moment emissary, started to grab hold.

The following enormous pattern was Napster, opening up the potential outcomes of data sharing and broadening the conceivable outcomes of the kind of media that could be traded on the web. Napster made music accessible on the web, and for nothing. Until chronicle names and specialists started to debate the conveyance of copyrighted material, Napster was the principle hotspot for media dissemination.

The following period of social media accompanied the rise of social systems administration locales. "Friendster" was the first of its sort yet was immediately bested by MySpace and after that Facebook. As the Internet turned into an essential device for regular day to day existence, individuals started to relinquish the dread of uncovering their genuine personality, for sure, many have put their full life in plain view for nearly anybody to take a gander at.

It is difficult to envision a world without social media now. Facebook, LinkedIn, Twitter, and the immense blogosphere are utilized for stimulation purposes as well as have turned into a noteworthy piece of business and political collaboration. So what's the following stage? There are lots of buzz about Google Wave and the plausibility it presents to give a stage to ongoing productivity and coordinated effort as opposed to simply discussing it.

The History of Social Media Websites

Man has consistently been a social creature and, thus, has consistently lived in complex social structures. The Internet added another measurement to this perspective through the idea of social media sites.

How It All Started

As the Internet saturated into each home, young people found another method for articulation using the Internet. One way youngsters found of imparting basic interests to other similarly invested adolescents was through MySpace. This method of articulation had no immediate checks or guidelines clipped on by grown-ups. In essence, guardians really felt more secure having their youngsters play on their PCs at home as opposed to celebrating outside.

Adolescents just as grown-ups observed MySpace be an uncommonly quick and reasonable method for speaking with each other. They could utilize Myspace - and now Facebook or Second Life- - to associate with each other, to impart records to each other, and to mentor each other into the satisfaction they had always wanted.

The notoriety of social systems administration sites developed with the requirement for the young people to have their very own space, away from according to their folks and other "capable" grown-ups. What came about was an incredibly solid and powerful method for correspondence that spread like out of control fire over the globe, increasing thousands, if not, a large number of individuals consistently.

Until a couple of years prior, despite the fact that a great many youngsters went through hours on MySpace, numerous grown-ups didn't know about its reality. Tragically, as social media sites turned out to be progressively prominent and across the board, predators started utilizing them as an instrument to target unfortunate casualties, and an ever-increasing number of individuals wound up mindful of the idea of social media sites, for good and terrible.

As the distinction of social media sites created and picked up unmistakable quality, their potential as cash producers went to the bleeding edge. Social media sites, for example, Digg, Second Life, Reddit, and Facebook, have now turned out to be famous for grown-ups and young people, and MySpace keeps on being broadly utilized.

How Social Media Websites Work

You start with your own space on a page that anybody can get to. This is your "relax" where you engage your Internet companions. There you place various bookmarks for locales that intrigue you, and you put in your remarks and additional connections (assuming any). You can likewise include individual photographs, a blog, and news about what's going on in your life. At the point when your companions visit your page, they can look at your preferred locales or photographs and leave their remarks there.

As such, you build up a social circle that is fun and keeps you refreshed in your field of intrigue. You can build without much of a stretch structure a system of online companions and referral sources by means of social media sites. Something other than a good time for young people, social media sites are perceived as a viable instrument for viral marketing, and they have really turned into a marketing vehicle for some people and associations. Numerous individuals today utilize social media sites to manufacture traffic to their own sites, advance their products, and build up a superior and more extensive client base.

CHAPTER THREE

SOCIAL MEDIA MARKETING

Introduction to Social Media Marketing

Do you have to get into Social Media Marketing (SMM) - Almost positively YES in light of the fact that a) different methodologies don't work so well any longer, and b) since it offers a lot more extensive reach, to an all the more intently focused on a group of followers? Also, it's free.

a) Other methodologies don't work anymore:

* Cold approaching the road - when was the last time anyone got welcomed in to make their pitch?

* Cold approaching the telephone - conversing with voice message isn't fun any longer.

* Print and other communication media - very costly and unproductive.

* Email - approved sender records and different channels send these to Trash.

* SEO your marketing website - Google positions sponsors first and substance (in online journals) next.

* AdWords - cost per snap is driven up by enormous brand spending plans and just Google profits.

Over there is the obstruction we as a whole need to meddling publicizing. Our cerebrums, our Firefox, or our Tivo, enables us to sift it through.

b) Social Media stages aren't proposed for marketing; however, help us get messages out there to individuals keen regarding the matter. The makers constructed these frameworks so networks could connect on the Internet. Individuals abstain from publicizing like every other person; however, as in other social spots, they are available to meet individuals and learning and sharing. Partaking in these networks, we can meet individuals who are purchasing what we sell.

Social Media Marketing is:

1. Progressively viable

2. More extensive reach to individuals who are intrigued

3. Free!

The Seven Secrets to Being Welcome

Beginning with SMM can seem threatening. These spots appear to be loaded with specialists who utilize their very own exceptional dialects. We need to compose and distribute stuff in manners individuals need to peruse. Above all else, it appears to occupy so much time.

However, it's simple if we adhere to the basic standards:

* Avoid Internet Marketing Experts like the plague. Destinations are commanded by these characters attempting to drive peruses to their web journals, in the expectation they'll click an Ad. They think less about SMM than we do, or they wouldn't act the manner in which they do.

* Find some authentic (there are a couple) SMM specialists and read what they liberally share in their web journals. An incredible beginning spot is chrisbrogan.com. Discover Chris's paper "Fish Where the Fish Are" for the clearest clarification.

* Sign up to destinations where your prospects, or individuals they know, hang out. Be social. Round out your profile as though you're joining a club. In Social Media, individuals like to know the

individual behind the business. It's much the same as gathering individuals at a mixed drink party.

* Write blog entries on stuff you truly get it. Make these posts short, to the point, and offer authentic ability. The goal here isn't winning a Pulitzer Prize - it's sharing your skill. Try not to profess to know something. Fakes are uncovered instantly.

* Write remarks in gatherings, sharing what you know with individuals who don't. Answer addresses posted with short remarks straightforwardly on the subject. Individuals keen on a similar subject watch the responses to questions. The inquiry turns into the point of convergence of a scaled-down network. Here you can address one inquiry and have ten individuals perceive your worth include.

* Don't make guarantees you can't keep. Terrible news about a product or administration will be the world over in a nanosecond and entrust the culprit to obscurity.

*, DO NOT SELL. There are a lot of boneheads who do, yet they're seen as Spammers. There's no compelling reason to sell. When we hear what we're saying, individuals in the market will need to purchase.

Anyone adhering to these guidelines will be welcome to exchange discussions and other gathering places.

Simple Steps to Global Presence

We have to think about the Internet as a turning plate. We can remain in the center and not move while it goes on around us. However, we know there's stuff going on out there. The edge is moving a lot quicker than the inside. It's each of the haze.

To participate in, we'll have to push toward the outside and be set up to move all the more rapidly. The further we get out there, the quicker we need to think and move. What's going on isn't close to the middle, it's out there on the edges. In this day and age, it's an instance of "be out there, or be square."

In B2B, the uplifting news is we don't need to get to the limits of what the masters are conjuring up. Our group of spectators, being more centered on business than reclassifying the world, assembles in spots where it's simpler to have an influence. Not so distant from the inside. Further, there will be openings, later on, so we should stake out a spot, yet we most likely aren't going to work together there - yet.

The vast majority of the destinations out there have been begun by individuals needing to get paid for promoting, somehow, and run the site for their own advantage. Why not begin at Front

Office Box User Group? - It's kept running for your advantage. You can deal with your own networks, get all your blog entries naturally sent to content wholesalers. Get your profiles filed via Search Engines, and exhortation from the Social Media Marketing gathering.

Next, go to Linked In. Here we find 25+ million experts, similar to us, needing to the interface for business: reconnect with past partners, get employment bids, and get help from their companions. Connected In has 1,000s of particular vested parties and posts questions and replies in 100s of classes.

Developing quick is a large group of extraordinary intrigue destinations utilizing Ning and Collective X programming. Both offer indexes of their destinations. There are 1,000s of Ning locales, some with 100,000s individuals, concentrated on unique intrigue or geology. Ning makes it especially simple for us to set up our own and keeps a predictable profile of us and our "companions" over every last bit of its destinations. Locate some intriguing gatherings, join and participate in discourses. You'll be acquainted with the way everything works-the client gathering's a Ning site.

Get a Google account. Post content in your Blogspot blog, distribute it in Google Sites pages, make recordings and distribute on YouTube.

Answer others' inquiries anyplace you discover them - especially at Linked In, Yahoo Answers, and Knol Debates. Individuals value the assistance, and Google is viewing - at this point, you're turning into a world specialist regarding your matters. (Worth recalling 99% of the substance on the web is disgorged trash - if your stuff is great it's anything but difficult to stick out).

Microblogging and What We Can Do With

At the outrageous edge of our plate, we come to microblogging with Twitter, Pownce, Yammer, Plurk and a couple of more - on the essence of it the best for nothing administration believable, with communicate distributing restricted to 140 characters and a large group of complimentary programming/services increase the value of it. The quantity of individuals joining Twitter is developing at a blinding rate, in light of the fact that the individuals are making the reason for it as they come. With Twitter, the insane people truly have assumed responsibility for the shelter.

Considerably farther, we come to Twingo. This is a site/administration giving individuals a chance to make their own networks, much the same as Ning, yet restricted to the 140 character post size. (It's brand new, so may require some an opportunity to fix a couple of things.)

Why limit messages to 140 characters? Since it slices to the mustard. Individuals out there need to profit by our understanding, not out scholarly abilities. The farthest point spotlights minds on the meat. Perusers can examine several posts in no time flat, picking ones they need to find out about.

Microblogging began with basic notices - what I'm doing now - between companions. At that point, it detonated with clients and advancement.

Presently news services screen Twitter presents on to discover what's going on. Columnists screen them to discover what individuals are thinking. Government officials are doing likewise and drawing in another open with their very own thoughts. Programming organizations are distributing administration notification to their clients. Brands needn't bother with client studies any longer; they simply screen Twitter.

Sales folks are observing Twitter discover who's keen on what, and what's being said about their rivals. This is the new wellspring of sales leads, and we don't need to search for them, they come to us.

In excess of a million early adopters are distributing news and assessments to the remainder of the world. The administration is so effective, engineers wherever are composing projects to include esteem - including Twitter Search, checking watchwords and sending each post utilizing them to our RSS peruser, and Twellow, an index of Twitter clients with in excess of 620,000 sections.

With Twitter, we can discover new companions and partners anyplace on the planet. We can learn of another chance, assess and choose inside only a couple of minutes.

We can be a great deal more productive in light of the fact that we have access to a lot more data and backing. It's a definitive inquiry and answer administration.

Social Media Marketing's Growing Popularity

Why utilize social media marketing?

A significant number of the present fruitful businesses have been around for quite a long time, sometime before the web was a feasible alternative in marketing a product. Regardless of the way that announcements, TV attachments, and radio and print notices have been powerful previously, they won't have the impact they once did in the present market. Various people never again check the paper for film times; they reference online scenes. Various people never again hand-form letters; they electronically draft messages. Many stay away from parking space sales when they can utilize Craigslist. While some may restrict the real factors, this country and the rest of the world relies upon development progressively more reliably. This isn't something to fear or stand upon; it is something to abuse!

For anyone brought into the world after 1980, it is definitely not hard to see the creating reputation of social frameworks, and it doesn't take a virtuoso to separate the course wherein our existence's social media market's predominance will continue moving. People from the age of 20 to 29 use social media more than some other age gathering, with 41% experiencing 11+ hours seven days on social media goals. Age 30 to 39 is the accompanying most standard customer base of social media, with 37% of them experiencing 11+ hours seven days on social media districts too. While the more energetic age bundles on these frameworks, organization areas will be continuously enthusiastic about social status, the more settled get-togethers will focus on advertising and publicizing. Normally, a large number of individuals have thought about Facebook, which has transformed into the greatest social frameworks organization site to date. Facebook has over 500 million of customers, half of which sign on in any occasion once consistently. Among the US web individuals, 72% are people from Facebook, with ages 18-24 seeing the quickest improvement? That is 36% of this present country's web customers visit alone website consistently! It would be phenomenally slippery another channel with that kind of impact. Twitter, LinkedIn, and online diaries are just two or three the other notable social frameworks available today, all giving amazing receptiveness to a tremendous get-together of people.

Social media is the snappiest creating advertising mechanical assembly, and any business not benefitting by its different limits could be asleep to its opponents. Staying and not misusing this vastly creating promoting contraption is an open entryway that associations are missing. Business is reliably growing along these lines should promoting endeavors in order to keep pace with the test. So then is there any valid justification why somebody wouldn't immediately draw in with social advertising? It can't be money, as most of these frameworks are free. It can't be a contribution since anyone can re-proper their social advertising for affordable. Most by far, just don't have the foggiest thought. They don't have the foggiest thought what it is, nor grasp its abilities. Most importantly, they are unaware of the positive money related improvement it will perhaps have on their association.

Social media advertising is the undertaking to convey various kinds of media over social frameworks organization advances, plain and direct. Two or three favorable circumstances of social media join extended introduction, extended lead age, getting of new associations, extended traffic, and promoting cost diminishes. All things considered, 88% of publicists using social media have to point by point extended presentation for their business. Essentially half of these individuals who used showcasing techniques through social media for a year or less declared new associations got. Customers who experienced 6 hours or less consistently watched their lead age addition, and 58% of business visionaries using social media promoting will undoubtedly observe advertising cost diminishes.

The web is outfitting this world with new items, capacities, and gadgets that have at no other time been possible. Social media promoting enables one to possibly affect hundreds, thousands, or even a considerable number of people for a limited quantity of the cost of out of date advertising methodologies. It is the commitment of the present agents to focus on the destiny of each market and the course it is going. Social media is a canny hypothesis for all intents and purposes of any association and will be progressively useful in the past; it ends up joined inside an association's indispensable action. Social media frameworks organization is simply going to create, and my best direction currently is to set up your brand at the most punctual open door through these strategies.

Steps to Success in Social Media Marketing

Social Media Marketing is right now a crucial piece of any business's advertising plan. Anyone with an item or organization that necessities raising can go to Social Media Marketing to introduce, share, gain input, associate with clients, and finally, Sell. Ask any business owner what or who are your best quality leads, and they'll likely say 'referrals.' Referrals are made from one individual contribution of their experience to another person inside their SOCIAL circle.

Additionally, this is the power of Social Media Marketing. By placing yourself or your business in a social space, you increase your chance of tolerating more business as a result of someone discovering, examining for, getting some answers concerning, or clearly being suggested to you. Regardless, like any advertising stage, there are continually certain principles to hold quick to and traps to avoid. Right now, focusing on the 4 phases to achievement in Social Media Marketing.

Stage 1: WHO?

Any particularly orchestrated promoting exertion must begin with the request, who are we concentrating on? If you are a clerk and you feature yourself to youngsters, how productive will your fight be? You have to acknowledge who is most likely going to require or incredibly better; NEED your item or organization.

At the point when you work out who you're concentrating on, EVERYTHING in your promoting material, whether or not on the web or separated, must be in the full-scale course of action with this goal showcase. This consolidates the printed styles used, pictures, language style, shades, offers, and all things considered mind science behind your campaign.

When it doesn't, you will presumably have little achievement with your Social Marketing exertion.

Stage 2: HOW?

The accompanying fundamental development to a successful Social Marketing exertion is to choose how you will show up at your goal advertise. All of the four rule Social Media destinations credit themselves to different showcasing openings. Dependent upon the kind of campaign you plan to begin will make sense of which Social site will be commonly fitting.

The four most notable Social locales are Facebook, YouTube, LinkedIn, and Twitter. In the event that you mean to use all of the four goals to feature your item or organization, it's major to have a cautious perception of each to ensure your campaign will be powerful.

Stage 3: OFFER

Without an offer or spurring power, a Social advertising exertion falls under the characterization of 'branding.' Additionally, in what manner may you measure branding? You can't.

A successful advertising exertion, either on the web or detached, should be quantifiable. In the event that you put 'x' proportion of time or money into a campaign, it should reestablish quantifiable results in dollar terms or leads made.

Your offer must consolidate these segments if it's to realize an arrangement or lead...

Stand-out - for what reason would someone take up your offer in the event that they can get an equal or similar offer elsewhere?

Uncommon - we regard things that are uncommon. For what reason is gold so critical? Since there's next to no of it.

Expiry Date - having an offer available all through the whole year won't make motivation in your possibility to 'get it right now before it's past the final turning point.'

Appropriate - your printed styles, shades, pictures, plan, etc. of your web showcasing must be in the course of action with your goal advertise.

Qualify - only one out of every odd individual that goes over your offer will be qualified. Despite requiring the money to pay for your item or organization, they ought to, in like manner, be impelled to make a move today (or whichever time apportioning suits your plan of action).

Stage 4: STRATEGY

A compelling Social Marketing exertion must-have in any event one frameworks set up to ensure the target showcase seeks after your business strategy.

What does your showcasing pipe take after each frame for each Social Media site? Will you have one system that just triggers eagerness for the possibility of having them visit your site? Will you have another procedure that goes straightforwardly for the arrangement? Something is said about an email showcasing procedure that allows the client time to create trust and motivation to purchase your item or organization? Will you have an ensuing telemarketing organization to fabricate the change paces of leads that come through?

These are very critical requests to answer and execute answers for in the event that you're to expand the eventual outcomes of your Social Marketing exertion. Various business owners acknowledge that they simply need to 'be' in Social Media for it to happen for them magically. They acknowledge that possibilities will somehow flood through their virtual approaches to get hold of their item or organization. This essentially isn't sensible.

A Social Marketing exertion ought to be joined with at any rate one regular deals and showcasing frameworks in the event that you're to intensify your results.

CHAPTER FOUR

USING SOCIAL MEDIA FOR BUSINESS

Social media marketing is now fundamental for the improvement of organizations lately. With the assistance of social media marketing, organizations can arrive at their prospects and clients in a practical and simple way. Whenever arranged and executed well, social media marketing is the least expensive, yet one of the best strategies for the advancement and development of any organization or brand. Brand building is one of the most significant parts of social media marketing, and even big names and sports clubs utilize the social media instrument for brand building reasons. In this way, it isn't amazing that numerous organizations these days employ masters devoted to social media advancement of their brand or organization. The organizations which are dynamic in social media marketing have walked in front of their rivals, particularly as far as the prevalence of the brand on the Internet. These days, it isn't unprecedented to see organizations connecting with their present clients, future prospects just as offering help and responding to inquiries through different social systems. Pretty much every rumored organization has a twitter profile or a Facebook page these days, and it helps their current clients and future prospects to cooperate with them effectively. A portion of the upsides of social media marketing for organizations and brands are recorded as pursues:

1. Organizations can utilize social systems administration sites for bringing issues to light about their brand and their well-known products. Numerous organizations these days utilize social systems for featuring and bringing issues to light about their top-rated products. A large number of them likewise organize extraordinary challenges, complimentary gifts, or uncommon advancements devoted to only a specific system, for example, Facebook, and so forth. Sites, for example, Facebook and Twitter, are probably the most visited sites on the planet. Thus, such social media marketing encourages an organization to build its brand reliability and to arrive at a huge new undiscovered market spreading everywhere throughout the world.

2. Organizations get an opportunity to connect with their current clients through the mechanism of the social system. The vast majority these days have accounts in social media destinations. Thus, it makes it simpler for organizations to take input from their clients straightforwardly through social systems. Organizations can expand their bonds with their clients because of such coordinated associations. The criticism got from their clients can help in upgrading the nature of the products as well. A great many people notice their different inclinations in their social media profiles. Thus, the inclinations of the clients can be effectively recognized by the organizations through such sites with the goal that future products can be equipped to those interests.

3. It is simpler for organizations to declare their new products through social systems administration sites. Most organizations these days post new declarations on Facebook, Twitter, and so on when they post the declaration on the site. Now and again, organizations allude to future products through social systems administration sites even before the products are propelled. Social Media is a modest yet amazingly powerful approach to dispatch new products to an enormous market. What's more, such declarations on social systems administration sites are rapidly gotten up to speed by columnists and website admins who are additionally present in such sites. Now and again, it is seen

that news channels and famous sites report the declarations made by organizations in social systems administration sites even before they get the public statement from the particular organization or brand.

4. The measure of individuals, including normal guests to the social systems administration sites, is huge. What's more, social media makes it simple to answer to a specific update straightforwardly or to remark on an update. In this way, through the mechanism of social systems administration sites, any individual can without much of stretch access or interface with the organization. Along these lines, social systems administration sites successfully evacuate a hindrance among clients and the organization. Individuals don't hesitate to express their suppositions here or to interface with the organization delegates without stressing a lot over legitimate implications.

5. Consumer loyalty can likewise be expanded if social media is utilized appropriately by an organization. As referenced before, numerous organizations offer help straightforwardly from their social systems administration pages. Facebook is an awesome model where a few organizations, including little ones without a legitimate help site, offer help straightforwardly from their authority Facebook Page. It is exceptionally simple to deal with their clients' issues in a straightforward way and within sight of

other individuals. Such goals help the organization in structure trust among different clients just as future prospects.

With the approach of present-day innovation and new strategies for marketing in an incredibly focused market, it is almost unimaginable for an organization to stand apart from others without the assistance of social media marketing. In this way, social media and social systems administration sites assume a critical job in the advancement of an organization in this cutting edge age.

Social Media Marketing Helps Businesses Thrive

The marketing model was to get whatever the number of eyeballs on your product or administration's message as could be allowed and trust that a level of clients buys. Business catalog, radio publicizing, standard mail, TV advertisements, magazine ads, and so forth are instances of these customary publicizing techniques. These customary kinds of marketing are never again successful; the same number of shoppers have turned out to be oblivious to the 'single direction' informing. The message has been overcompensated, and individuals never again trust promoters. An ongoing study found that lone 14% of individuals trust ads, while 76% of individuals trust shopper suggestions. In like manner, more advertisers started looking for elective approaches to associate with potential buyers.

Marketing on the Internet was initially made famous by using Websites and streamlining those locales through Search Engine Optimization (SEO) strategies. While still a beneficial system, SEO has been refreshed by Web 2.0 procedures, for example, social media marketing. Social media marketing is when organizations use Web 2.0 stages, for example, web journals, social systems administration destinations (like Facebook, Google+, Foursquare, Twitter, and YouTube), and other developing web-based marketing instruments. The advantage stages versus conventional methods for promoting, and even customary site marketing, is that it includes 'two-way correspondence,' where clients are enabled to produce substance and businesses are boosted to speak with their clients.

The era of broadcasting your product to the majority and seeking after a reaction is no more. Organizations or persons would prefer not to buy from anonymous, nondescript organizations. In addition to the fact that consumers are focusing on the 'man behind the drape,' yet they likewise need to comprehend what others are stating about your product or administration. An ongoing report reasoned that 80% of US Internet utilizing mothers were affected by listening in on others' conversations from loved ones when settling on a buy choice. No other media stage takes into consideration independent ventures to profit by shopper informal publicizing like social media marketing.

Advantages Of Social Media Marketing

• Increased New Customer Acquisitions - The principle bit of leeway of social media marketing is that you will have the chance to interface with systems of potential clients that you would some way or another be not able gone over using other customary marketing strategies and even SEO.

• **Word of Mouth Marketing** - Word of mouth marketing has consistently been the most persuasive approach to produce sales. With social media marketing, you can make raving fans who will intentionally advance your product and services to their systems of companions. Obviously, if your product or administration is poor, you may endure the invert advantages of this.

• **Brand Awareness** - Branding your business utilizing social media marketing is a lot more straightforward, quicker, and more affordable to accomplish than the conventional publicizing medium or even site marketing.

• **Customer Retention** - Web 2.0 stages are the ideal spots to speak with your clients about new products, unique advancements, or just to teach them on your business. Through steady, FREE correspondence, you can stay with you before your client's eyeballs, which will thusly prompt recurrent business and referrals. Keep in mind, the way into this sort of correspondence is to be content-rich; don't utilize these roads to pitch your product or administration.

• **Rapid Results** - The viable and fruitful execution of a social media marketing plan will make practically immediate outcomes for your business. This expansion can be evaluated through expanded site traffic, expanded lead procurement, and at last, expanded sales. In contrast to radio or TV ads, where your clients vanish once the ads go off the air, these web 2.0 stage advantages will proceed with a long haul as long as the correspondence and refreshing of your social media nearness is kept up.

More Businesses Are not Using Social Media Marketing

Truth be told, most businesses don't have the foggiest idea of how to make or actualize this sort of system. What choices do entrepreneurs have when trying to make and execute a social media marketing plan?

Contract a representative while utilizing the time, involvement, and services of others is a keen method to work together, commonly this system comes up short. Why? At last, it is up to the entrepreneur to make the arrangement and deal with the representative. Most business proprietors don't comprehend web 2.0 enough to make an arrangement and haven't a piece of information on how to deal with the representative. Additionally, paying a representative expands your work costs, your finance imposes, your advantage, and so on...

Redistribute re-appropriating is a superior option in contrast to enlisting a representative as you won't need to enlist, train, oversee, and pay a worker to play out these capacities. Notwithstanding, there is a cost for these advantages. Redistributing these services can be extravagant. I've realized social media organizations to charge over $1,000 to make a Facebook Fan Page. This undertaking takes, probably, 20 minutes to set up. Once more, the issue rotates around training. Except if you see how social media marketing functions, at that point, you shouldn't enlist or re-appropriate the assignments except if you're willing to overpay.

The truth is learning the fundamentals of social media, making an arrangement, and executing the arrangement is an errand that each business proprietor is equipped for performing. Finding the correct preparing programs that will tell you bit by bit the best way to make and oversee web 2.0 stages is foremost as is using programming that will enable you to deal with the majority of your records from one straightforward area. With a tad of interest in training, you can make your own special web. You can also locate an across the board do it without anyone else's help social media dashboard that will enable you to play out your web 2.0 marketing in under 10 minutes per day.

Utilizing Social Media for Business

Utilizing social for business has turned into the most well-known pattern to advance with the utilization of the Internet. There has been not at all like social media previously or since the beginning of the Internet for business marketing. It is a pattern that every single present-day business must contemplate as a major aspect of their special plan and as a method of promoting today. The universe of client assistance and the open association has been changed by the approach of social systems, however soon, it might turn into the favored method of correspondence with clients of various sorts.

Social Marketing utilizes online social systems to advance and promote an organization to potential clients. Clients can wind up intuitive with the organizations they use through fan pages and connecting to sites or sites through the social systems. There are such a large number of social systems accessible to businesses and the open today, which they are the most helpful approach to get to data about one another. The social systems likewise help clients feel that they are getting progressively close to the home connection with the organizations through social media correspondence.

Social Media Marketing takes into account a lot of speedier correspondence among organizations and their clients, yet additionally, it fits a lot more extensive base of potential clients from their companion's systems. It enables organizations to publicize themselves with insignificant speculation and is the most financially savvy approach to advance any cutting edge online business. This is found in enterprises, free businesses, and even home businesses today.

The utilization of online associations through social media is the most current pattern in publicizing for organizations everywhere throughout the world. Private companies would now be able to go after their market with a lot of bigger organizations, yet they can do it without having colossal measures of capital for promoting spending plans. This is an incredible equalizer in the advanced data age, and social media is causing unrest in the manner organizations to work together. Any individual who has a cutting edge organization must exploit social media, or else they are probably going to lose potential business to those that do.

Utilizing Social Media for business can change the manner in which the cutting edge organization utilizes the Internet, yet in addition, can change the manner in which client support is taken care of. The client of today can connect with current organizations straightforwardly, which makes their experience substantially more close to home. It can establish a long term connection on the cutting edge client and make an association with them; however, it will likewise help keep them returning to the organization that gives them top quality client care. The eventual fate of the business is, by and large, socially intuitive on the web.

Motivations To Use Social Media For Business

There are such huge numbers of motivations to utilize social media for business that it is difficult to pick which ones are the most significant! We did a touch of work, and here are the best five reasons why social media is an unquestionable requirement for businesses nowadays.

1. Circumstances are different! Already, business circles and social circles were kept independent. Presently those lines have obscured, and clients or customers need to draw in with businesses in a manner that was incredible just a couple of years prior - clients need a customized administration from an organization they can identify with, an organization that is social, much the same as their clients. You must ensure they can!

2. It is reasonable! You can set your social media represents business purposes yourself, yet after that, it is truly practical to connect with experts and do a legitimate social media marketing for your business. There is no charge for huge numbers of the

services offered by social media locales, so there's no reason not to manufacture an association with your customer base.

3. It manufactures your notoriety. You can set up your business as one that is reliable, and advance yourself as somebody with aptitudes, understanding, and information. Setting up yourself as a specialist in your field used to be practically unthinkable without broad media inclusion, grants, and promoting. Presently it's as basic as reacting to customer inquiries and offering guidance on the web. You essentially can't purchase this type of brand mindfulness in some other manner, and that is one of the most energizing parts of social media for business.

4. Evoke client input. Social systems administration permits you not exclusively to give data out, however, to get data back too. So you can utilize it to get extraordinary criticism from various sorts of clients. You never again need to experience the agony of center gatherings or extensive overviews - rather, use Facebook and Twitter to increase a fantastic comprehension of what your customers need, and adjust your business in like manner.

5. Drive individuals to your site. Being dynamic socially is an incredible method to drive individuals to your fundamental site, giving you a more prominent shot of changing over your presentation to sales. This is doubly valid if your clients can buy from you on the web. Higher traffic to your site additionally leads

to a superior web index rank, which thus gives you considerably more introduction - which demonstrates that social media truly is a triumphant methodology.

Instructions to Use Social Media for Business

Figuring out how to utilize social media for business/sales is the central calling of the cutting edge advertiser. Nonetheless, business proprietors need to comprehend the guarantee that social media are publicizing and marketing holds for the advancement of their products/services and brands.

So what is it about social media that is so significant and effective? Basically, social media marketing is probably the ideal approach to get a more noteworthy portion of the market. This is, for the most part, since purchasers are currently going to social media at whatever point they have to purchase something. To guarantee you draw in a greater amount of these shoppers, you have to redo your profiles, accounts, and on different social channels with the goal that they can purchase from you.

Consider the accompanying strides to expand your social media reach and draw in more clients:

1. Comprehend Your Prospect

Before you join any social system to cause sales for your business, to guarantee you comprehend your customer base. Social media possibly works when your prospect and customers are on these channels.

Along these lines, you ought to completely examine the market. At that point, discover what number of your objective clients are utilizing such locales as LinkedIn, Instagram, Twitter, Facebook and Snapchat. When you have this data, you can feel free to begin interfacing with your prospects on the individual channels utilizing social media for business.

2. Make a Persona

Invest some energy with the channels you are going to utilize. At that point, develop your record using your business brand as an online persona. Contact your prospects, have a discussion with them, and become familiar with their desires and standards.

The persona you make must fall off looking proficient, dependable, and courteous. Develop your organization and discussing your industry. Retweet them, remark on their posts, share those you discover fascinating, and answer their inquiry.

When you add to this online discussion, you will increase the value of their systems. From that point forward, it may be reasonable for them to give locate a shot increasingly about you. Now, guarantee you don't besiege them with the pitches you have arranged. Instead, they become more acquainted with them well and recognize their specific needs. Along these lines, when the opportunity arrives for you to utilize social media for business/sales, you will know precisely how to approach them.

3. Construct Relationship

This is significant if you are to stay in business as time goes on. Great relationships consistently transform into trustworthy leads. Individuals will, in general share a ton of data on social media. In this way, you should screen them and tune in to what they need to state. In the long run, you will be in a superior situation to draw in with them in an increasingly significant manner.

In the wake of building up the relationship, you can begin educating your prospects regarding how your products/administration may be something that they need or need.

4. Speak

The terrible thing one can do while marketing on social media is to compose your prospects and add a pitch and connections to your products. Instead, advise them that you have a few arrangements that may support them. Along these lines, they realize you care about them.

On the other hand, make a gathering of Facebook identified with your products/administration and welcome every one of your prospects to it. At that point, start sending focused on messages to the generally dynamic gathering individuals. You can likewise join the gatherings your customers are in on LinkedIn. Draw in with them, answer their inquiry, and demonstrate that you are a specialist in taking care of the issues they appear to have.

Twitter additionally has vast amounts of chances to start an exchange with your customers. Tune in to the tweets your prospects convey and use them to trigger essential and productive discussions.

Far beyond all, figure out how to listen more than talk. This is indispensable for the achievement of any social media crusade. It will give you earlier learning into your prospects and help you think of marketing pitches and methodologies that will get individuals to converse with you and start putting orders for your products and administration. Attempt it today and perceive how well it will function for your business brand.

CHAPTER FIVE

THE FACEBOOK ADS STRATEGY

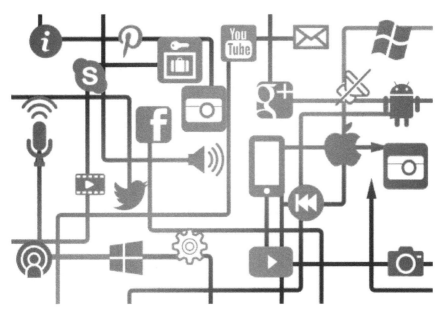

Facebook is right now, the most important social systems administration site on the planet. The system will most likely keep up its top situation for a considerable length of time to come thinking that there is no immediate challenge in the skyline that may thump it off the top spot. With regard to traffic, Facebook is presently in a group of web mammoths like Google, YouTube, and Wikipedia. There's no denying the way that Facebook is among the present most persuasive sites. Because of this tremendous ubiquity, Facebook has additionally pulled in consideration of businesses, of all shapes and sizes. It has turned into a typical internet marketing apparatus. Pretty much every company out there is utilizing it to advance products, services, occasions, and causes. If you have a business and you are not on Facebook, you are passing up a ton of advantages and openings. Facebook has its very own publicizing project to take into account these businesses that need to expand the introduction of their products and services. This promoting system is called Facebook Ads.

Facebook Ads work simply like any self-serve web-based publicizing program. You set up your ads, finance them with enough cash, and at that point, distribute them live on the social system. Presently these ads can take various structures. If you are a Facebook client, at that point, you know about the numerous ways you can connect with substance in the site. These creative exercises incorporate remarking on posts, loving posts, preferring pages, and participating in applications or games. These are the place the Facebook ads come in, other than obviously the customary advertisements that you see on the sidebar of your profile or record. The ads you make will rely upon what you are attempting to accomplish. Do you need more likes for your Facebook page? Do you need individuals to share your page's substance? Or on the other hand, would you most like to guide more traffic to your external site? These are only a couple of the things you have to consider when working with Facebook's publicizing program.

Here are a few hints on how you can utilize Facebook ads for the best outcomes:

1. Use pictures well in your ads. If you investigate the advertisements appearing in Facebook's sidebar, the ads with the best images stand apart from all the rest. Gain from this and search for an outwardly satisfying picture to use in your advertisement. Ensure that you have the rights or consent to utilize the map. Utilize the images of individuals, however much as could reasonably be expected.

2. Focus on your ads. With regard to focusing on ads, Facebook is unmatched. You can focus on a crowd of people by area, sex, age, relationship status, instruction, interests, and so on. So relying upon who you need to reach, you should utilize these choices when setting up your ads. This ensures your ads are seen by the suitable individuals.

3. Have a go at pivoting ads. This is to test which sorts of ads convey the best outcomes. Track their exhibitions, assemble information at that point, figure out which advertisements to continue running.

4. Compose persuading and intriguing advertisement duplicate. This is the content that goes with the pictures in your ads.

What's the Difference between FB Ads and Google AdWords?

We've shrouded this inquiry in detail before, yet here is the short answer: Generally, individuals use Google to take care of an issue, and they use Facebook to peruse pages and spend time with their companions.

This implies as opposed to looking into 'watchwords' as with AdWords; you will concentrate on descriptive terms that individuals are utilizing to portray themselves, their interests, and their leisure activities.

Also, because there is less challenge for publicists on Facebook, for the most part, the expense per snap is lower than utilizing AdWords.

Facebook Ads = Lower CPC + Higher Quality Traffic

What Types of Ads Can I Run on Facebook?

Standard ads or supported stories.

Standard Ads

These are the standard ads you find in the correct sidebar of Facebook. The primary segments of the usual promotion are:

• Headline

• Image

• Content

• Link

As a sponsor, you choose precisely what you need the development to resemble and to say.

Supported Stories

Supported stories transform clients' activities into paid ads in the correct sidebar.

When somebody communicates with your business on Facebook, you, as a publicist, can transform this social activity into a paid advertisement. This is an incredible method to use the intensity of social media and an online word of mouth marketing.

Who does Will see My Facebook Ad?

This is maybe the BEST part of Facebook ads. The appropriate response is: Pretty much anybody you need!

Facebook enables you to focus on your optimal customer or client and publicize legitimately to them. You can focus on clients dependent on:

• Age (and even birthday)

• Location

• Gender

- Workplace
- Interests and pastimes
- Education level

Also, substantially more.

When you select which focusing on alternatives you'd like, Facebook will convey your ads straightforwardly to clients meeting your criteria.

What are My Payment Options for Facebook Advertising?

Likewise, with numerous other internet promoting choices, you can pick between CPC (cost per click) or CPM (cost per thousand impressions).

If you are chiefly intrigued by clients navigating to your site or page, you'll most likely need to go with CPC. This choice enables you to demonstrate the most significant sum you'll pay for each navigates you get.

Nonetheless, in case you're increasingly keen on getting your brand out there and merely having your advertisement seen by whatever number eyes as could be allowed, CPM can be a decent decision. This alternative enables you to demonstrate the amount you're willing to pay for 1000 individuals seeing your advertisement.

Exploiting of Facebook Ads

As we all in all know, it's getting progressively difficult to 'be seen' on Facebook since this powerhouse organizes has advanced toward a remuneration to-play model over ongoing years. Facebook ads and paid decisions despite everything remain a convincing technique to concentrate on your ideal client and extend the scope of your huge Facebook revives, despite the way that various customers are not energized at paying for this decision.

On a logically positive note, Facebook is continually trying to convey the best to its customers and has starting late revealed specific enhancements that give businesses the edge concerning coming to centered clients. Is it sheltered to say you are up on the most immediate Facebook Ad improvements? If you aren't, you may leave behind the augmentation of your group. This is what's new with one of the most standard social media stages.

Increased Ads - Too specific organizations and individuals, it may appear to be a non-issue, but when you have what you truly need shoppers to see, you need to pull out all the stops. You are considering that Facebook made the correct section ads greater and bolder. This increases the value of your promoting effort since it gives a superior impression. Presently you have more space to exhibit the entire story for clients. Fewer ads on the page mean more consideration regarding the ones that show up.

Exploit the area and make an eye-catching advertisement that will prompt a higher active visitor clicking percentage. Transfer your inventive notice on News Feed and the correct section to ensure you arrive at your intended interest group.

Progressively Frequent Exposure - Remember how your mother, for the most part, needed to reveal to you something twice before you heard her? Since early August, promoters have had the option to utilize a single advertisement twice around the same time. This is a change from the past once everyday top. You can likewise embed ads two times per day from a page that an individual isn't associated with; once more, an expansion over the once a day by day top. If an individual is related to a page, the ads from that page can, at present, be embedded into News Feed.

What this implies for us is potential clients will see your promotion twice in a day. It doesn't build the number of ads for the customer; just the recurrence a similar development is seen. Facebook is continually investigating roads to make the Facebook experience better for buyers and businesses. These are only a couple of the progressions that have been actualized as of late.

Overseeing Ads in a hurry: As of July 2014, promoters have another approach to deal with their Facebook ads in a hurry with Ads Manager on cell phones. Utilizing Facebook (iOS, Android, and versatile site) applications, advertisers can now:

• Pause or resume crusades

• Edit spending plans and calendars

• View bits of knowledge

• Respond to alarms

Advanced Posts: If the idea of making and actualizing a Facebook Ad still causes you to wince, there's consistently the super-basic Promoted Post choice to fall back on. Advanced Posts are individual page posts that get extra paid reach in News Feed among fans and companions of fans because of utilizing the page's Promote catch. It's easy to use, has incredible investigation, and enables the client to choose and spending utilizing a sliding scale rapidly.

Motivations To Power Up Your Facebook Ads

In case you're searching for brisk and exceptionally compelling approaches to contact a large group of spectators, at that point, you have to take a gander at Facebook ads truly. Why? Well, if you read on, we'll take a gander at five of the most compelling motivations why more than 2 million businesses and an advertiser at present utilize the stage, and why you ought to consider it for your business as well.

Reason 1 - It's PPC

PPC (or 'Pay Per Click') is likewise the arrangement of the other famous publicizing system, Google, AdWords. The intrigue of

PPC is that you don't pay anything if no one is tapping on your promotion. You are possibly paying when they do, which means you get a free presentation for your brand, and you won't pay a dime if your advertisement doesn't urge individuals to visit your site or whatever else you may advance. Also, via cautiously separating individuals who you don't need tapping on your promotion with skillfully picked content, you can nearly ensure a positive profit for your venture.

Reason 2 - Facebook Ads Fit Any Budget

Facebook ads aren't only for major corporate sponsors. Any size business or solopreneur advertiser can without much of a stretch manage the cost of them paying little heed to spending plan. You set the sum you are eager to pay each time somebody snaps, or, even better, you let Facebook make the offering for you (that is my main event). Regardless of whether you just put in a couple of dollars seven days despite everything, you'll locate a lot of movement from your ads.

Reason 3 - Facebook Ads Are Highly Targeted

A favorable position that Facebook has over Google is that it gives you a chance to target explicit socioeconomics, psychographics, and even practices and exercises. As it were, you can decide to just demonstrate your promotion to ladies, for instance, who are single, more than 34 years of age, who like pooches and watch the Food Network.

This information enables you to abstain from squandering cash on individuals who aren't in your intended interest group. And keeping in mind that Google AdWÐ¾rdÑ• is focused in an alternate manner (it gives you a chance to concentrate on individuals who are scanning for specific subjects), it doesn't provide the same incredible focusing on control. Facebook likewise enables you to target individuals by their exact area.

Reason 4 – It's Social

Another incredible preferred position of Facebook ads over Google AdWords is that it consolidates the intensity of Facebook's social viewpoint. Individuals can like your ads and offer them, or you can utilize them, to direct individuals legitimately to your Facebook page to get more likes there. Furthermore, if somebody's companion loves your post or your page, Facebook will let them know along these lines, bringing significantly higher validity and 'social verification' your way. If social media marketing is a significant piece of your system, at that point, these are profoundly synergistic.

Reason 5 - It's Super Simple To Do

Beginning with Facebook ads is staggeringly quick and straightforward. Truth be told, you can have an advertisement battle fully operational quickly to start creating income. Ads aren't the best way to fabricate your business nearness on FB.

Approaches to Build an Online Business With Facebook Ads

Marketing procedures and battles for advancing your business online don't need to require a gigantic spending plan. Making mindfulness among individuals through advertisement, Google PPC advertisements, leaflets, and numerous such mediums can cost a great deal of cash. To chop down these costs would be anybody's fantasy, and this fantasy presently could be satisfied by advancing your online business through Facebook ads.

Alongside the Facebook profile and fan pages, Facebook ads are ending up being a wellspring of innovative advancement of the online business. These ads are shown intermittently alongside the visibility of each client, and these ads have been incredibly useful in making mindfulness among the clients about the online business.

Facebook ads give the accompanying chances to advance the business:

1) At this exact second, the Facebook individuals add up to around 400,000,000, which will keep on expanding after some time. So you can envision the measure of introduction you will have through the Facebook social ads. The number would naturally

decrease to the real specialty, giving you a complete thought regarding the interest of your product.

2) The Facebook promotion, alongside demonstrating your ads on various profiles, additionally tracks and reports the advancement of your ads on the social systems administration site.

3) The extraordinary thing about Facebook ads is that it will give you the knowledge and record of how often your advertisement has been clicked.

4) Facebook ads bolster the content-based advertisement. However, you can likewise innovatively make a picture to give the message of your online business to individuals. You can utilize the marked line of your organization in the image to upgrade the marketing.

5) The Facebook ads give two alternatives on the installment for the ads' continuous show ups. These two choices are: pick either pay per snap or pay per impression in your nearby cash.

Take a gander at the favorable position Facebook social ads could give you, and you would not need to surge around with hoardings and TV advertisements to advance your online business. The top reason companies to incorporate corporate America are utilizing

Facebook ads is a direct result of the fabulous open doors that are accessible to advertisers through the statistic highlights Facebook gives when structuring ads. Using this statistic information, you can have your ads just appear on pages having a place with or being seen by only those individuals who fall inside your real market specialty.

If you are out to pull in forthcoming clients and build up your online nearness and introduction, you deserve it and the eventual budgetary fate of your business to get the hang of all that you can about Internet marketing.

CHAPTER SIX

USING THE FACEBOOK ADS FOR BUSINESS GROWTH

Facebook for business development is a new issue at present and most likely will, in any case, be five or quite a while from now, why? Since it works! If you comprehend what you are doing. It is viable, and it is useful, and it's straightforward to actualize. With right around 1 billion clients using Facebook for business advancement, it's hugely a straightforward choice. In essence, you either do it, or you let your opposition take the majority of the traffic, Fans, and benefits from you.

For what reason Is Using Facebook For Business Essential?

There are a horde of reasons why executing Facebook for business is the ideal approach to get your business off the ground, in this article I need to attempt to audit only the absolute most significant advantages and a portion of the potential downsides.

The Pros of Using Facebook For Business

1. Usability. So all things considered, if you can set up an email address and browse your email usually or if you use web banking in any capacity, you can utilize Facebook. Those two models are set up basically in a similar way as pursuing a Facebook account. In essence, it is a straightforward arrangement of steps that are anything but difficult to pursue, and there are a lot of instructional exercises on the net or YouTube if you are uncertain about the best way to begin.

2. Information in Minutes. Presently state you've chosen to attempt disconnected publicizing utilizing the frequent flyers, pamphlets, and business cards in your nearby neighborhood, this can get pretty tedious most definitely, and can likewise pause for a moment before you see any outcomes or reaction for your endeavors. With Facebook marketing, you can have a battle set up and have traffic heading off to your site inside minutes. If you are, state, making an announcement or needing to run radio or TV advertisement, this kind of marketing can likewise be expensive, yet it very well may be quite a while under the steady

gaze of you can indeed pass judgment on the viability of your promoting.

3. Incredibly Accurate Targeting. At the point when a client pursues a Facebook account, they enter their age, nation, and city, and in some cases, road address, different preferences, and an entire host of various factors. You can focus on all or any of these that you wish, which is amazingly ground-breaking for a business. Utilizing Facebook, for instance, in the self-start venture specialty, you can indeed limit your market by further by deciding just to demonstrate your ads to state, homemakers between the ages of 25-50. At that point, you can make a promotion explicitly intended to focus on this precise statistic and, after that, guide them to an offer that suits them precisely. It removes the majority of the vulnerabilities of publicizing, and you don't need to go for the "shotgun" approach.

4. Spending limit As Necessary. If you possess a little garments store in Iowa, you can spend around $30 bucks or somewhere in the vicinity and perceive how your outcomes go for your Facebook promoting and after that choose from that point. It is dependent upon you to choose the amount you need to spend and if you will put more on this road or not. If you see that getting the outcomes that you need - wonder why. You can generally attempt to target various socioeconomics or change your promotion. Maybe you are merely utilizing an inappropriate wording in your ads, and so

forth. Whatever you choose, you can generally attempt again with another little spending plan and perceive how that performs.

The Cons Of Using Facebook For Business

For every one of the activities, there is an equivalent and inverse response, and that is valid on the web as well! Here is a portion of the drawbacks of utilizing your Facebook for business.

1. You Need To Feed It Cash. Facebook isn't a not-revenue driven association. Utilizing it costs genuine cash, not as much as conventional promoting, however, it's cash no different. You'll have to pay for every guest that snaps on your promotion, otherwise known as. Pay Per Click. The truth is, best Facebook advertisers utilize some sort of paid promotion. Much the same as rentals are most elevated in spots with the most pedestrian activity; certain ads will cost more to run contingent upon how rewarding those specialties are.

2. You Have Competition. Although Facebook runs a tight delivery in many specialties, you will have rivalry if you need to utilize Facebook for your business. This is something you most likely know, yet it can imply that you pay more for your ads if you are in a profoundly aggressive market.

3. It Does Take Some Time. Although it is moderately inactive traffic once it is set up, you do need to invest the energy in the

first place to set up those ads; discovering pictures, thinking of the features and content just as enhancing them to get some high navigate rates. This is work that can be redistributed, in any case, if you are an independent venture, this is something you should do yourself.

Like some other wellspring of publicizing or free marketing, there are great and terrible focuses on utilizing Facebook for business. In any case, when you contrast it and other online techniques, for example, article marketing, AdWords, blogging, and gathering marketing, you will rapidly observe that utilizing Facebook to showcase your organization can yield quicker and more noteworthy outcomes.

Facebook - A Serious Strategy For Serious Players

With a client base of just about a billion people and the accurate focusing on accessible, you can make Facebook promoting work for you as the vast players do. It's merely an issue of improving your battle suitably, changing your ads around when vital, and changing your objective market until you have adjusted it. It might be challenging to see your cash getting spent and getting no arrival; however, utilizing Facebook represents business development, and productivity is much the same as some other technique for advancement. In essence, you have to test it out, track the outcomes, reach a determination, and afterward settle on a choice about where to go from that point.

Five Ways to Succeed With Facebook Ads

Do you realize that feeling directly after you've planned that extraordinary promotion for your business, posted it on Facebook, and are sure it's the answer for all your income needs? You recognize what comes straightaway... nothing. The truth is out because most promoters on Facebook are essentially discarding their cash with ads that will never be seen or followed up on by their target group. Here are five hints to support you and your business conquer this very fundamental issue.

1. Portable Only Ads

Something like seventy-five percent of all Facebook clients gets to Facebook on telephones, tablets, and other cell phones. When you make a Facebook promotion, you are allowed to choose where the advertisement will run - news channels, side, or portable. One procedure that numerous promoters are utilizing is to part their focusing between their portable battle and work area crusade as opposed to making a different battle for each. Simply ensure you have a versatile greeting page set up if you run mobile ads.

2. Ads for your versatile application

If you have a portable application for your business, Facebook enables you to follow the download option of your application downloads, which can be an extraordinary method to make your very own locale, since you currently have direct access to those clients. For a startup engineer or business in development mode, there are unmistakably vast amounts of potential here. Just don't misuse it.

3. Retargeting

Hardly any individuals know the term; however, almost all have experienced ads pursuing us around the web (or around Facebook). Suppose you are on a webpage that sells shoes, regardless of whether you make a buy or not, all things considered, you will see ads for the shoes you were taking a gander at all around the edges of the web as you peruse somewhere else.

Indeed, Facebook enables you to retarget your ads utilizing their custom spectator apparatus. You essentially need to insert a code (which they give) in your site and start fabricating the rundown of guests to whom you need to advertise or urge an arrival visit to your website.

4. Investigation with page posts

One of the manners in which you can publicize on Facebook is by advancing posts on your fan page. It's always essential to push natural page posts that have had a high level of commitment and sharing among Facebook clients. This will, in a flash, add a social setting to your intended interest group and give the most astounding ROI. Furthermore, more critically, it will urge Facebook to demonstrate a higher amount of your presents on natural traffic going ahead.

5. Turn your inventive structure

Switching up the imaginative segments of your ads has, for some time, been training in publicizing. What's more, when you advertise on Facebook, it's the same. Clients see your ads on different occasions, and to maintain a strategic distance from them getting to be oblivious to your substance; it's insightful to change a component or two so they continue looking.

Advantages Of Having A Facebook Page For Your Business

There are many open doors with regards to social systems administration, and Facebook is the greatest and most surely understood. Nearly everybody knows about Facebook and individual profiles. To personal profiles, you include companions. Those companions offer posts, trade messages, and interface in an assortment of ways.

You can likewise make a Facebook page for your business. The objective is to get likes. These preferences mean fans, and afterward, you connect with those fans, so they share your posts, and therefore, more individuals come and like your page; thus, it keeps on developing.

A Facebook page offers numerous advantages to a business. In this article, I need to see ten positions to having a Facebook page for your business.

1. Your Facebook page can drive focused on traffic to your business site.

2. You can convey and cooperate with your fans; similarly, you would with email. At the point when an individual likes your page, they are naturally included and starting there; it is anything but difficult to speak with them. It does not have any difference what several fans you have, talking with them requires no more work. One message arrives at all of them.

3. The more fans you have quicker the quantity of fans develops. It's called viral development, and you can profit altogether from it. This is because every one of your fans likewise has a system of individuals whom they convey and that more significant gathering can see the pages that your fan likes.

4. Facebook has a high page rank, so your Facebook page will show up in Google and other web crawlers. Your site is additionally a decent place for backlinks.

5. The more fans or likes you have, the more popular your product or administration will be, and thus the more likes or fans you will get. This development will be exponential.

6. Your Facebook page is an incredible hotspot for input on your products or services. It additionally permits a setting for the top to bottom exchanges on products or services. These talks will be unquestionably more coming to than any promoting that you will do through practically some other medium, and the majority of the exchange won't originate from you.

7. Your Facebook page can be an astounding apparatus if you use it as a client care framework for your business. You will rapidly find that your clients will bolster one another.

8. The coming of Facebook informing and Facebook email has furnished other methods for speaking with your clients or prospects.

9. Facebook has various social modules that you can use to add extra usefulness to your site. By the method, for instance, one such module enables guests to your site to remark in a Facebook remark box on your website, and those remarks in a split second appear on your Facebook page.

As a business proprietor consistently vigilant for better approaches to advertise your products and services, you'd need to consider Instagram for your social media marketing plan. As one of the world's quickest developing social systems, Instagram has more than 100 million dynamic clients around the globe, producing 40 million pictures every day. If these figures don't intrigue you, we don't have the foggiest idea what else would! This picture-based social system gives innumerable of conceivable outcomes to brand marketing.

You, at long last, chose to put it all on the line and marked your business up for an Instagram account. Approach to go! This is one of the most captivating social networks out there today. To take advantage of the majority of its marketing potential, you need to contribute a ton of time. What happens when you end up without sufficient opportunity to spend for you?

With Instagram, similarly as with some other social media account, if you are not going to be a functioning member, at that point, you should not join.

This visual social system was not made in light of proficiency, making it one of the most disappointing parts of a brand's social media marketing technique. All in all, how would you ensure that you can incorporate Instagram without the majority of the disappointment that accompanies it?

Here are some useful hints on the most proficient method to benefit from the time you spend on the social system without sucking up the majority of your time.

Utilize a booking application

If you have been on social media long enough, at that point, you realize that there is a pinnacle time for posting. It is diverse for each brand and generally depends on when your crowd is the most dynamic.

Do your examination and discover when that pinnacle time is for your supporters. This makes it well on the way to see a commitment from your group of spectators when you post.

The perfect time to post on Instagram isn't continually going to be the most advantageous for your calendar. For instance, how might you ensure that you are posting those pictures at 5 p.m. each Friday when you have part of the arrangement set up during that time?

Necessary arrangement: utilize a booking application. Locate the one you like and line up the presents you need on include consistently or month. Timetable the date and time you need each post discharged. And after that, go on with your day.

React to remarks with assistance

A significant piece of making brand dependability on social media is to set aside an effort to answer to your devotees' comments. They need to realize that their comments are being recognized. This can be hard when your following develops and you begin to get a ton of remarks on your posts every day.

Fortunately, you can utilize the assistance of applications to make it simple to answer back.

Cross-post with one application

In some cases, you need to share your Instagram post over the majority of different systems that you are utilizing. In any case, how might you do that without investing a ton of energy on your telephone?

Utilize the If This, Then That application. IFTTT is a fabulous apparatus for helping brands cross-post their substance without going in and physically post. With this application, you make a kind of "formula" that will spare you time on social media. Mostly, you make a recipe of what you need to happen when you accomplish something different. With this application, you can have the pictures you share on Instagram to be shared on Twitter, for instance, naturally.

The present innovation, explicitly the number of available applications, makes it so natural to assume responsibility for your social media marketing and make it fit into your calendar. This is particularly useful with regard to the tedious parts of Instagram.

Approaches To Effectively Use Instagram

Instagram is presently utilized by a vast number of individuals around the world, and for a valid justification: taking pictures and imparting them to your companions has never been simpler! Nonetheless, Instagram can be utilized powerfully, for systems administration as well as for marketing purposes also. If you have a business and you might want to advance it in the online condition, at that point, this can be an extraordinary advancement apparatus. There are five of the ideal approaches to use Instagram adequately:

1. Hashtags are Like Magic!

Twitter uses them, even Instagram also utilizes them, and as of late, Facebook has executed hashtags also. Instagram clients associate principally using hashtags; this is the reason you have to figure out how to utilize them to your most significant advantage. This viewpoint can be especially helpful for businesses who are searching for devotees, as it enables them to make their substance accessible, and it will likewise trigger a viral impact that will profit the market over the long haul.

2. Photographs And Videos Can Tell A Story

A picture can merit a thousand words, and everyone realizes that. Instagram is about movies, yet taking random pictures won't make you extremely far, particularly if you intend to utilize Instagram primarily for marketing purposes. Truly outstanding, quickest and most effortless approaches to expand brand mindfulness and to help sales is to post photos of your product consistently: they don't need to be proficient, they simply need to feature the primary highlights and elements of the product being referred to and to speak to varieties on the audience.

The same goes for recordings: you can send records in real life, or you can make live product audits. Notwithstanding your decision, recordings and pictures are probably going to turn into a web sensation, as individuals love media documents more than content, and they are probably going to recollect them throughout the years. If you possess another business and you need to become well known, at that point, pictures and recordings will prove to be useful!

3. Challenges

Individuals love complimentary gifts, limits, and a wide range of special offers, this is the reason you can never turn out badly with a problem. A challenge is a success win: your clients will get a free product or administration, while you find the opportunity to expand brand acknowledgment. One extraordinary approach to utilize Instagram for challenges is to urge individuals to share their very own photos of your product, and to reward the most suggestive or unique picture. Simultaneously, you can utilize different instruments that enable you to effortlessly install an Instagram feed or a hashtag feed into your site.

4. Monitor Your Success

Following the accomplishment of your Instagram, the marketing effort is necessary. Luckily, there are numerous exhaustive and easy to understand applications that enable you to follow the client's development, to see which are your most mainstream posts, to decide when is the ideal time to post content, etc. As unimportant as these subtleties may appear from the start locate, they can have any kind of effect.

5. Interface With Your User

Staying in contact with your clients is significant, particularly for small and medium ventures which have a restricted objective market. You can demonstrate to your clients that you care about their input by basically answering to their remarks or questions. This won't just pull in client produced content. However, it will likewise improve believability and increment the perceivability of your business. Try not to disparage the intensity of your Instagram devotees, as they can add to the achievement of your business!

To whole it up, these are five of the ideal approaches to utilize Instagram to build sales and lift income adequately.

Instagram Marketing; Merits and Demerits

When you are finding more customers, individuals go to social media. Lots of sites and business proprietor disregard Instagram as it's a little activity when contrasted and different destinations. In any case, this is a slip-up, and a keen business person needs to utilize Instagram if the individual needs to discover more customers. Given this, there are a few downsides. Here are three geniuses and three cons of using Instagram.

Merits:

An image is profitable: As is frequently stated, words usually can't do a picture justice. Consider it, when running an organization, one will need to utilize pictures to show off their product or administration. This is particularly significant when selling sustenance, weight reduction products, or whatever other things that individuals love to take a gander at and appreciate. Notwithstanding, one can take it further and hotshot travel goals or any number of items. This is perhaps the best tip for utilizing Instagram for business as an image will genuinely indicate guests the genuine estimation of a product or administration.

Viral: Without any uncertainty, when utilizing the Internet to showcase a product, administration, or thought, one will need it to become famous online. If a site or thought turns into a web sensation, one will profit and discover a lot of new and energized guests. Consequently, when utilizing Instagram, one needs to ensure they give a genuine incentive to a guest. At that point, and at precisely that point, one can see the photograph become a web sensation, which will bring about a ton of new guests to the website.

They take the necessary steps for the organization: Finally, as referenced, when one offers a photograph with their companions, etc., it can become a web sensation. Not just that, when utilizing Instagram, the devotees will do the more significant part of the work. Given an organization offers a fascinating photograph, it will probably become a web sensation. At last, one ought to pursue the best tips for utilizing Instagram for business. That way, the adherents will do the legwork.

Demerits:

More active group: Now, when hoping to discover new customers, one will, as a rule, need to pursue a more seasoned group. Honestly, while a lot of youngsters and youthful grown-ups use Instagram, not every one of them has the money to spend. In any case, there are opportunities to get them snared and returning when they are more established. In any case, when searching for the best system for Instagram, one must recollect that not all individuals can spread out any money.

Not business-disapproved: When following their preferred VIP on the web, many individuals are not keen on anything besides burning through idle time. This means, while on Instagram, many individuals are hoping to take a break on the train and have no expectation of spending any cash.

Not quickly recognized the name: While any semblance of Facebook and Twitter are acclaimed, many individuals don't think about Instagram. This is changing, however, not rapidly, and a brilliant business visionary ought to understand that the individual in question needs to pursue the best technique for Instagram if they need to discover accomplishment as it's not as simple as utilizing other social media locales.

When maintaining a site or business, one needs to utilize Instagram. While not the best game around the local area, it's useful to use this social media site to discover new customers from everywhere throughout the world.

CHAPTER SEVEN

USING TWITTER FOR BUSINESS AND BRAND PROFITABILITY

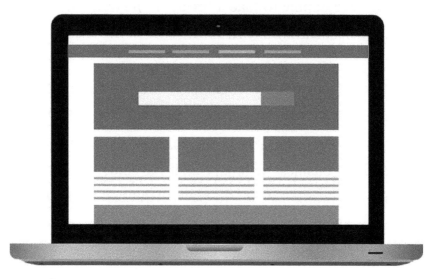

Brands on Instagram

The well-known photograph sharing application, Instagram, offers its 50 million clients the chance to move toward becoming armature picture takers with a one of a kind photograph altering list of capabilities that has detonated in fame in the course of the most recent year. In any case, Instagram has not just given an imaginative new medium to wannabe picture takers; however, for brands too. Brands have exploited opportunities to provide buyers a masterful, in the background, take a gander at what their products and services bring to the table.

Today, a few brands are utilizing Instagram to give shoppers off-camera takes a gander at games or style appears. A few brands have even enrolled exceptionally compelling Instagram clients for publicizing purposes. Here are a couple of brands that are adequately utilizing Instagram for marketing, branding, and promoting goals:

1. Red Bull: From the usual social media locales like Facebook and Twitter to the new and strange social applications like the popular video sharing application, Viddy, Red Bull is unquestionably an industry head with regards to internet marketing - and their Instagram nearness is no exemption. Red Bull posts an "everyday marvelous" photograph and keeps up the convention of "Flying Friday" to keep fans and adherents locked in. Red Bull doesn't stop with merely posting drawing in substance; the brand has likewise been known to "Like" different clients' photographs too.

2. Puma: Rather than basically commending shoes, Puma's Instagram was set up to feature all the cool places that shoes take you. Panther has been known to send powerful Instagram clients to huge occasions over the globe and take pictures. Panther even sent some fortunate and compelling Instagram clients to Abu Dhabi so they can Instagram the Volvo Ocean Race. Since Puma doesn't have the accompanying of some different brands (like Red Bull), this procedure of utilizing persuasive clients to photo occasions was a decent method for guaranteeing more individuals saw the photos.

3. Tiffany's: Tiffany's embraced Instagram as a significant aspect of its battle about genuine affection. They utilized a notable design blogging couple to take previews of romantic tales in Paris and New York and them on Instagram. Tiffany's likewise allowed couples the chance to present their very own photographs utilizing Tiffany's downloadable Instagram channel. Past is directly fusing Instagram into their genuine romance crusade, Tiffany's likewise utilized the photograph sharing application to give fans an inside take a gander at how adornments are made.

Even if Instagram is as yet a genuinely new mechanism for web-based marketing, numerous brands understand the intensity of and points of interest in utilizing the photograph sharing application for marketing purposes. Even though it might require a lot of imagination and thought to work Instagram into an organization's social media procedure, those that have done so have seen astounding outcomes and been incredibly acknowledged by clients on the stage.

Building Brand Awareness and Followers Using Instagram Marketing

With the coordination and developing significance of common sign to Google calculation, increasingly more are urged to utilize social media stages to soar their publicizing endeavors. One of the scenes that have been increasing extensive consideration from SEO masters and web advertisers is Instagram. In any case, similar to some other business procedure, you can't simply hop into the fleeting trend and get results. Realize the correct method to do Instagram marketing; at that point, manufacture brand mindfulness and addition more devotees.

Instagram has stood out in making the web dynamically visual, making dedicated picture takers from typical customers and brand stars from businesses who have seen the capacity of such a stage. Photo sharing has exhibited to be a remarkable technique to attract a not too bad after, increase customer relations, and animate unique participation and talk from customers. To welcome all these promising focal points, what does it require to put forth your marketing attempt a triumph?

1. Set up and manage your record expertly. If you are not redistributing social media improvement, you should put aside the push to set up and afterward manage a career expertly. Consider how you would require people to review and see your

business. One extraordinary Instagram marketing system to research is that of Burberry's-a British indulgence style brand. Among the photos that they offer are taken during their events, behind the scene. Along these lines, they cause the supporters to welcome the "experience" through insider photos of remarkableness and energy. This incorporation ignites interest and sharing.

2. Set up schedules. No web customer would need to seek after a record that uploads 30 photos in a steady progression, consistently. Regardless of the way that flooding your feed with all that you have in your camera can be luring thought to make the brand stick, this move can simply provoke disturbed fans who'll decide to unfollow your record and despite indicating your posts as spam. Revolve around quality and imaginativeness, and your one single photo would have the choice to bring your message across over more productively than the most extended article you can make.

3. Move Actual Photos. The achievement of your Instagram marketing exertion lies seriously in the creative mind of your photos. Never populate your channel with pictures or compositions relating to news, events, or progressions. Offer veritable, original photos, and if you have to fuse some substance, by then, that is what the caption is for. What's more, if you are

experiencing serious difficulties making sense of what to post straight away, here are a few thoughts for the substance system:

• Images of your products in different sets or backgrounds.
• Images of individuals, popular or normal, utilizing your products-can be the standard thing, real to life, clever, or offbeat.

4. Hashtags. In social media streamlining, hashtags fundamentally help arrange posts. These can likewise be utilized to make networks inside the photograph sharing stage that holds similar interests. Another approach to expand the utilization of hashtags is through arranging challenges with prizes in question.

Tips To Boost Your Instagram Marketing

A huge number of individuals internationally are presently utilizing Instagram. Instagram has made it less complex to take pictures and offer them with sidekicks, and various people value doing this. You can also use Instagram in an inexorably powerful way for marketing. Instagram is a phenomenal unique instrument to propel your business on the internet.

Photos have a thousand words, and Instagram is about pictures. If you are into Instagram for marketing purposes, by then, you ought to appreciate that self-assertive photos don't work. You need to post photographs of your product, ceaselessly. Posting photographs of your products is presumably the best techniques for growing your brand care and lift sales of your products. The key is having the entirety of the photographs included in the key features and primary components of the product you are progressing. The photographs should offer a monstrous group on Instagram.

Accounts additionally are critical in Instagram marketing. You can make and grant a video to your delegates to propel the present product. You can similarly choose to do a live product overview video and offer it on Instagram. Pictures and accounts are more addressing various people than content records. Media reports stand higher chances of turning into a web sensation as people share them. They are in like manner more foremost than content records. Make photos and accounts that exhibit your brand story and characteristics. So pictures and chronicles are noteworthy on the off chance that you have to improve your brand and sales.

Use quality media

To improve your detectable quality, you need to make an offer astounding photos and chronicles in your feeds. Where crucial, search for master help or urging from an image taker. Regardless, you can use a mind-blowing camera to take sharp pictures. Endeavor to get your photos, most ideal situation focuses. Adjust your photos for better results. Nowadays,' mobile phones are outfitted with photo modifying gadgets consequently. Instagram, too has a couple of photo modifying instruments. Apply this mechanical assembly for your Instagram marketing reason.

Partner with followers

Staying in contact with your customers is basic, particularly for doing business with a little bit of the general business. You can start by exhibiting your clients that you are stressed over their info. You can achieve this by explaining their requests and comments. This will improve customer made substance and legitimacy similarly to advance the detectable quality of your products and business. Your Instagram disciples can, in a general sense, sway the achievement of your undertaking, and you should remember them.

Use hashtags

Hashtags are huge in Instagram marketing. You need to use them because Instagram customers collaborate using hashtags. Hashtags empower customers to make your substance open and are critical if you have to extend your supporters. You can likewise misuse inclining types of hashtags, particularly if the hashtags are related to your product. This is important that Instagram customers can utilize the hashtags to search for posts.

Use hashtag that is branded

Join your business name in your hashtags. Use epic hashtags for a particular restricted time fight you run. Notwithstanding the way, this advances your fight, yet it moreover gives an exceptional hashtag to your clients to partner and bestows to various individuals.

Have a kindhearted attitude to everyone

While finishing your Instagram marketing, you need to understand that Instagram is a system made out of people with moved contemplations, emotions, and establishment. Consistently be all around arranged to everyone and worth their chance to interface with you on your page. Ceaselessly promise you to check out your clients.

Be dynamic

Post on any occasion once steps by step to keep awake with the most recent and assurance your fans revived with the present happenings. You can test posting at various events of the day to see which time your posts do best.

Consistency

Consistency is basic in Instagram marketing in this social media era. Ensure to be consistent in your postings and develop a theme that is obvious in your posts. Mention to your followers what's in store from you.

Association your Instagram and Facebook accounts

Interface your Instagram and Facebook records to improve your marketing power. Nowadays, you can have an Instagram tab on your Facebook page. This empowers you to share your Instagram presents on your Facebook followers if you have a fan page.

You can associate with friends and the world by methods for Instagram. Instagram can be used for marketing purposes. Instagram marketing can improve your brand's detectable quality, increase sales, and along with these lines, earnings. Consider the recently referenced Instagram marketing tips to gain ground.

CHAPTER EIGHT

SETTING UP SOCIAL MEDIA PAGES

Setting up profiles for your organization's social media channels can be an overwhelming undertaking because every stage has it is very own character and profile prerequisites.

The following is a manual for setting up your organization profiles on Facebook, LinkedIn, Twitter, and Instagram. It will assist you in preparing the data and materials you need ahead of time so that you can stay with your or brand steady over the majority of your social media stages.

Step by step instructions to Set Up Your Facebook Page Profile

Facebook gives you a chance to advance your brand with Facebook Pages. Try not to befuddle your profile with your page profile since it's an infringement of Facebook's strategy to utilize your profile for business. If you've effectively tragically used your profile for business, you can fix it by changing over your profile to a business page.

This is what you have to set up your Facebook page:

• Profile Photo: This ought to be a 170 x 170 px logo. Facebook says you may show signs of improvement results with a PNG rather than JPG.
• Wall ("Cover") Photo: This ought to be 820 x 312 px picture if conceivable, yet requires at least 400 x 150 px.
• Page name
• Location
• Hours of activity
• Type of business
• Summary of your business

Make a Call to Action

You have the chance to make a CTA with Facebook's "make an offer" instrument at the highest point of your business page. What activity do you need guests to take when they arrive on your page? Will you offer a product rebate or a free digital book in return for an email information exchange?

For instance, The Manifest's principle invitation to take action on its Facebook page is, "Find out More." At the point when Facebook guests click the CTA, they are brought to our landing page, where they can pursue our pamphlet or examine the most recent substance.

Check Your Facebook Page

Get your Facebook page checked to build your authenticity and possibly improve your hunt rankings. It's speedy and simple to get a confirmation identification on your business page:

1. Click "Settings" while in the ordinary site visit.

2. Select "General" from the left-hand segment.

3. Click on "Get checked" close to the highest priority on the rundown.

4. Enter your telephone number, and they'll immediately call or content you a code.

5. Enter your mystery code in the spring up the structure.

Facebook offers a free instructional class if you'd like to get familiar with setting up your business page.

Step by step instructions to Set Up Your Instagram Profile

Before you set up Instagram for your business, make certain your Facebook business page is rounded out effectively. Since Facebook claims Instagram, you utilize a similar stage to make your Instagram business record profile.

Start by making a business record profile and afterward changing over it to a business page. This is a significant advance since it enables you to:

• Enter your business telephone, email, and physical area
• Place a "contact" catch on your page so clients can contact you
• Gain access to your page's Insights

This is what You Need to Set up Your Instagram Profile

• Logo: You just have a 160 x 160 px hover to show off your logo. Dissimilar to Facebook, clients can't snap to augment the picture, so make sure it's unmistakable and conspicuous.

• Business Description: You have 150 words to depict your business, brand, or administration. Hashtags are welcome, but on the other hand, they're connected, so they remove clients from your page. Use them astutely, if by any stretch of the imagination.

• Your Website's URL: This is the main possibility you'll need to incorporate your URL. Settle on a choice on whether you'll incorporate your site, a presentation page, or an email buy-in structure.

• Social Accounts: Instagram allows you to interface your other social records, similar to Twitter and Facebook. Make sure that you associate coordinating business accounts if you utilize this element.

When you've set up an essential business account, you'll convert it to a business page and round out your page profile. Here's the ticket:

1. Log in to your business' open record (you can have up to 5 Instagram accounts).

2. Access your record settings with the apparatus symbol.

3. Select "Change to Business Profile."

4. Select "Proceed as" to associate with your Facebook account.

5. Choose the Facebook page you need to associate with your Instagram account.

6. The data from your Facebook page will, at that point, naturally be added to your Instagram page.

7. Be sure your contact data is current (telephone number, email, area) so clients can connect with you.

If you need to get familiar with rounding out your profile and advancing your business on Instagram, go to the Instagram Business Blog for accommodating recordings, tips, and thoughts.

The most effective method to Set Up Your LinkedIn Profile

LinkedIn is a business-to-business organization and is evaluated as the most mainstream social channel among B2B businesses and second for B2C businesses.

Your LinkedIn profile contains individual data about you so you can coordinate with different businesses. You likewise have the alternative to make a LinkedIn "organization page" and "grandstand page."

An organization page at LinkedIn is the place you educate individuals concerning your brand and post news, updates, and marketing-related substance. It's additionally used to post openings for work and hotshot your organization's culture.

A LinkedIn exhibit page is the place you post explicit point substance and manufacture a network of connected supporters. This is what you need to set up your LinkedIn company page. You can make a LinkedIn organization page by choosing the "Work" tab in the upper right corner. At the base of the rundown, there is the choice to "Make a Company Page."

To make an organization page, your own LinkedIn profile needs to meet the accompanying prerequisites, among others:

• The profile must be in any event seven days old

• Must be a present worker of the organization and the organization position is recorded on your profile

• Have an organization email address affirmed and included your LinkedIn account

This is the thing that you'll have to make a LinkedIn organization page.

• Company Page URL: It must contain in any event one non-numeric character, and can't have more than one back to a back hyphen or start/end with a hyphen.

• Company Description: This must be between 250–2,000 characters, including spaces.

• Logo: This is prescribed to be 300 x 300 px.

• Cover Image: This is prescribed to be 1536 x 768 px.

You can become familiar with setting up your LinkedIn profile through Linkedin Learning. You need a superior record to get to the courses. However, it may merit speculation. It offers an enormous choice of instructional exercises, driven by specialists.

The most effective method to Set Up Your Twitter Profile

Twitter enables you to set up different records, so if you, as of now, have an individual record, it's alright to include another for your organization. Twitter profiles are short and basic, so pick your words cautiously and have your SEO catchphrases prepared.

This is what You Need to Setup Your Twitter Profile

• Profile Picture: This ought to be your logo, and the prescribed size is 400 x 400 px.

• Header Photo: This ought to be 1500 x 500 px.

• Username: This is organized like @yourcompanyname.

• Description: You have 160 characters to depict your organization. Think about whether you need to incorporate a subsequent URL or potentially your SEO catchphrases here.

If your organization is of open intrigue (identified with music, news-casting, business), you might need to make it a stride further and get confirmed by Twitter.

Getting confirmed demonstrates that you are who you state you are and enables work to trust with your group of spectators.

Make a Memorable First Impression

Social media can be a fun, fulfilling, and productive experience if you approach it admirably. The initial step is rounding out your profiles with consideration. Treat them as though they are individual presentation pages for your business.

Keep in mind, for some individuals, this will be their initial introduction to your brand. Take as much time as necessary, and round out whatever number subtleties as could be allowed to help fortify your notoriety and set up your social media methodology for development and benefits.

CHAPTER NINE

PRESENTING YOURSELF AS A SOCIAL MEDIA MANAGER - HOW SOCIAL MEDIA HELPS BRAND IDENTITY

One of the most striking advantages of such media for an association is the entry it gives to convey its brand. The chance to connect with clients, both existing and forthcoming, is monstrous. This isn't in separation from other potential increases. Different advantages of having a social nearness may incorporate contender and market understanding, notwithstanding client relationship with the board, and direct sales. In any case, any online social exercises will affect the brand personality, so all exercises must be considered in this unique situation.

Before seeing how online networks and their related stages can influence brand mindfulness, it is fundamental to comprehend the social media services that are available to you. There are hundreds, if not a great many firms that offer help and instruments to enable you to handle this generally new zone of marketing, and these can be outlined in three classes: assessment, the board, and preparing.

Assessing an organization's social nearness will mean breaking down the discussions and patterns that are important to your area and brand, just as providing significant understanding and information related to your product or administration. Online media stages give an exceptionally open stage to all business exercises, including that of your rivals, so rival examination likewise adds to the learning picked up. This procedure of assessment enables a business to comprehend the effect that social media has on its tasks and picture, and the picked-up understanding accordingly adds to the marketing strategy, which will eventually impact shopper feeling and conduct.

The administration of an organization's social systems administration could incorporate making and refreshing records on stages, for example, Facebook, Twitter, and channels, for example, YouTube, and posting pertinent, modern substance as notices, tweets, or various media content. Reacting to remarks and inquiries in a promising way with significant answers is likewise basic to guarantee that your online nearness is functioning and drawn in one. Services may likewise incorporate after and loving pertinent posts and points, making and keeping up an organization blog, visitor blogging on different locales, and talk room or discussion control. The act of refreshing substance and overseeing guest connections makes discussion stages, fabricates networks, and can prompt referrals and proposals - all essential for drawing in with the purchaser and imparting that brand personality.

Preparing and consultancy assume a key job in the services that are on offer, so as opposed to depending on an outside source to deal with all your locale exercises, there is a consolidated methodology. From bespoke, singular preparing to increasingly nonexclusive courses and learning occasions, business proprietors can be taught concerning how best use the accessible online networks, just as assistance make techniques and introduce certainty and information so staff can execute them legitimately.

How precisely can these social media services influence your brand? Pinpointing the components that give a brand it's distinct, and that decides its prosperity, which causes us to comprehend the job that social marketing will play in its observation. There are five key angles to a fruitful brand that should be considered.

1) Vision. A brand's vision ought to be open and comprehended by everyone. The very awesome means to accomplish this is through unique and pertinent correspondences and substance.

Online people group give the phase on which this message can be passed on, and giving the stages are overseen in like manner, they will empower predictable and clear correspondence of the vision.

2) Values. The estimations of a brand characterize the individuals and culture encompassing the association behind it. They will directly affect the buyer's basic leadership process, regardless of whether it be through expanded sales, fortifying a fan base, or sharing and suggesting. A brand's qualities may not generally be in a split second self-evident. Yet, since social media takes into consideration communication and commitment between a brand and the purchaser, these qualities can be shared and communicated straightforwardly.

3) Target showcase. Fundamentally, a brand realizes its objective market, all together that the group of spectators can identify with its vision and qualities, and in this way, be sure enough to get tied up with the product or administration, making the request. Through compelling assessment of a brand's online nearness, it is then conceivable to focus on, become more acquainted with, and afterward spotlight marketing endeavors on the intended interest group. Clients of online social systems share an abundance of data about their preferences just as significant statistic pointers, offering the association a very much focused on a group of spectators.

4) Prominence. Website design enhancement and third party referencing are tied in with standing apart from the group. Yet, unique, imaginative, and attractive substance shared on social systems, and online networks will likewise make your brand stick out and thus increment acknowledgment.

5) Permanence. A brand needs a life span to be fruitful, and client faithfulness is vital to this. Significant and proceeded with commitment with prospects, fans, and clients will concrete the connection between a shopper and the brand. Brand sturdiness leads to rehash custom, securing net revenues thus.

Painstakingly considered branding has consistently been a significant piece of marketing procedure, however, the appearance of social systems administration, purchaser produced substance, and viral sharing has implied that there is a lot more noteworthy open door for brand observation and personality to be translated by the masses. Used social media will fortify a piece of the pie through better brand mindfulness, and by exploiting the different social media services on offer, you can guarantee that your brand is seen correctly by the suitable individuals.

The most effective method to Make Social Media Work For Your Brand

A portion of those has a large number of clients billions on account of Facebook. Your business is only grain in the rice pack. Fear not, here are a few different ways to make social media work for your brand:

Pick Wisely

It is anything but a savvy thought to endeavor to have a nearness on such a large number of social stages. Every stage works uniquely in contrast to the others and ought to be dealt with interestingly to get the most out of it. Treating things interestingly requires some serious energy and care, so except if you have a devoted individual or group for social media (and motivation to behave a nearness on a ton of locales), pick carefully. Social media resembles a child don't fly out octuplets except if you have enough sustenance to go around. Most brands can discover use out of Facebook and Twitter, and for a great deal of littler brands, those two will be sufficient to give you a nearness in the social world and not take up your entire day. Brands that sell exceptionally visual or outwardly motivating products, for example, retail locations, get-away bundles, and so on. Ought to be on Pinterest. Stick like there's no tomorrow. There are a lot of other mainstream and valuable locales like LinkedIn, Google+, Youtube, and a bunch of others that merit investigating. The key here is to pick the social systems that are directly for your brand and have a solid nearness on them.

Drive Website Traffic

One of the most significant things to originate from utilizing social media is the capacity to direct people to your site. The best ways are by connecting to your site's blog entries or other substance, and by running challenges/giveaways that have a housed point of arrival on your site.

Connect Often

Utilizing your picked social media destinations every day will make a bigger after and a more grounded nearness. By checking and posting often, you can collaborate with fans, clients, and all-out aliens to prop the discussion up or kick it off. It's an extraordinary extra client assistance device for any brand, and an incredible method to stay aware of patterns.

Be Diverse in Media, Consistent in Voice

The best thing you can do in all the disarray is kept your message completely clear overall systems. They may all have diverse fundamental purposes, (photograph sharing, blogging, and so forth.) however figuring out how to utilize those various media while keeping your message reliable will enable you to contact your crowd regardless of where they invest the vast majority of their energy regardless of whether it is 40% of the workday on Facebook.

Being different in media will enable you to hit a more extensive assortment of your crowd with their favored media types. Blend it up-connection to blog entries, post photographs, how-to recordings, infographics, or whatever will draw in your group of spectators. Regardless of how you state it, keep your character predictable. You've picked your organization's voice for a reason, so keep the message clear.

Step by step instructions to promote a Brand with Social Media

Something remarkable is occurring today. Publicizing doesn't work any longer as it used to. Before now, getting some TV time or placing an advertisement in a paper was viewed as keen and powerful. Yet, these days the vast majority, particularly the young, spend a ton of their inert time socializing on the web and even get their news on the web. This isn't an altogether abnormal event since man since the initiation of time has been a social being. What is uncommon is the fast rate at which correspondence has been improved through the across the board utilization of the Internet, which makes our computer-generated simulation today.

As of March 2013, there were more than 1 billion Facebook clients, more than 200 million dynamic clients, and accessible in 35 diverse languages. Over 346 million individuals read it writes internationally, and 184 million individuals are bloggers themselves. Twitter has more than 200 million enlisted clients who all things considered tweets a normal of 3 million tweets for each day, and YouTube asserts more than 100 million watchers for every month. LinkedIn has more than 200 million individuals in more than 200 nations and domains.

It's not all fate and despair. To advance your brand, you don't need to attempt to outspend the greatest organizations any longer; presently, you outflank them with viral recordings. You might not need to burn through thousands on sterile center gatherings; you have your market's heartbeat readily available with a fast Twitter look. The universe of social media is an amazing spot to connect with existing clients, extend your compass to new showcases, and to keep up great associations with different brands.

Today, through the approach of new web advancements, it is simple for anybody to make and, in particular, circulate their very own substance. A blog entry, tweet, Facebook page, or YouTube video can be created and seen by millions practically for nothing. Promoters need not pay wholesalers or distributers gigantic totals of cash to communicate their messages; presently, they can make their very own intriguing substance that watchers will rush to. More shoppers are associated than any time in recent memory, and consistently your organization isn't drawing in them in social media is a squandered chance. Along these lines, jump aboard.

Before we begin, let us juggle our brains on the meaning of some key terms. Media can be essentially characterized as a stage where you can share thoughts. Conventional media, for example, TV, papers, radio, and magazines, are single direction, static communicate innovations that are ending up less compelling marketing apparatuses today. Social media, not at all like its antecedent is another stage where we can share thoughts; make statements we like and don't care for; discover individuals that offer regular interests, etc. Instances of social media are websites, Facebook, Twitter, Pinterest, Google+.

Thinking about the accompanying as meager techniques for you to advance your brand with social media:

Be Authentic and Genuine
Social media ought to be utilized as a virtual medium to showcase your physical personality. Similarly, as your physical picture is remarkable, your virtual picture must be special moreover. Being bona fide gives you consistency with your clients, which would rouse brand devotion and subsequently increment consumer loyalties. This is genuine because the vast majority purchase from

who they like and trust other than the other way around. Social media gives you the intensity of information sharing, and by utilizing it suitably, you will help assemble trust in your association while indicating others the incentive in your business.

Be Open

Social media is about transparency and sharing. Businesses attempting to assemble their brand online must discover their clients first and ceaselessly connect with them in quite a while, advising their clients about their brands. These discussions ought to be two-route between the businesses and their clients to guarantee sufficient input for the two gatherings. Organizations should be cautious because these discussions presently occur in the front of a huge number of individuals, and they're documented for a considerable length of time to come.

Be Alive and Responsive

Social media permits constant correspondence between the various gatherings included. It's anything but an extraordinary encounter for news to show up. It has been as of now spread on social systems administration destinations before they show up on the customary news media like paper and TV. So also nowadays, clients like it if you can react to their needs and difficulties at the earliest opportunity. The inability to react on time could leave your clients looking for elective arrangements from your rivals.

Screen your brand

Regardless of whether you're a nearby business or a global brand, it is conceivable that individuals are now discussing you on the Web. Yet, before you can engage in those discussions, you need to begin tuning in. After you start listening, then you can begin reacting to what is being stated, where it is being stated, and who is stating it. Checking social media ought to be a progressing procedure anyway, and you should exploit different social media stages to make sure nothing gets lost in an outright flood the right (or wrong) story can begin from anyplace and burst up in your face. You would prefer not to get found napping.

Spread the news

Your own "pledge of mouth" is your best marketing device. Tell everybody. Everybody! Tell every one of your companions, relatives, and collaborators that you are beginning a social media battle and are transparently broadening your quest for customers. The more individuals think about this energizing arrangement, the more probable the news will get-go along to the ears of your forthcoming customers. The best exposure you can get is free, so ensure you amplify on all the free attention that you can get.

CHAPTER TEN

HOW TO USE SOCIAL MEDIA TO PERSUADE CUSTOMERS

Social media has been the appropriate response that advertisers have been searching for to raise their endeavors. Since the appearance of the web, they think about it as a speedy marketing ground to be persuasive—with a solitary snap; their substance can arrive at a more extensive degree around the globe, their message can be more than once executed and conveyed in an inventive way.

Advertisers utilize social media effectively for their different marketing endeavors. As per the Social Media Examiner's 2014 Social Media Marketing Industry Report, 92% of advertisers demonstrated that social media is profoundly pertinent for their businesses; and this finding is generally higher than 86% from a year ago's outcomes. With different social media stages accessible, most advertisers bounce into the temporary fad by posting in a flash. However, all they get are paid preferences, with no commitment by any means. Is this what we need to accomplish?

To win the marketing impact game, fusing the science and craft of influence is an unquestionable requirement. How would you do it?

Here are 11 keys of influence for your social media marketing endeavors

1. Give and Receive

We can impact other individuals' choices by honing our relational abilities and joining enticement to it. Use influence methods to express the genuine and certifiable similitudes among you and your group of spectators to associate with them.

Influence your group of spectators through the rule of correspondence: react to some help given to you by returning it to a similar degree or significantly more prominent. Start by unmistakably distinguishing your intended interest group, your purpose behind affecting them, and what they truly need. At that point, respond by furnishing your clients with free significant substance, for example, a digital book, free download of applications or projects for a specific timeframe, or welcome to your occasions and training that clients may discover profitable. This will make clients visit your site consistently, and share your substance in their social media handles as their appreciation to what you have given them.

2. Connect With People's Emotions—Through A Story

Individual's romantic tales. They like stories that issue to them, particularly if they can without much of a stretch identify with it. When you get profoundly of their feelings, you have the ideal chance of convincing them to look at your site, which will, in the end, lead to their buy. You have the job to pass on a decent story that will contact straightforwardly into individuals' souls and psyches and summon the right feelings without hard-selling your product.

Coca-Cola propelled its "What is Happiness" battle, relying upon the possibility that you can discover satisfaction when you wouldn't dare to hope anymore. It centers on various endearing stories that satisfied individuals as a result of a jug of Coke shared. Battles this way, when infused with appropriate social media marketing endeavors, are a certain flame hit that will build changes for your business. Consider the top feelings to tap when making a substance to create the correct sort of substance for the correct feelings of your clients.

3. Consistency Counts, All the Time

They state that it is simpler to keep a current client, as opposed to pulling in another one. Be steady in what you state to your clients with the goal that they remain on your side. Consistency additionally means higher transformation rates and leads you to your steadfast clients.

Start by offering a free preliminary for your product for a specific time to check their consistency. Attempt to guide your clients to your mailing list membership, online classes, or articles in a reliable manner. After they have encountered these from your site, they will feel progressively dedicated to acquiring. Each site visit or snap, regardless of how little, can be their little strides of consistency.

4. Show People That You Are Their Option

Every day, individuals are looked at with decisions. Some of the time, we feel solid with our inclinations, however frequently, we are stuck between two similarly solid alternatives. In this circumstance, we will, in general, research how others are picking to have a social confirmation that one is working and one isn't.

Since individuals pursue patterns, influence your clients by including sentences, for example, "9 out of 10 individuals favor this... "To apply this guideline in your next marketing movement. One genuine model for this is Amazon: they use star evaluations, suggestions, and remarks to help individuals in their basic leadership on a specific product. This is another ideal method to influence your clients to visit you consistently.

5. Increment Your (Like)ability

Research says that we are bound to tail somebody whom we like. There are loads of components to be considered, for example, how an individual looks or talks, and how he conducts himself. Also, we will, in general, purchase something from somebody we knew—companions, family, and individuals whom we gaze upward to, as opposed to from an outsider. This is valid, notwithstanding for social media marketing.

Impact your clients better by being increasingly amiable on the web. Be progressively empathic with your substance production by consolidating pictures or recordings that your clients can without much of a stretch identify with. This will build the likelihood that individuals will like you, and your change rates will go higher. Do mull over the correct utilization of SEO and substance marketing procedures to more readily contact your crowd. Be increasingly inventive with your "about" page and demonstrate your likenesses among you and your customers. When done appropriately, individuals will feel that you speak to them, and they will feel a solid association with your organization's brand.

6. Yell out The Authority

Expert in social media implies that you have built up a decent association with an outstanding brand, particularly if they left positive remarks. Gladly yell it out to the remainder of the world through social media. This will indicate to clients that your business is dependable. Construct a more prominent impact by exhibiting your accomplishments locally and all-inclusive, and offer your substance that has been distributed in solid on the web and disconnected productions.

Likewise, incorporate an exceptionally compelling individual for your tributes. This can enable when individuals are dubious of a specific brand. Adidas throughout the years has constantly utilized noticeable figures in their battles, for example, Lionel Messi, to push for a specific brand message. Individuals are bound to pursue these expert figures, even in social media, so you have to feature them in your marketing techniques.

7. Be Limited To Gain Their Unlimited Attention

Being rare or restricted in your product or services is not a terrible thing, particularly if your offering is of high incentive to your customers. This influence standard tells individuals that they're going to pass up something profitable if they don't choose or act rapidly.

Weave this with your methodologies by telling individuals that you have restricted time with a compelling visitor. For instance, if you have Tim Cook in your online course, tell everybody through social media that he just has 1 hour for the said occasion. Individuals will run towards your site along these lines. Likewise, give due dates for the accessibility of a specific product or administration. Ticketmaster offers bunches of occasion ticket bargains temporarily. Being restricted builds the odds that individuals will routinely beware of you as long as you give individuals that they need, in great quality.

8. Offer the Power of Influence

Verbal exchange joined with social media is a ground-breaking mix for your business. The Digital Marketer: Benchmark and Trend Report for 2011, directed by Experian, uncovers that 54 percent of grown-ups in America expressed that informal still impacts them intensely with regards to their buy choices.

Offer the intensity of impact by giving your clients straightforward stages to give criticism and associate it with their social media handles. Since people are always considering proposals from individuals they know, they will be intrigued to tap on your site to acquire data about your organization when they see a positive remark or post from their companion talking about your brand.

9. Connect More to Persuade More

Brisk commitment with individuals is one of the characteristics that social media gloats. Seeing this preferred position, you have to utilize successful social media marketing methods for better commitment. A social media brand commitment can't keep running on a single direction correspondence. If individuals associate with you, they expect straightforward cooperation or a "like" from their post referencing you and your services.

If you disregard both positive and negative messages, it can give a sign that you couldn't care less or you don't esteem them who support your brand. Check the most well-known social media stages that your clients are using and set an ordinary time for commitment, to keep them to ceaselessly the benefit of your products and services.

10. Use Power Words

Words are amazing. The Ultimate Terms hypothesis expresses that words have "unique importance inside each culture and convey control where they are utilized." If you use words appropriately in your strategies inconspicuously and lightly, you can influence individuals all the more viably.

The hypothesis partitions words into three classes. God terms to pass on gifts, penance, or permission (for example esteem), Devil terms inspire nauseate (for example, extremist), and Charismatic terms are legitimately connected with immaterial things (for example, commitment). Terms can change, particularly when utilized inappropriately, so you have to keep an eye on the motivation behind why you are utilizing it. Power words can likewise be coordinated to a particular thought or idea, for example, wellbeing, wellbeing, control, and comprehension.

11. Keep an eye on Your Progress Regularly

Successful influence additionally includes the correct assessment of your advancement with regards to your social media marketing endeavors. It is prescribed that you direct quarterly audit to check whether you are compelling and to measure whether it is delivering client transformations.

To make changes, one ought to consistently break down the traffic and leads being produced from every social media stage that you are utilizing. If it is inadequate, at that point, modifications to your influence ought to be finished.

These keys of influence for your social media marketing endeavors can enable you to win the marketing game by connecting more and affecting more your crowd. Be progressively enticing without sounding edgy to address your clients' issues to construct an enduring association with them as your steadfast clients.

Approaches to Be More Persuasive With Social Media

How might you be powerful with customers on social media? The strategies underneath and break down how they can best be connected to a social media crowd are as follows.

1. Response – The Oldest Trick in the Book

The response is based upon the hypothesis that if you give something like a blessing and, at that point, approach the beneficiary for some help, they'll react in kind.

For instance, Dropbox will give you 2GB of extra room for nothing. However, the organization requests that you give back where it's due by offering the support of companions, at that point, rewards you with another 250 MB of room. That is correspondence.

Another normal social media procedure is to give away digital books. For instance, after a client has downloaded a free digital book, urge that individual to buy into your blog, Facebook Fan page or Twitter account — "Since you have the book, okay personality tailing me on Twitter?"

2. Social Proof – Don't Be Left Behind

With regard to deciding, we frequently seek other individuals for pieces of information. This is called social verification. Here are a couple of markers of social confirmation in the social media world.

- Subscriber or adherent tallies – Are many individuals following this blogger? At that point, you presumably ought to tail him as well.
- Reviews – If you see that a book has more than 500 audits and a normal four stars, you are bound to get it than a book with no surveys.
- Comments – Blog posts with many remarks propose that it is an excellent (or questionable) post. You are more enticed to perceive what's happening.
- Share checks – If you see an article has been tweeted multiple times, you are bound to peruse it than an article tweeted multiple times.

Primary concern: When it comes to social media, an enormous group of spectators is brilliant.

3. Preferring – Never Met a Stranger

That is to say, do individuals like you? Here are a couple of thoughts on how this deals with the social web.

• Be warm and amicable - Whether you're on LinkedIn or Google+, converse with individuals how you would connect with them at a mixed drink party.

• Give individuals things they need – For instance, if you realize someone is searching for research examines on portable application marketing. You run over some data, share it with that individual.

• Be gracious – Unfortunately, it's extremely simple to give everything hangs a chance to out on the web, yet you shouldn't do that. If you can't utter a word decent, don't utter a word by any stretch of the imagination.

• Be amusing – If you have a comical inclination, display it on the web. Individuals love to chuckle, even in expert settings.

4. Specialist – Why You Must Listen to Me

What does the specialist resemble in social media? Keeping up associations with understood brands can just help. For instance, if any of your articles have been distributed in well-known disconnected or online productions, show that substance on your social media accounts.

If you've at any point distributed a book or manufactured a fruitful organization, you are viewed as an expert and built up an application? You are a specialist.

Feature your remarkable accomplishments in your social media collaborations, and you'll have a more prominent impact on your group of spectators.

5. Shortage – Last Chance to Be Popular

The shortage is another method for saying you have a restricted stock of something. With regards to social media, mesh shortage into your endeavors.

• Limit your operations on the web – Having a 30-minute Q&A on Twitter each Thursday. Individuals flood him with inquiries during that time since they know he's not accessible something else.

• Time your associations – Online consideration is rare. Like this, distinguish the best occasions to collaborate with your social media networks. Ace social media timing, and you'll expand your social media execution.

• Use due dates – Force individuals to act rapidly by constraining to what extent a product, opportunity or offer is accessible.

6. Responsibility and Constancy – Don't Go Back on Your Word

This is the place everything meets up. During the whole procedure of associating with your social systems utilizing the above strategies, you ought to always request little duties.

For instance, request that individuals share a digital book before they download it. When they download, help them to remember their dedication!

Push those responsibilities because the vast majority despise their very own irregularities. If they focus on something, they will probably do it.

AFFILIATE MARKETING FOR BEGINNERS 2020

INTENSIVE COURSE FOR BEGINNERS TO LEARN ABOUT AFFILIATE MARKETING. LEARN IN 30 DAYS HOW TO CREATE YOUR FIRST PASSIVE INCOME WITH THIS FANTASTIC BUSINESS!

CHAPTER ONE

INTRODUCTION

Affiliate marketing is the point at which an online retailer pays you a commission for traffic or deals produced from your referrals. Affiliate marketing is a kind of performance-based marketing in which a business rewards at least one affiliate for every guest or client brought by the affiliate's marketing endeavors. Affiliate marketing covers with other Internet marketing strategies somewhat because members frequently utilize standard promoting techniques. Those techniques incorporate paid search engine marketing, search engine optimization, email marketing, content marketing, and (in some sense) show promoting. Then again, affiliates here and there utilize less universal procedures, for example, distributing audits of products or administrations offered by an accomplice.

Affiliate marketing is usually mistaken for referral marketing, as the two types of marketing utilize outsiders to drive deals to the retailer. The two types of marketing are separated, be that as it may, by the way, they drive sales, where affiliate marketing depends absolutely on monetary inspirations. In contrast, referral marketing depends more on trust and personal connections. Promoters often neglect affiliate marketing. While search engines, email, and site syndication catch a significant part of the consideration of online retailers, affiliate marketing conveys a much lower profile. Affiliates keep on assuming a critical job in e-retailers' marketing procedures.

Affiliate marketing helps to adapt your substance by advancing other organizations' products utilizing affiliate joins. At the point when someone purchases a product or administration dependent on your referral, you win a little commission on that buy. Right now, acquaint you with the rudiments of affiliate marketing and talk about how it functions by and by. We'll likewise give you how you could profit by utilizing it and give you some assistance in the beginning. How about we start! Adapting your website doesn't need to be a troublesome or bargaining try. It very well may be staggeringly fulfilling, both from a financial and imaginative perspective. Also, it does not require much of the legwork associated with different strategies for bringing in cash on the web.

Affiliate marketing includes advancing products from outer sellers on your website. While definitions once in a while change, there are commonly three or four gatherings associated with an affiliate arrangement. Since these terms can be confounding, how about we pause for a minute to explain the 'who' of affiliate marketing:

• The affiliate. Otherwise called 'the marketer,' this is the person running a site that contains affiliate joins. The member gets a commission on each buy made by guests who found a product by clicking on one of their connections.

• The customer. This is a guest on the affiliate site, who clicks on an affiliate interface and finishes a buy (regardless of whether that is the first thing being advanced, or something different from a similar organization).

• The network. This alludes to the inside or outsider stage that the affiliate program is operated on. This means they are giving the connections that the affiliates use and paying the member their bonuses.

• The shipper. This is an organization that sells products being advertised by the affiliate. By and large, the dealer and the network are the equivalents, as individual organizations run their affiliate programs. For straightforwardness, we'll be joining these last two substances all through the remainder of our conversation here.

If that despite everything sounds somewhat befuddling, we should take a gander at a run of the genuine mill case of how an affiliate deal may function:

1. An affiliate shares a blog entry on websites. The post maybe that of a survey of a couple of shoes sold by a dealer.

2. At the base of the post, the affiliate incorporates a connection that prompts the tennis shoes' product page.

3. A buyer peruses the blog entry and, charmed by the audit, clicks on the affiliate connect.

4. Once on the vendor's website, the buyer chooses to buy tennis shoes.

5. The vendor procures a benefit off of the deal and offers a segment of that cash with the affiliate.

You may be interested in how the dealer realizes which affiliate is liable for the buy. That is the simple part as each member is given a special connection that tracks every product they advance. This lets the trader track all referrals and guarantees that they realize how a lot of cash they've earned gratitude to each affiliate and what to pay them consequently.

How Affiliate Marketing Can Benefit You

The possibility to acquire cash by mostly sharing connections most likely sounds enticing as of now. Affiliate marketing incorporates an entire host of favorable circumstances past the conspicuous one. Let's investigate a portion of the ways being an affiliate marketer can profit you and your site.

Above all else, it's a generally safe and reasonable business. The absolute minimum for beginning as an affiliate is having a blog, a website, or even only an online life profile. This makes it an efficient strategy for acquiring cash. It likewise implies you don't need to submit a great deal of money in advance since you can begin little and develop your marketing endeavors after some time.

Another exciting portion of affiliate marketing is that it leaves you alone inventive and give something precious to your crowd. Since you can utilize affiliate connects anyplace, you can set up an audit site, distribute long-structure articles, or even produce video content. Since you're advancing other organizations' products, you don't have to stress over making, delivering, and supporting the things yourself.

Affiliate marketing additionally allows you to pick what you advance. It will also offer you the advantage of being critical. If you get to choose definitely which projects to work with, however much of the time, you'll even select the individual products and administrations you need to advance. You generally have full authority over what's highlighted on the website.

Affiliate marketing can be worthwhile (you, although remember that it is anything but an easy money scam). Since you're acquiring a percentage of each deal you allude, there's no most extreme roof for income either. This implies if your affiliate site takes off in a significant manner, you might wind up making an extraordinary easy revenue.

Considering the entirety of that, you ought to have a genuinely clear thought regarding whether affiliate marketing is something you'd prefer to engage with. For some individuals, the advantages represent themselves. Before you begin posting affiliate joins, there are various things you'll have to tolerate as a primary concern.

How Does Affiliate Marketing Work?

Affiliate marketing is a straightforward 3-advance procedure:

1. You prescribe a product or administration to your devotees.

2. Your devotees buy the product or administration utilizing your affiliate interface.

3. You get paid a commission for the deals made utilizing your affiliate interface.

Beginning with Affiliate Marketing

Presently you know the essential meaning of affiliate marketing and how the procedure functions, so how about we talk about how to begin. Many would-be affiliate marketers don't set aside the effort to design and instead pursue each affiliate marketing network or affiliate marketing program they can discover.

They end up overpowered and over-burden.

Try not to resemble them.

Take as much time as necessary and work through these seven stages if you need to set yourself up for progress.

Complete the initial four stages before you even consider advancing a single product.

1. Discover Your Niche

Do you say "nitch" or "needs?"

Whichever way you say it, choosing a niche will give concentration to businesses and help with the content. It will also make it easier to make focus on marketing efforts.

For specific individuals, picking their niche is the hardest piece of going into business, yet it doesn't need to be that way. To choose your niche, it just takes posing a couple of inquiries:

• What am I enthusiastic about? Ordinarily, the things we're energetic about are things we're likewise definitely learned about, which makes it a lot simpler to create content.

• Is this point sufficiently large? Is there enough to the subject to make up to 100 blog entries? If not, you may battle with search engine optimization or experience difficulty creating authority.

• Is the niche oversaturated? Is there space for another affiliate in the niche? Before hopping into an excessively popular niche and attempting to contend with people who've been around for some time, perhaps check out another slot.

• Is there cash right now? Money isn't all that matters, indeed. In case you're keen on a few points, and one is a money-maker. However, one isn't... pick the money-maker.

You can look at a niche on an affiliate retailer like ClickBank to check whether it merits investing energy into it.

What you're searching for is products that have a high Gravity score, better than average standard pay per deal, and that would fit in generally with your substance. In case you're discovering a lot of products you would have the option to expound on, you've found a profitable niche!

2. Design a Website

When you've found out the right niche that you're ready for, you're prepared to fabricate a website and blog. WP-Beginner has an incredible manual to assist you with picking the best blogging stage that will make this procedure significantly simpler.

The essential focal point of your webpage will be your blog. However, there are a few pages that you ought to consider including (and some that are a level out MUST for affiliate marketers):

1. About: Make it personable and let individuals find a workable pace a bit.

2. Contact: This ought to incorporate all contact data that you need to impart to your perusers, publicists, or potential accomplices.

3. Disclaimer: If your site is adapted, this is the place you share its how.

4. Privacy Policy: Let clients know whether you gather any data about them and how that data is utilized.

5. Terms of Service: This is a legitimate page restricting your risk in case of abuse of data or administrations gave on your site. It additionally subtleties client duties in regards to copyrights and trademarks.

6. Custom 404 Page: A custom 404 page goes far toward improving the client experience.

7. Advertise: If you plan on selling nearby promotions, incorporate a page for publicists with data about accessible spots, month to month sees, crowd socioeconomics, and a contact structure. It's critical to ensure that your arrangements are clear and forthright to maintain a strategic distance from disarray and to assemble trust with your crowd.

3. Make Quality Content

Since the system of your page is all set, you have to make content.

Some affiliate networks and affiliate programs expect you to as of now have set up content, site traffic, and month to month sees at a specific level before they'll acknowledge you as an affiliate, so make sure to peruse the qualification prerequisites for the particular networks and projects you're thinking about before you apply.

This doesn't imply that you need to make 100 blog entries before you can even consider turning into an affiliate marketer. Yet, you ought to have in any event 5 in number posts as of now on your webpage with progressively booked.

4. Develop Your Email List

Indeed, email is as yet the #1 correspondence channel for marketing. It, despite everything, conveys a wild $38 return for each $1 spent.

Am I not catching this' meaning to you? That it's 3800% justified, despite all the trouble to put some time and cash into developing your email list.

Probably the most effortless approaches to develop your email list is by adding a popup to your site:

Try not to stress if you've never done email marketing; we've all found a good pace. We have a tenderfoot's manual for email marketing that will take you from zero to computerizing your email marketing effort in the blink of an eye.

In case you're hoping to step up your email marketing efforts, look at these posts on diminishing you're withdraw rates and portioning your email list like a genius.

5. Pick Affiliate Products to Promote

If you've accomplished the work to pick a niche, picking affiliate products to advance ought to be simple! Pick products that fit your niche and identify with your substance.

Where do you get thoughts for products to advance? Anyplace, truly:

Advance Products you Already Use

What do you, as of now, use and love? There's most likely an affiliate program for that.

Make a rundown of the entirety of the products and administrations that you use and hit up Google to discover their affiliate programs. At that point, compose surveys and plug in the affiliate joins.

6. Join an Affiliate Marketing Network

Affiliate marketing networks are online commercial centers where retailers list their products, and affiliates can discover products to sell. The marketing network goes about as a go-between. As the affiliate, you ought to never need to pay to pursue an affiliate marketing network.

Here are a couple of the more popular affiliate networks out there, yet there are such a large number of more than this:

• ShareASale

• CJ Affiliate

• ClickBank

• Amazon Associates

This WordPress module lets you dispatch a completely working affiliate program from beginning to end in only a couple of moments. You'll have the option to effectively follow outbound connections, clicks, payments, and deals from your simple to-utilize dashboard, personalized to incorporate just the information that is critical to your objectives.

7. Track Your Results

You can utilize MonsterInsights to handily follow the performance of your affiliate products on a WordPress site.

To begin, you'll have to introduce and enact the MonsterInsights module. At that point, interface your WordPress site with your Google Analytics account.

When actuated, you'll go to Insights » Settings in your WordPress dashboard and select the Tracking tab. s

There are a few segments to the tab. We begin in the Engagement area where you can see that Enable MonsterInsights occasions following defaults to Yes, which is the thing that we need.

CHAPTER TWO

THE BASICS OF AFFILIATE MARKETING

Affiliate marketing is the procedure by which an affiliate gains a commission for marketing someone else's or organization's products. The affiliate essentially searches for a product they appreciate, at that point, advances that product and acquires a bit of the benefit from every deal they make. The arrangements are followed using affiliate joins starting with one website then onto the next.

Since affiliate marketing works by spreading the duties of product marketing and creation across parties, it figures out how to use the capacities of an assortment of people for an increasingly successful marketing technique while furnishing benefactors with a portion of the benefit. To make this work, three unique gatherings must be included:

1. Seller and product makers.

2. The affiliate or publicist.

3. The purchaser.

We should dive into the intricate relationship these three gatherings offer to guarantee affiliate marketing is a triumph.

1. Vender and product makers.

The vender, regardless of whether an independent business person or enormous endeavor, is a seller, dealer, product maker, or retailer with a product to showcase. The product can be a physical article, similar to family unit merchandise or assistance, similar to cosmetics instructional exercises. Otherwise called the brand, the merchant shouldn't be effectively engaged with the marketing. However, they may likewise be the publicist and benefit from the income sharing related to affiliate marketing.

2. The affiliate or distributer.

Otherwise called a distributer, the affiliate can be either an individual or an organization that engagingly advertises the merchant's product to potential buyers. As such, the affiliate elevates the product to persuade buyers that it is significant or useful to them and persuade them to buy the product. If the purchaser ends up purchasing the product, the affiliate gets a bit of the income made.

Affiliates regularly have quite a certain crowd to whom they advertise, for the most part sticking to that crowd's advantages. This makes a characterized niche or personal brand that enables the affiliate to draw in purchasers who will be well on the way to follow up on the advancement.

3. The shopper.

Regardless of whether the shopper knows it or not, they (and their buys) are the drivers of affiliate marketing. Affiliates share these products with them via web-based networking media, web journals, and websites.

At the point when customers purchase the product, the vendor and the affiliate share the benefits. Now and then, the affiliate will decide to be forthright with the shopper by revealing that they are getting a commission for the business they make. On different occasions, the shopper might be unmindful of the affiliate marketing framework behind their buy.

In any case, they will once in a while pay more for the product bought through affiliate marketing; a lot of the benefit is remembered for the retail cost. The shopper will finish the buying procedure and get the product as ordinary, unaffected by the affiliate marketing framework in which they are a huge part.

How Do Affiliate Marketers Get Paid?

A fast and economical technique for bringing in cash without the issue of really selling a product, affiliate marketing has an evident attraction for those hoping to build their pay on the web. Be that as it may, how does an affiliate get paid after connecting the dealer to the shopper? The appropriate response is muddled. The buyer doesn't generally need to purchase the product for the affiliate to get a payoff. Contingent upon the program, the affiliate's commitment to the dealer's deals will be estimated quickly. The affiliate may get paid in different manners:

1. Pay per deal.

This is the standard affiliate marketing structure. Right now, the shipper pays the affiliate a percentage of the deal cost of the product after the purchaser buys the product because of the affiliate's marketing procedures. As such, the affiliate should get the speculator to put resources into the product before they are redressed.

2. Pay per lead.

An increasingly mind-boggling framework, pay per lead affiliate programs, repays the affiliate dependent on the change of leads. The affiliate must persuade the purchaser to visit the shipper's website and complete the ideal activity — regardless of whether it's rounding out a contact structure, pursuing a preliminary of a product, buying into a bulletin, or downloading programming or documents.

3. Pay per click.

This program centers on boosting the affiliate to divert customers from their marketing stage to the trader's website. This implies the affiliate must connect with the buyer to the degree that they will move from the affiliate's site to the vendor's site. The affiliate is paid dependent on the expansion in web traffic.

Why Be an Affiliate Marketer?

What are the motivations to turn into an affiliate marketer?

1. Easy revenue.

While any "ordinary" work expects you to be grinding away to bring in cash, affiliate marketing offers you the capacity to bring in cash while you rest. By putting an underlying measure of time into a crusade, you will consider consistent with being at that time as customers buy the product over the next days and weeks. You get cash for your work long after you've completed it. In any event, when you're not before your PC, your marketing abilities will gain you a consistent progression of salary.

2. No client care.

Singular merchants and organizations offering products or administrations need to manage their shoppers and guarantee they are happy with what they have bought. On account of the affiliate marketing structure, you'll never be worried about client service or consumer loyalty. The total employment of the affiliate marketer is to connect the merchant with the purchaser. The dealer manages any buyer objections after you get your bonus from the deal.

3. Work from home.

In case you're somebody who detests heading off to the workplace, affiliate marketing is the perfect arrangement. You'll have the option to dispatch crusades and get income from the products that dealers make while working from the solace of your own home. This is a vocation you can manage while never escaping your night robe.

4. Financially savvy.

Most businesses require startup charges just as an income to fund the products being sold. Be that as it may, affiliate marketing should be possible effortlessly, which means you can begin rapidly and absent a lot of issues. There are no affiliate program charges to stress over and no compelling reason to make a product. Starting this profession is generally clear.

5. Helpful and adaptable.

Since you're turning into a specialist, you get ultimate freedom in defining your objectives, diverting your way when you feel so slanted, picking the products that intrigue you, and in any event, deciding your hours. This comfort implies you can enhance your portfolio if you like or spotlight exclusively on primary and direct battles. You'll likewise be liberated from organization limitations and guidelines just as sick performing groups.

6. Performance-Based prizes.

With different occupations, you could work an 80-hour week and still acquire a similar compensation. Affiliate marketing is simply founded on your performance. You will get back what you put into it. Sharpening you're looking into abilities and composing drawing in battles will mean direct enhancements in your income. You'll at long last get paid for the extraordinary work you do!

7. Try not to underestimate the power of SEO.

There's a huge amount of natural traffic you can get from search engines if you do SEO properly. The days when Search Engine Optimization was tied in with duping Google are no more. Today, it is tied in with improving your website for guests. Individuals normally search for data on the web. That is the reason you ought to become familiar with the nuts and bolts of on-page SEO, catchphrase research, and third party referencing to be the data source they discover first. Who wouldn't have any desire to rank #1 for terms, for example, "best product" or "product survey" in Google?

Normal Types of Affiliate Marketing Channels

Most affiliates share regular practices to guarantee that their crowd is locked in and open to buying advanced products. In any case, not all affiliates publicize the products similarly. There are a few diverse marketing channels they may use.

1. Influencers.

An influencer is a person who holds the ability to affect the buying choices of a huge fragment of the populace. This person is in an extraordinary situation to profit from affiliate marketing. They, as of now, gloating an amazing after, so it's simple for them to guide buyers to the dealer's products through web-based life posts, websites, and different collaborations with their supporters. The influencers, at that point, get a portion of the benefits they assisted with making.

2. Bloggers.

With the capacity to rank naturally in search engine questions, bloggers exceed expectations at expanding a dealer's changes. The blogger tests the product or administration and afterward composes an extensive survey that convincingly advances the brand, driving traffic back to the vender's website.

The blogger is granted for their impact getting the message out about the estimation of the product, assisting with improving the merchant's deals. For instance, my article on the best email marketing administrations incorporates product surveys, and affiliate connects all through.

3. Paid search centered microsites.

Creating and adapting microsites can likewise collect a genuine measure of deals. These destinations are promoted inside an accomplice site or on the supported postings of a search engine. They are particular and separate from the association's principal site. By offering progressively engaged, important substance to a particular crowd, microsites leads to expanded changes because of their basic and direct source of inspiration.

4. Email records.

Despite its more seasoned starting points, email marketing is as yet a reasonable wellspring of affiliate marketing pay. A few affiliates have email records they can use to advance the vender's products. Others may use email bulletins that incorporate hyperlinks to products, procuring a commission after the buyer buys the product. Another technique is for the affiliate to manufacture an email list after some time. They utilize their different crusades to gather messages as the once huge mob; at that point, convey messages concerning the products they are advancing.

5. Enormous media websites.

They are intended to make a tremendous measure of traffic consistently; these destinations center around building a group of people of millions. These websites elevate products to their large crowd using standards, and relevant affiliate joins. This strategy offers superior presentation and improves transformation rates, bringing about a first-class income for both the vendor and the affiliate.

Tips To Be A Successful Affiliate Marketer

1. Build up compatibility.

When starting your affiliate marketing vocation, you'll need to develop a group of people that has quite certain premiums. This permits you to tailor your affiliate crusades to that niche, improving the probability that you'll change over. By building up yourself as an expert in one zone as opposed to advancing an enormous exhibit of products, you'll have the option to market to the individuals destined to purchase the product.

2. Make it personal.

There is no lack of products you'll have the option to advance. You will be able to see the varieties of products that you put stock in, so ensure that your battles based on really significant products that buyers will appreciate. You'll accomplish an amazing change rate while at the same time building up the unwavering quality of your image.

You'll likewise need to get great at email effort to work with different bloggers and influencers. Utilize a device like ContactOut or Voila Norbert to assemble individuals' contact data and send personalized messages to accumulate visitor blogging and affiliate openings.

3. Begin evaluating products and administrations.

Concentrate on evaluating products and administrations that fall inside your niche. At that point, utilizing the compatibility, you have made with your crowd and your position as an expert, explain to your perusers why they would profit by buying the product or administration you are advancing. Nearly anything sold online can be assessed if there is an affiliate program. In essence, you can survey physical products, computerized programming, or even administrations booked on the web, similar to ride-sharing or travel resort booking. It is particularly powerful to contrast this product with others in a similar classification. Above all, ensure you are producing point by point, articulate substance to improve changes.

4. Utilize a few sources.

Rather than concentrating on only an email crusade, additionally invest energy bringing in cash with a blog, contacting your crowd via web-based networking media, and in any event, investigating cross-channel advancements. Test an assortment of marketing techniques to see which one your crowd reacts to the most. Utilize this system. For more data, you can look at this article on the most proficient method to begin an effective blog this year.

5. Pick crusades with care.

Regardless of how great your marketing abilities are, you'll get less cash-flow on a terrible product than you will on an important one. Set aside the effort to read the interest for a product before advancing it. Try to research the vendor with care before collaborating. Your time is worth very much, and you need to be certain you're spending it on a gainful product and a merchant you can have faith in.

6. Remain current with patterns.

There is not kidding rivalry in the affiliate marketing circle. You'll need to ensure you keep steady over any new patterns to guarantee you stay serious. Moreover, you'll likely have the option to profit by, in any event, a couple of the new marketing methods that are continually being made. Be certain you're staying up with the latest on all these new systems to ensure that your change rates, and in this way income, will be as high as could reasonably be expected.

The Top Affiliate Marketing Trends of 2020

1. Improved affiliate announcing and attribution.

Lots of affiliate programs operate with last-click attribution, where the affiliate accepting the last click before the deal gets 100% acknowledgment for the change. This is evolving. With affiliate stages giving new attribution models and announcing highlights, you can see a full-pipe, cross-channel perspective on how individual marketing strategies are cooperating. For instance, you may see that a paid social crusade created the principal click, Affiliate X got the second click, and Affiliate Y got the last click. Then, you can strategize your affiliate payments, so Affiliate X gets a percentage of the kudos for the deal, although they didn't get the last click.

2. Influencer niches are turning out to be hyper-focused on.

Before, huge affiliates were the backbone, as catch-all coupons and media destinations offered traffic to hundreds or thousands of publicists. This isn't such a lot of the case any longer. With shoppers utilizing long-tail watchwords and searching for quite certain products and administrations, influencers can use their hyper-centered niche for affiliate marketing achievement. Influencers may not send publicists immense measures of traffic. However, the crowd they do send is believable, directed, and has higher change rates.

3. GDPR is changing how personal information is gathered.

The General Data Protection Regulation (GDPR), which produced results on May 25, 2018, is a lot of guidelines overseeing the utilization of personal information over the EU. This is constraining a few affiliates to acquire client information through select in assent (refreshed security strategies and treat sees), regardless of whether they are not situated in the European Union. This new guideline ought to likewise remind you to follow FTC rules and unmistakably reveal that you get affiliate commissions from your suggestions.

4. Affiliate marketers are getting more astute.

Shippers getting an enormous percentage of their income from the affiliate channel can get dependent on their affiliate accomplices. This can prompt affiliate marketers to utilize their significant status to get higher commissions and better arrangements with their promoters. Regardless of whether it's CPA, CPL, or CPC commission structures, there are a ton of lucrative affiliate projects, and affiliate marketers are in the driver's seat.

Best Affiliate Products for Beginners

As you're getting moving, there are three explicit kinds of products I prescribe beginning to showcase. These are ones that will give you the most obvious opportunity with regards to achievement in developing your business and making commissions at a convenient time.

The most effective method to promote an Affiliate Offer

Alright, presently, the most significant part. At this point, you ought to have a decent feeling of what affiliate marketing is, have a thought of what products you need to elevate, and realize how to get your affiliate joins for them. In any case, if you don't have the foggiest idea how to advance them properly, it doesn't generally make a difference presently, isn't that right? Probably not. Right now, going to take a gander at probably the least demanding and best approaches to advance an affiliate offer.

Affiliate Marketing with Product Reviews

If you've developed a great deal of trust with your crowd, product surveys are an awesome method to create a few deals. This works for every one of the three kinds of products you can advance, and I've personally observed accomplishment with each.

The key to an effective product survey is trustworthiness.

I'd commonly just audit things you like, yet if there are disadvantages or easily overlooked details that trouble you – be forthright about them. A great many people realize that no product is perfect, so if you set desires and are unguarded with them, there's a decent possibility they'll get it at any rate.

Ensure you remember the accompanying things for any product survey:

1. A clear feature highlighting your ideal catchphrase ("product name audit" for example)

2. Clear connections for where to purchase at both the top and base of the page

3. A clear proposal

4. A personal tale about how you utilize the product or why you suggest it

Affiliate Marketing for Every Beginners

As we've just referenced, affiliate marketing has a generally low hindrance to passage. To assist you with beginning rapidly, we're going to walk you through the initial steps for transforming your site into an affiliate marketing achievement.

Stage 1: Choose a Suitable Affiliate Niche

In case you're beginning another affiliate site, you'll have to consider what niche you will work inside. Your site's niche figures out what sort of substance you make, who your intended interest group is, and which sorts of products you will advance.

Normally, it's significant to pick a monetarily suitable niche. This shows that you have to place a subject that enough individuals will be keen on. That may appear to be precarious, yet there are, in reality, a ton of choices you can look over. Performing watchword research is likewise a savvy thought at this stage, to discover what catchphrases are driving the most traffic using search engines.

In any case, this progression isn't just about finding the niche that pays the most. You should focus on a niche that suits you personally for effectiveness. If you, as of now, have some information and enthusiasm for your picked region of the center, you'll be in a situation to make legitimate and drawing in substance to oblige your affiliate joins.

You'll likewise have a superior comprehension of your intended interest group's needs and wants. This is basic since it encourages you to manufacture trust with your guests. If they have an inclination that they can depend on your judgment and proposals, they'll be bound to click on your connections and make buys dependent on your recommendations. Hence, the best niche will have a lot of potential buyers and will be something you can make proficient and dependable substance about.

Stage 2: Find and Sign Up for the Right Affiliate Programs

When you have a niche and site all set, it's an ideal opportunity to search for affiliate programs. As we referenced already, numerous projects are run legitimately by a dealer, to advance their own organization's products.

While selecting which projects to pursue, you should initially take a gander at what products they need you to advance. Above all, they'll have to offer products that are famous in your chosen niche. Subsequently, search for brands that address your objective market and check whether they offer affiliate programs. If your webpage is in with running websites, you could search for the web has with their affiliate programs.

Usually, it's likewise essential to discover programs that will pay you well. All things considered, you're investing a great deal of energy into advancing the traders' products, so you should see a decent amount of the benefits. Before you join, it's likewise a savvy move to research each program and see what experiences different affiliates have had.

You may even think that its helpful to search out an affiliate network, for example, Wealthy Affiliate. There, you can get guidance and help from the individuals who have been distributing and marketing for quite a while. This can be especially useful when you're an amateur. At that point, in a couple of years, you may be the one helping another learner begin.

Stage 3: Add Affiliate Links to Your Site

Now, you've pursued the best affiliate programs in your deliberately picked niche. Presently it's an excellent opportunity to indeed find a workable pace, implies sharing your affiliate joins. How you execute these connections on your site will shift, contingent upon what kind of substance you're making.

For instance, in case you're running a survey site, it bodes well to put principal affiliate connects inside your audits. The easiest method for doing this is simply to incorporate them as content connections in the substance itself. Notwithstanding, this methodology can be viewed as deceiving since it's less confident that you're advancing the products being referred to.

A superior method is to keep your connections somewhat isolated from your fundamental substance.

Some affiliate projects will likewise give you resources, for example, pennants, that you can use to advance products. This may be increasingly appropriate if you need to keep your marketing and substance unmistakably isolated.

Similarly, as with your niche, your way of dealing with actualizing connections will rely upon your site's motivation. Don't hesitate to experiment with various procedures; however, consistently recall that your attention ought to be on offering some benefit to your crowd. If you flop in that task, guests won't trust you, click on your connections, or return later on. Ensure you compose quality substance, in this manner, and watch out for your changes to perceive what's working (and so forth).

At last, we by and by the need to pressure the significance of unveiling your affiliate joins. This is an essential piece of conforming to the support rules given by the FTC. Damaging these rules could prompt lawful activity, which is usually something you'll need to stay away from, no matter what.

Like this, you ought to give data about your connections' tendency and reason, which you can do by making an 'affiliate divulgence' articulation. The notification ought to be unambiguous, and noticeable anyplace affiliate joins are utilized. This will keep your site in the clear, and help to advance trust with your crowd.

A Few Last Affiliate Marketing Tips

If you track with the methodologies above, you'll be making affiliate deals instantly off of your blog.

To improve your odds considerably more, I have a couple more tips for you.

Utilize Pretty Link

Affiliate joins are commonly genuinely revolting. They're long connections that frequently go to an optional area, and are entirely evident that they're an affiliate. Download the Pretty module Link to make your contacts look substantially more benevolent.

Build up a Good Relationship with an Affiliate Manager

Most significant affiliate programs for physical products or administrations will have an affiliate supervisor, whose sole occupation is to assist you with creating more deals.

You'll have to demonstrate to them that you have some potential, however, give a valiant effort to get them on the telephone before you begin doing any significant advancements. They'll have the option to provide you with a decent feeling of what works, what doesn't, and conceivably even give you a lift in commissions. One call about multiplied my payments for one is facilitating organization specifically.

Affiliate Marketing Alternatives: Four Other Online Businesses to Supplement Your Affiliate Marketing Business

• Freelance Writing – The least demanding approach to begin a business on the web, begin constructing a few aptitudes, and building trust in your capacity to effectively accomplish something like affiliate marketing.

• Niche Sites – Once you get the nuts and bolts of affiliate marketing down, you can genuinely focus on rehashing the procedure and making niche destinations on a wide range of various subjects.

• Blogging – A large segment of each excellent affiliate marketing website is the blog, take that range of abilities and make an interpretation of it into another business.

• Physical Products – Want to make a physical product that integrates with your niche and afterward sells it on the web? If you need to work at it, there's a considerable amount of chance here.

CHAPTER THREE

ONLINE WORK TOOLS

There are a vast amount of these apparatuses presented each day; these are only a couple of our top picks:

1. Adblock Plus

AdBlock Plus strips Flash advertisements, pop-ups, and inserted activities on any site you see, including Facebook and YouTube. It additionally squares malware to secure your PC. Accessible for IE, Firefox, Safari, Chrome, and Android OS.

2. Aura

Aura offers note, screen catch, and an image cutting instrument to assist you with recollecting relevant data or motivation found on the web. Their suite of tools permits you to catch and offer substance from locales through an augmentation on different internet browsers. Their cut-out apparatuses provide heaps of adaptability to find different parts or even whole site page scrolls.

3. Blog Social Analyzer

Blog Social Analyzer lets you check your blog or another organization's RSS channel to locate some essential realities, for example, Alexa, MozRank and Domain Authority, and to perceive how a lot of online networking sharing is going on. Use it to assess yourself or to check whether offers are basic on a blog you're considering visitor posting for. This one is an essential online apparatus and doesn't require a module or expansion.

4. Disengage

Disengage prevents destinations from following your developments on the web. It squares outsider treats, gives you command over site contents, and shields your protection from prying "eyes." The free form runs on Chrome, Firefox, and Opera.

The superior rendition is accessible for Mac, PC, iOS, and Android.

5. dotEPUB

Date pub spares online articles and transforms them into epub documents you can open later on an assortment of eReaders or practically any cell phone. Accessible for Chrome and Firefox, additionally as a bookmark on different programs.

6. Evernote web clipper

Evernote web clipper lets you get almost anything on the web and set it back into an Evernote scratchpad. It matches up overall gadgets with your record to review significant web bits. What is particularly extraordinary about this instrument is its capacity to feature critical data and include notes while including the passage. Accessible for IE, Firefox, Safari, Chrome, and Opera.

7. Ghostery

Ghostery is like Disconnect, giving you labels, web bugs, pixels, and reference points that are remembered for pages to follow your online conduct. Ghostery approaches a library of 4,500 contents and screens more than 2,200 trackers, giving you a move call of the promotion networks, conduct information suppliers, web distributers, and different organizations intrigued by your action, letting you deny them from gathering your data. Accessible for IE, Safari, and Opera.

8. Hootlet

Hootlet lets you watch a hashtag (HootFeed in HootSuite) with live updates directly from your program while surfing different pages. You can likewise plan presents on different social stages, including Twitter, LinkedIn, Pinterest, Instagram, YouTube, Google maps, and the sky is the limit from there. Accessible for Firefox and Chrome.

9. HoverZoom

HoverZoom extends thumbnails on mouse-overs to full-estimate pictures. HoverZoom takes a shot at destinations like Facebook, Tumblr, and Amazon for simple amplification and a quicker perusing experience. Accessible for Google Chrome as it were.

10. GIPHY

GIPHY delineates your substance, email message, or blog entry with the perfect energized GIF quickly. It is a search expansion that permits you to type in catchphrases to search, select, at that point intuitive into Gmail, Facebook, Twitter, Slack, Hipchat, and the sky is the limit from there.

11. TooManyTabs

TooManyTabs tidies up your work area by sorting out the tabs you have open. You can sort out bookmarks by creation time, space, or title, see every tab's substance, and reestablish as of late shut tabs. Accessible for Chrome as it were.

12. Grammarly

Grammarly is an augmentation that improves and triple check your internet composing. It surveys spelling, syntax, and even plagiarism. It underlines and proposes remedies almost any place you compose on the web, including Gmail, Facebook, Twitter, Tumblr, and LinkedIn. Accessible for Chrome, Safari, and Firefox.

13. Canva

Canva is a visual communication programming where you can without much of stretch prepare illustrations for web-based life, introductions, and additionally utilizing their pre-stacked formats or by making your own. There are free pictures, vectors, and textual styles to effectively and rapidly make proficient looking designs. Takes a shot at Chrome, Firefox, Safari, Internet Explorer and Microsoft Edge.

14. PlaceIt

PlaceIt is a mockup generator that permits you to put plans or pictures on a mockup without messing around in Photoshop. It has an enormous assortment of photographs and recordings to browse, including clothing and different gadget screens. New pictures are included much of the time by their staff picture takers.

15. Found's SEO Audit Tool

Found's SEO Audit Tool permits you to survey SEO mistakes on your site page in short order. You should simply reorder your space and click a catch. A report will stack that gives blunders, alerts, and triumphs concerning your SEO strategies. You can send out the information into a PDF so you can address the discoveries.

16. MeisterTask

MeisterTask is a venture the board apparatus that permits you to mind map undertakings and see your entire day initially. You can organize projects dependent on which to concentrate on for the afternoon, immediately message colleagues, and even imprint task connections in classifications: identified with, copied, or blocked. This instrument incorporates Google Drive, Dropbox, Slack, and the sky is the limit from there.

You are beginning your online business.

If you have decided to work at home as opposed to having a regular office work, odds are you'll like to work for yourself while accomplishing on the web fill in also. These online employments will let you deal with your own time, understand your latent capacity, and, as a rule, gain significant cash.

Maker (selling your specialty on the web)

If you are capable of any specialties or plan, there is certainly a business opportunity for your craft. Unquestionably, you can sell your manifestations in disconnected occasions like artworks fairs or Christmas markets. Be that as it may, trading on the web will presumably be increasingly gainful and may even transform into full-time online work, mainly if a portion of your specialty is computerized.

Some incredible stages for selling your work on the web:

• Facebook is the brightest spot to start. Make a page for your product or brand, welcome all of your contacts to join and think about a test with free giveaways. Like this, you will get the message out about your product and get your first fan base. You can, in like manner, add a shop to your Facebook page or join Facebook Marketplace that enables buying and selling straightforwardly in the application.

• Etsy is the most acclaimed stage for exhibiting carefully assembled things. Regardless of whether your fine art is advanced, you can sell it here. A few models are wedding greeting layouts, superior banners, diaries, objective organizers, and plans for the day, structure maps, and so on.

• If your craft is less substantial, you can make your online store with Sellfy. Innovative business visionaries utilize this instrument to sell digital products like video or photograph presets, digital books or copywriting formats, liveliness, jingles, beats, or sewing designs.

Sell T-shirts, banners, mugs, caps, or even sacks with your plan or wonderful statements. Outsourcing administrations like Printful handle all the printing, bundling, marking, and in any event, sending in your place. You simply need to transfer plans, draw in purchasers, and afterward get your benefit. A few clients have announced acquiring over $1,200 in three weeks with this administration.

Product analyst on YouTube

The vast majority of us have checked a product survey on YouTube before buying. Can you be on the other side of the screen and offering your product audit recordings? Fortunately, you can audit products in your preferred niche – be it tech, excellence, home stylistic theme, wellness, or some other.

Here are a few different ways to acquire by putting product surveys on YouTube:

• YouTube promotions – if you get a lot of perspectives, publicizing can be a decent wellspring of salary.

• Affiliate marketing – place an affiliate interface in the video portrayal and get a percentage of the deal.

• Get paid to deliver supported surveys – get enlisted by brands to do explicit product audits. Websites like Famebit and Grapevine are a decent spot to search for paid sponsorships.

With time, you can develop your audience, gain impact, and work out more arrangements surveying products that you love.

Affiliate marketer

Affiliate marketing is the way toward helping another website to sell their products or administrations through uncommon affiliate joins. At the point when you pursue an organization's affiliate stage, you'll get your one of a kind connection or connections, that will gain you a commission each time a client clicks on them (or purchases something in the wake of clicking).

Numerous bloggers use affiliate marketing as an online work to gain cash from their composition. You don't need to be an essayist to take in substantial income along these lines – you can advance affiliate connects on your YouTube channel, web-based life, Facebook gatherings or discussions, blog entry remarks, and so forth. The greatest reward of affiliate marketing is that it liberates you from the duties of conventional deals models, such as having a product, website, or deals engine.

Blogger

As portrayed above, affiliate marketing is a boundless wellspring of salary for bloggers. In any case, you can procure cash as an essayist utilizing different ways as well. Some different approaches to win as a blogger (other than affiliate marketing):

• Placing advertisements on your blog and getting paid each time a guest clicks on them.

• They are writing audits about other organizations' products or administrations. Ensure they are significant to your audience and that they are not your solitary substance.

• Offering extra paid substance inside your articles (e.g., downloadable digital book, online meetings, or related products).

• You are doing content marketing for your clients. You can either compose articles for your customer's blog, or pitch visitor presents on respectable stages, including connections to your customer's webpage. Your client will pay you for getting the message out about their administrations and improving their positioning in search engines.

• I am writing for different web journals and news sources that pay visitor supporters.

The huge advantage of blogging is that you needn't bother with any spending limit to begin it – just great composing abilities and expertise in a niche theme or an interesting experience.

Affiliate

Exchanging implies discovering minimal effort in things that you can sell for additional. This can be available online work if you have extraordinary abilities or information that lets you find out products that are less available to others. In this manner, they would be glad to pay more to have these products brought to them by you. For instance, you might be a master in discovering forte things, incredible carport deals, or old pieces. Or then again, you might be a middle person between states or nations – recognizing something modest in one spot and offering it to another audience.

You can even begin by selling the things you have at home and never again need. For exchanges, you can either make your online store or sell stuff on destinations like eBay.

Picture taker

If you love taking photographs, you can rapidly transform this leisure activity into a wellspring of salary. Here are a few different ways picture takers can procure cash on the web:

• Teach photography. Offer valuable hints and procedures that hopeful picture takers couldn't want anything more than to catch wind of.

• Sell banners or advanced work of art. See point No—1 (Selling your specialty on the web).

• Sell your photographs on stock websites. Shutterstock, iStock, and BigStock are the most well-known photograph databases. The amount paid for each download is commonly low, so you should wager on the amount and transfer new groups of photographs consistently. The way to getting saw on stock websites is including numerous important watchwords that individuals would search for.

• Offer your photography and photograph altering aptitudes on specialist stages (see the accompanying area about Finding on the web deal with consultant stages)

Website analyzer

Numerous websites lose cash because of a poor UI, lousy route, and hazy duplicate or terrible structure. Accordingly, organizations search for individuals to test and survey their site before propelling it. Much of the time, you'll have to talk your musings for all to hear and record your screen activities as you peruse the website. For the most part, tests take between 5-25 minutes to finish, and the pay is an average of $10 per test.

Here's a rundown of stages that join website proprietors and analyzers and can offer great online work to do on aside.

Finding on the web take a shot at consultant stages

If you aren't prepared to wander into your own online business, offering your administrations on specialist stages is a decent spot to begin online work. Probably the most well-known specialist stages incorporate Fiverr, Upwork, and Freelancer. Other than joining these stages, there are different approaches to locate your first clients. For instance, using your companions and expert contacts; by sharing your portfolio on your internet based life; or by connecting with organizations straightforwardly (e.g., offering a copywriting administration to a website with an imperfect duplicate).

On the whole, characterize your ability and make it your calling.

Publicist, interpreter or editor

If composing is your quality, you can undoubtedly transform it into a wellspring of pay. You may be underestimating acceptable composition – everybody can write, isn't that so? Numerous individuals are not talented in making deals messages, thorough portrayals, or even internet-based life posts. There's an enormous audience glad to re-appropriate such undertakings.

Additionally, numerous business visionaries compose their website messages or blog articles that simply need altering and editing, or interpretation for different markets. All you have to do to catch that customer base is offer them your abilities and experience. Express your subject matters in your resume and provide instances of your work – along these lines, you'll stand apart from the opposition.

Web or Graphic creator

In our advanced period, visual depiction works are more requested than any other time in recent memory.

If you have some structure aptitudes and experience, these are only a few sorts of online work you can do:

• Website and presentation page structure

• Logo structure

• Mobile application structure

• Business cards and corporate gifts

• Ads, pennants and marketing materials

• Leaflets, pamphlets, digital books

• Packaging structure

• Presentation structure

• Diverse delineations

Other than specialist stages, there are different dependable approaches to bring in some additional cash with your plan work.

Language guide

Individuals have been anxious to learn new dialects since old occasions. Fortunately, it's a lot simpler to ace another dialect today than it was hundreds of years or even decades back. Doesn't make a difference if your native language is English or any of the world's 7000 languages. You make certain to discover understudies ready to learn or rehearse with you.

Far superior if you, as of now, make them instruct experience. If you don't, add a particular component to your resume. For instance, you may remember some social realities for your course, or make your classes' additional enjoyment, casual, or adaptable for any hour of the day – whatever is your thing.

Voice over

Various businesses are searching for male or female voices to portray their marketing or explainer recordings. Moreover, book recordings, web recording introductions, TV/Radio advertisements, instructional exercises, and even phone messages all require proficient voice overs.

If you have astounding vocal aptitudes in your local language, there's an immense open door for you to win cash with them. The best part – this activity is anything but difficult to do as all you need is a PC, a great amplifier, and alive with respectable acoustics.

Client assistance delegate

Numerous organizations are hoping to re-appropriate client care – particularly if their customer base is worldwide and they can't furnish nonstop help with their group. If you are into helping individuals or might want to construct experience right now, your administrations on specialist stages is a decent spot to begin.

Email, web-based life, and talk support just as lead age are the most widely recognized undertakings of a redistributed client assistance delegate. Nonetheless, the more extensive the scope of administrations you offer, the higher your possibility of getting contracted. For instance, you can include information passage occupations, web-based life the executives, report planning, and different obligations to your resume.

On the opposite side, you can function as a riddle shopper assessing the client care nature of other online shops and websites. Psyche that to have this as a genuine online work, you'll have to do a lot of secret shopping.

Expert, consultant or mentor

If you are an expert in truly any region, some individuals need to get your point of view and gain from your experience.

These are only a few instances of various zones you can counsel on:

• Business and Entrepreneurship

• Marketing and deals

• Freelancing

- Relationships

- Health and Fitness

- Fashion and Style

- Parenting

- Interior structure

- Writing

Investigate the classifications on consultant stages and offer your recommendation during the ones pertinent to your calling or experience. For instance, if you have dealt with an independent company, offer your meetings under Business or Marketing classifications.

Bookkeeper

Planning and funds are the bad dreams of numerous business people; no big surprise incalculable businesses are searching for approaches to re-appropriate these perplexing errands. If you are acceptable with numbers and make them account experience to appear, your customer base is without a doubt out there.

Shockingly better if you have lawful information, such as setting up a business, getting ready agreements, or enrolling your trademark. This might be an aptitude applicable in your area, yet at the same time profoundly requested.

Menial helper

The elements of a menial helper can go from straightforward assignments like information passage or interpreting discussions to progressively complex web research and examination, lead age, Photoshop alters, travel arranging, top to bottom LinkedIn search, and bookkeeping.

Start by characterizing your expertise and offering it on one of the consultant locales. The more extensive your range of abilities and the better your audits, the more probable you are to bring home the bacon from this sort of online work. Menial helpers in the United States procure $15.57 per hour.

Web-based life director

This activity is now and again recorded under a menial helper. In any case, as web-based life, the board is a profoundly requested expertise, bosses regularly search for it independently. If you are an authority of web-based life, you can make administration bundles that businesses could purchase from you. Essential online networking the executives' month to month bundle could include:

• Setting up an online networking profile (if vital)

• Monitoring 3-5 online networking stages, by noting remarks and messages

• Creating substance and posting a few times each week

• Adding applicable hashtags, pictures, and connections

Internet-based life the executives is a generously compensated kind of online work that is sought after. It is likewise an entirely adaptable activity as you can plan the posts whenever and anyplace.

If you pick this way, think about working with a few clients simultaneously to boost your pay.

CHAPTER FOUR

THE MINDSET TO BE SUCCESSFUL

In this day and age, having a triumph mindset is significant. It permits you the adaptability to see the various prospects and steps expected to take care of business. Regardless of whether it's in sports, business, the scholarly world, or amusement; Individuals with a triumph mindset consistently appear to make sense of how to get things going, despite apparently unthinkable odds. Some true instances of individuals with a triumph mindset are those with troublesome childhoods who have proceeded to make stunning things out of themselves. We've seen pioneers who've figured out how to battle extraordinary conditions and secure achievement. They've all had a similar shared characteristic, a point of view or conviction framework called the achievement mindset.

In a fixed mindset, individuals accept their fundamental characteristics, similar to their insight or ability, are fixed attributes. They invest their energy recording their knowledge or ability as opposed to creating them. They additionally accept that ability alone makes achievement—without exertion. These kinds of individuals feel crushed after a disappointment and step away from difficulties outside their customary range of familiarity.

In a development mindset, individuals accept that their most fundamental capacities can be created through devotion and challenging work—cerebrums and ability are only the beginning stage. This view makes an adoration for learning and flexibility that is basic for extraordinary achievement. These sorts of individuals see difficulties and disappointments as chances to learn and develop. They persist despite misfortunes. This mindset is a sign of accomplishment and achievement.

We, as a whole, have a few shades of both development and fixed mindsets, contingent upon the circumstance. Developing a development mindset will improve your capacity to prevail in all everyday issues. Learning a development mindset makes inspiration and productivity in the realms of business, instruction, and sports. It influences how you lead, oversee, parent, and appear seeing someone. Consider how you last moved toward a test: with interest for what you could realize or by pondering how you may show up if things turned out badly? If the last mentioned, it may be the ideal opportunity for a mindset change.

The Success Mindset: Top 3 Aspects

We here at Acquirent think three things characterize this achievement mindset:

1. A Growth Mindset

A development mindset is accepting that you can turn out to be better and improve with time and practice. Having a fixed mindset is imagining that there are parts of your personality and range of abilities that can't be enhanced past your current state. One model is knowledge. A development mindset accepts that a person can raise their IQ or information with study and practice. In any case, somebody with a fixed mindset takes that your IQ is the thing that it is. If you are awful at math, it doesn't make a difference in the amount you practice; there are ideas that you will not be able to get a handle on.

2. An Inward-Looking Propensity

N a nutshell, this is simply the capacity to search internally. It is challenging to have a triumph mindset without mindfulness. Ensure you are pointing fingers at yourself in all circumstances, even great ones. Might you be able to have accomplished something other than what's expected that would permit you to improve later on? Some significant inquiries to pose to yourself are:

• What did I gain from the circumstance?

• How am I developing?

• What might I be able to have done?

Asking yourself these inquiries keeps you continually looking forward and pushing ahead.

3. Positive Possibilities

Our third part of having a triumph mindset is accepting positive opportunities for yourself. This isn't visually impaired good faith and doesn't mean you ought to take that you can do everything. For instance, if you are 5'5" and trust you can dominate, that doesn't mean you can do it. In any case, if you can understand the real chance that you can improve your shot, bit by bit, you can grow as a bounce shooter. This is the conviction that positive changes can occur when we find a way to get it going.

It takes practice to embrace a triumph mindset for the individuals who don't as of now have one. If you trust you can change your viewpoint, at that point, you can begin by investigating yourself and making sense of the means you can take to adjust your psyche toward an increasingly fruitful perspective.

In deals, this could begin with defining objectives or tuning in to your calls. You may choose to adjust your contents, follow up additional, or take a shot at your tuning in. Whatever it is, you should begin with trusting it is conceivable to show signs of improvement, at that point, give yourself the time and commitment to improving.

Why it's a higher priority than any time in recent memory to develop your development mindset.

These circumstances are just going to turn out to visit progressively. At no other time has the universe of work been assaulted with such a lot of progress, change from all edges, change that implies that businesses and the individuals that work inside them must adjust, test, learn and challenge themselves on a close to everyday schedule.

For most, this implies operating outside of our customary ranges of familiarity all the more regularly. It means a move from working in set circles where we realize we can perform well, rings in which there's no perceived danger of disappointment or of looking dumb. A transition to managing various divisions and outside accomplices and providers all the more routinely, to cooperating with individuals who we may esteem more educated than us, individuals we are bound to see as a risk.

Thus, to be effective in this day and age of work, and later on, we should all show signs of improvement at thriving in these sorts of testing circumstances, rather than giving the story access our heads dominate. We should improve at persisting with those issues we would have once slowed down finished – surrendering at last. We should enhance at looking for motivation from the individuals we would have once avoided. We should all move our mindset to see the world and everything in it as a ceaseless chance to learn. Since, when we do, we're unmistakably more probable future-evidence our aptitudes and expertise.

Managers perceive this as well, with many trying to pull in contender to their businesses who are unmistakably ready to put time and exertion into building up their capacities, as opposed to the individuals who accept their abilities in specific zones are fixed, never to be extended and improved. These are the individuals who can genuinely assist them in driving their businesses forward.

Things being what they are, how might you move from a fixed to a development mindset, and become progressively employable simultaneously?

Fruitful Affiliate Marketing

It tends to be hard to win a consistent pay from affiliate marketing, and significantly increasingly hard to stand apart among different marketers advancing similar products. When you've developed a website, blog, pamphlet, or online life, there are steps you can take to get useful and create a progressively dependable income stream.

1. Know your accomplices. Research each affiliate program you consider joining with the goal that you will see how and when you'll be paid.

2. Build trust. Purchase the products you plan to advertise so you can personally authenticate the quality. You'll be decided by the product or administration you advance, so center around the nature of your image and suggestions, not merely the winning

potential. Your adherents will come to confide in your proposals and be bound to purchase from you.

3. Have a brand. Pick affiliate things that coordinate your niche and the substance of your blog. Try not to depend on SEO or web-based social networking alone to drive individuals to your website and affiliate referrals. Comprehend who your objective market is, the place you can discover your audience, and how to allure clients on your site.

4. Use assortment. Blend and match affiliate promotions, so you don't overpower your guests (content-inserted affiliate interfaces, as a rule, have the best click-through rates over picture joins.) Consider utilizing a lead page and pipe framework to showcase your affiliate business. Draw possibilities to your email list with a free offer and incorporate connects to your affiliate product pages.

5. Know the lawful prerequisites. Most guests will presumably comprehend that notices lead to your pay. Yet, if you compose a survey or utilize an in-content connection as a suggestion, you should expressly express that each buy utilizing that connection can produce income for you. This isn't merely an acceptable business: it's additionally legally necessary. If you don't unveil affiliate or income-producing joins, you could confront legal and monetary penalties.6

6. Track your traffic and income. Screen the accomplishment of your affiliate programs, primarily if you work with a few unique ones. Realize which projects are the best and which products reverberate with your adherents so you can design future battles.

Like some other sort of home business, achievement in affiliate marketing relies upon contributing the time and exertion to develop your business and manufacture associations with your clients and accomplice brands.

If you choose to seek after affiliate marketing, comprehend that it is anything but a quick or programmed business model. Be that as it may, it is conceivable to gain dependable and legitimate pay as an affiliate marketer.

The most effective method to switch your mindset and become increasingly fruitful

I'm no expert right now, having perused around this subject and thought about my own experience. I believe there are a couple of things you can begin doing today to develop your development mindset and help secure your future profession achievement:

1. Become progressively mindful: Reflect on what your run of the mill reaction is when confronted with specific difficulties, what triggers you to change into a fixed mindset and how might you come back to a place of development? Do you stress over not being 'adequate' or question your capacity to discover an answer for an issue you believe you don't have what it takes to understand? Do you feel overpowered and dread disappointment, so concentrate on different errands, assignments that you know you're generally acceptable at? When given input, do you think your guards go up? What I'm attempting to state here is that you have to think about how you feel at those key 'trigger' minutes, tuning in to the voice in your mind and what it's letting you know. At the point when you do, you'll have the option to choose those unhelpful self-constraining stories going around in your mind, accounts that you'll have to quietness if you are to move from a fixed to a development mindset in any meaningful manner.

2. Comprehend that your mind works like a muscle, it very well may be prepared: This marvel is known as neuroplasticity, as has been clarified by Professor and Neuroscientist Michael Merzenich, the man generally acclaimed as the dad of the idea of cerebrum versatility. Experiments have indicated that not exclusively is the cerebrum intended to change, yet additionally, it's working can be improved at any stage. Merzenich clarifies right now the human cerebrum works a lot of like a muscle,

requiring difficulties to develop. You accordingly can't anticipate that your mind should develop in case you're continually doing things likewise, and not testing it. Instead, Merzenich says that you have to remain in 'challenge mode.' Simply consider the way toward getting fit; it takes reps and practice to manufacture muscle, the cerebrum is the same. To create expertise in a particular territory, comprehend that it's not your cerebrum that is preventing you from doing only that, it's your mindset.

3. Reliably pick testing errands as opposed to safe ones: Overcome your dread of disappointment or looking dumb, disregard any self-question you have, and center your time and vitality around those undertakings you perceive to be more troublesome than others on your plan for the day. At the point when you do, attempt to decipher and handle these from a mindset of development. Honestly, you may fall flat. In any case, all the while, you'll get the hang of something vital to you that you wouldn't have done something else – including what you can do next time to guarantee you improve later on. With a move in mindset and working on receiving this mindset, you can rapidly grow your abilities as you're beginning to move toward each new test with energy and certainty, rather than with evasion and dread.

4. If you think somebody is superior to you, don't consider them to be a risk: Instead, change how you feel to find how you can gain

from them. This person you perceive to be compromising or scaring may have technical expertise that would assist you with leaping forward on one of your activities that have been on stop – or perhaps they simply have a specific method for getting things done, of acquiring answers to an issue that you had never thought of. Begin to move your intuition to understand that everybody you experience is a chance to take in something or understand things from with an improved point of view – that is not something to feel undermined by that is something to grasp.

5. Comprehend that you're not going to ace another ability medium-term: Remember we're never tantamount to us can be at a given aptitude when we begin rehearsing it – rather, it takes work and effort to ace. In this way, at whatever point you take on another test or set out on learning another ability, quit squeezing yourself. Rather, comprehend that you will experience battles toward the start. Pick something that you can't do right now – that one thing that you've generally had an inability to think straight about. Invest energy rehearsing it. Try not to stress over not being accepted at it straight away, or about another person is better. Simply center on your learning venture, beginning little and building your abilities a little bit at a time from that point. After some time, you'll begin to see improvement. In essence, this will fortify your tendency and certainty with regards to getting the hang of, which means you're unmistakably bound to proceed on that venture, as opposed to rescuing at the primary obstacle.

6. Put forth an informed attempt to commit time and exertion (and don't surrender): Just think about all the abilities you could have added to your repertoire, that your fixed mindset is preventing you from creating – those things that could have won you that advancement before or are so significant to developing your organization. Try not to come up with the rationalization that you "need more time," to create them, or "that is another person's activity"– rather, cut out the time. The most elevated accomplishing individuals in history valued this. Simply take a gander at Albert Einstein, who saw that "it isn't so much that I'm so savvy, it's simply that I remain with issues longer."

Along these lines, for your vocation achievement, this is the ideal opportunity to move your perspective, to hinder those harming considerations that hover in your psyche, those contemplations that can deny you of the chance to construct new aptitudes – abilities that could help secure your future employability.

How to Develop Mindset For Success

Achievement isn't a move that you make; it's a lifestyle. If you need to achieve extraordinary things, enormity must be reflected in everything that you do.

Consequently, paying little heed to what it is you need to achieve, the way to progress must start by receiving the correct mindset.

Coming up next are five hints to build up the perfect mindset for progress.

1. Characterize What Success Means

The initial step to building a mindset for progress is to characterize succeeding.

Defining objectives for yourself makes it simpler to think of a strategy to accomplish your aspirations, and will persuade you to make that arrangement. It likewise gives you a standard against which to gauge your advance and change your system. You should consequently characterize life or professional objectives and afterward consider what you have to do to accomplish them. Take a stab at defining SMART Goals in every aspect of your life that you need to change.

What's more, make momentary every day or week, making a point to adjust them to your more extensive positions. In case you're experiencing difficulty figuring out where to begin, look at my Goal's Quickstart Masterclass to assist you with defining and accomplish any objective.

2. Keep in contact With Your Intuition

The second means of building a mindset for progress is to keep in contact with your instinct.

Many accept that achievement implies settling on determined choices dependent on exact information. While you should attempt to be as experimental as could reasonably be expected, such information isn't always accessible. Regardless of your particular way, you will probably need to settle on a choice sooner or later during your life or vocation where there is no measurable answer.

Right now, you must have the option to tune in to your instinct. Even though it's anything but a perfect wellspring of data, our abilities can frequently sift through issues more rapidly than a cognizant idea can.

This will permit you to settle on definitive decisions in troublesome circumstances.

3. Continuously Keep A Positive Attitude

Keep in mind the estimation of an inspirational mentality toward accomplishing your objectives. Regardless of the way you follow, it very well may be anything but difficult to get disheartened by brief mishaps or disappointments to achieve explicit objectives. Positive reasoning methods are recognizing these misfortunes as learning openings. This makes it simpler to beat little frustrations and keep endeavoring toward your goals.

Constructive reasoning likewise will, in general, make you an increasingly lovely person to be near, permitting you to draw in help from other people who can help you en route.

4. Make a move

You have to move your considerations without hesitation. Notwithstanding positive reviews, a mindset for progress additionally requires your speculation to be productive. At whatever point you are considering your objectives or obstructions to accomplishing them, you should have the option to recognize precise moves you can make accordingly.

The more promptly you can move a thought or want into a viable activity, the simpler it will be to gain ground toward your objectives.

5. Assume Complete Liability

A mindset for progress implies having the option to assume liability for all that you do, regardless of whether fortunate or unfortunate.

If you commit an error or mischief, somebody, along your way, assuming liability lets you contain the harm and save your notoriety. It likewise urges you to consider how you could stay away from that botch later on.

Similarly, if you achieve something, you need to guarantee duty regarding it. At exactly that point will others understand what you can do and bolster you on your way to progress.

Ways to Develop Your Mindset for Success

Top performers realize what they need and make a steady move towards it. They center on its most significant tasks. They persistently improve their abilities. Their smart personalities make passionate states, inspirations, and convictions that lead them to progress. Their mindsets direct them towards propensities and activities that produce their ideal outcomes.

1. Accept you'll succeed

Our conduct is steady with our convictions. If you accept you'll succeed, you make a successful move that draws you nearer to your objective. You assess the accessible choices in search of the most encouraging route forward. You persevere through difficulties since you're sure you will outperform them and proceed with the excursion towards progress.

Individuals respond contrastingly to comparable circumstances, dependent on their convictions. At the point when confronted with misfortune, one person comprehends it's a typical piece of the procedure while someone else whines that "things never go directly for me" and surrenders. The primary person developed a psychological structure that prompts a productive reaction to the misfortune.

If you accept there's a response to a problematic issue, you send your mindset to find that answer. You center on the conceivable outcomes and arrangements that will drive you forward. Then again, if you accept the issue is unsolvable, you direct your mind to locate the best reasons accessibly. Convictions direct our conduct. We can choose beliefs that push us towards our objectives rather than opinions that keep us down.

We will act reliably with our perspective on who we are, regardless of whether that view is precise or not.

2. Beat each snag in turn

At the point when we append to the result, we intellectually surge towards the end goal. Right now mind, we put an enormous focus on ourselves to succeed. We fixate on all the snags we may confront. We don't grasp gradual advancement and development. We need to track to the compensations of progress quickly. We can't viably deal with ten impediments without a moment's delay. Our psyche doesn't have the foggiest idea where to coordinate its consideration. Our consideration disperses, and our productive vitality disseminates.

We can beat each challenge in turn, however. We can systematically break down each challenge from all points. At that point, we can create procedures to assault the test in a manner that is well on the way to succeed. We focus on an arrangement and flood ahead. There's a long excursion ahead with numerous pinnacles and valleys. However, we don't have to discover answers for issues until we face them.

Separating the objective and concentrating exclusively on the following test is feasible. This mindset produces steady activity, which means monstrous advancement after some time.

3. Just contend with yourself

Displaying the mindsets, techniques, and activities of the individuals who have just achieved what we're seeking after is significant. Through demonstrating, we maintain a strategic distance from a portion of the missteps others made, making a course for progress. We find a demonstrated outline that abbreviates the time it takes us to arrive at our objectives. While gaining from others encourages our development, intellectually contending with them produces negative results. At the point when we measure ourselves against others, we look towards increasingly effective individuals. This leads us to feel deficient and question our capacity.

At the point when we move our ideal models and contend just with ourselves, we focus in on our way. We're not worried about what every other person is doing any longer. We're essentially attempting to improve from where we were yesterday. We're centered on enhancing our aptitudes and outfitting ourselves with the apparatuses we have to accomplish our objectives. We measure achievement dependent on our benchmarks rather than how others characterize achievement.

4. Focus on the best choices

As we become increasingly useful, we have more chances and demands. A of the open doors is great. If we express yes to most choices, we rapidly feel focused and overpowered by the volume of work and responsibilities. By disapproving of options that don't line up with our most significant objectives, we give ourselves the opportunity and space to entirely focus on the incredible preferences.

It's challenging to accomplish eager objectives. It's a lot harder to achieve these objectives when we have a lot on our plate. We gain steady ground on numerous undertakings without completing a large portion of them and betting everything on a couple of large ventures one after another until finish brings about gigantic movement. At the point when we finish them, we can proceed onward to the following arrangement of excellent choices that are pausing. We can accomplish all that we need. We can't accomplish everything simultaneously.

A business must include, it has some good times, and it needs to practice your innovative senses.

5. Build up a development mindset

Fruitful individuals have confidence in development. They accept their abilities will improve as they gain experience. They recognize they will discover guides, systems, and assets that will create the outcomes they need.

The development mindset prompts more outstanding commitment with challenges, perseverance, certainty, and eagerness to gain from botches. If we are confident that we will conquer these difficulties, we gain from them and continue attempting until we locate an effective strategy. The qualities related to a development mindset are a formula for progress.

At the point when we pick the development mindset over the fixed mindset, where we are today gets insignificant. The main thing that issues is the place we're going.

The Six Pillars of a Successful Mindset for Entrepreneurs

Being effective in business today is unique about it was ten years prior. As a business visionary, you are confronted with numerous difficulties and deterrents of the cutting edge age, including innovation to adjust to, web-based business to comprehend, and new and inventive approaches to secure clients. And these are advancing each day. Be that as it may, your ability to beat every one of these difficulties and to push ahead is basic to the accomplishment of your business. However, you have to sift through your psyche first.

The enterprise begins in your mind, and you need the correct mindset before you can develop an effective business. Find these six realities about the winning mindset that advances enterprise and discover what noteworthy characteristics can assist you with getting effective.

1. Positive Thinking

You can consider it an easy decision, yet this doesn't change the way that we have issues with it. A constructive clinician and hierarchical expert proclaim that "individuals will, in general, have a subjective inclination toward their disappointments, and pessimism." This implies human minds are bound to search out antagonism and assimilate it more rapidly to memory than actual data.

They state you can't accomplish your objectives without positive reasoning. Being sure is substantially more than merely being upbeat, and uplifting mentality that produces feelings, for example, satisfaction and happiness can make genuine incentive in your life and assist you with building aptitudes that last any longer than only a grin.

Your inspiration is both the antecedent to progress and its aftereffect. It has been demonstrated that the effect of positive feelings on the cerebrum causes you to feel and see more prospects throughout your life. Besides, positive reasoning will upgrade your capacity to assemble aptitudes and create assets to utilize further down the road.

So as should be obvious, positive reasoning and positive feelings help with enterprise, however your whole life as well. In any case, you can get yourself together and take a shot at your personality to change your perspective. Somewhat, you can get this going by overseeing zones of shortcoming to at long last increment the positive speculation in your life. For this attempt contemplation, expound on the positive experiences that you possess every day and calendar some energy for play and fun routinely.

OK, so we realize that positive reasoning is basic here; however, we should jump into different fundamentals of the business visionary's mindset.

2. Sensible Approach

Keep in mind; no one anticipates that you should transform into an unadulterated self-assured person who takes a gander at only the good in everything. Being practical is sufficient here.

Best business visionaries aren't hopeful in any way. They keep a sound separation in the tranquil occasions, and they don't get overexcited when everything functions admirably, and they are alarmed continuously and prepared for the war times so that you should simply change your approach and discover that there is no strength when you're growing a business.

3. You Must Be a Visionary Leader

Consider good examples, for example, the authority of Nelson Mandela, Henry Ford, or Alexander the Great. Despite the distinctive life purposes and missions they had, would they say they weren't all persuading in their dealings?

They were all visionaries. These are the best instances of visionary pioneers throughout the entire existence of humanity. Without the vision and the feeling of direction, defining a durable objective that everybody can move in the course of would not be conceivable.

Each pioneer needs enthusiasm about his specific plan to get sound. A business visionary isn't merely somebody who begins an organization for starting the organization, yet the individual takes care of a current issue. Here, each progression towards improvement and development is motivated by the incredible vision and desire for advancement.

At any rate, it should look that way. Visionary pioneers know their strategic feel it's solid calling from the time they were conceived. They ought to be able to look forward into the future more distant than others, foresee drifts and have a steadfast spotlight on an objective that may be accepted by others to be inconceivable.

At long last, they should attempt to push their plan as far as possible. At the point when you are a business person that drives a tech startup, and you effectively procure individuals for your group, you would do well to be a visionary. Having energy that means an away from of your organization structure is imperative to persuade individuals to go along with you and battle for the thought.

Since you can't persuade somebody regarding thought or business procedure when you don't have one, at the point when that is the situation, the best masters will detect it rapidly, and they will flee from you. We need those visionary heads to make products and administrations that carry an improvement to the world, and carry genuine incentive to individuals and tackle existing issues.

4. You Must Be a Persistent Leader

"Ability, virtuoso, and instruction mean next to no when persistence is inadequate."

Everything lies in proper assurance. The discourse was to show the need for persistence when attempting to accomplish goal-oriented or even unthinkable objectives. Persistence is the principal righteousness of the innovative mindset and one of the most basic factors in progress. An extraordinary achievement only from time to time comes without the exertion, and a lot of assurance.

Regularly the distinction between the individuals who succeed and the individuals who didn't lie in having the persistence to continue standing when everything else breakdown. It's anything but difficult to be persistent when all is well. Yet, we talk here about being persistent in the hours of an emergency when nothing is working out in a good way when the way is troublesome, and an answer isn't self-evident, and you appear not to draw near to your objectives by any means.

Persistence is the capacity to push ahead after a disappointment and having the internal certainty that encourages you to stand firm, prop up when it pours, defeat the snags and endure it until the minute when the sun turns out. It may get tested, yet it never gets annihilated; thus can generally go about as a wellspring of assurance and self-control to point higher and consistently seek after the advancement.

5. Consistent Learner

Million-dollar pioneers must output the world for signs of progress, and have the option to respond in a split second since this world progressively requires searchlight knowledge.

Searchlight knowledge is pivotal to envision what is coming straightaway and prevail with regards to developing prospects.

Therefore, nowadays, the best business people and pioneers become the best students. They should remain alert and constantly hungry for new information, abilities, and thinking designs that enable them to extend the scope of devices they use to gain the ideal ground and change or make what's to come. The best chiefs are normally interested and engaged with gaining from others, particularly the individuals who have just strolled a comparative way.

While perusing books isn't sufficient, you need genuine models and good solid examples. There is no better method to figure out how to turn into a fruitful business person than to gain from tutors, genuine, capable business visionaries. It's fundamental to encircle yourself with more intelligent individuals than yourself who can rouse you to turn out to be better and show the correct methods for beating difficulties and hindrances in your way.

6. Allure in Leadership

Martin Luther King Jr., Mahatma Gandhi, and Winston Churchill were known as unique, appealing, and helpful pioneers, and we expect this was an establishment of their achievement in authority.

All in all, what precisely comprises being a magnetic pioneer?

Appealing pioneers are extraordinary communicators that are outstandingly verbally expressive and fit for conveying on a profound, passionate level, contacting and stimulating forceful feelings in individuals.

They give the individuals around them a positive inclination, causing them to feel slanted to work with and adhere to guidance. Alluring pioneers are equipped for intriguing and motivating individuals around them and usually work admirably at advancing their ideas, associations, or manifestations.

The main concern

How about we abridge the six credits fundamental to a mindset of any practical business visionary.

These are, individually:

1. Positive reasoning that lets you make open doors for development and confidence in your favorable luck

2. A sensible methodology that gives you a sound perspective regardless of what occurs

3. A solid vision that pulls in individuals to battle for your thoughts

4. Persistence that pushes you ahead when everything else breakdown

5. Alertness to change and the insight to envision what is coming straightaway

6. The charisma that gives everyone around you a positive vibe to unite them.

7. On these occasions, while turning into a business visionary has gotten so natural, those mainstays of an enterprising mindset are considerably more essential than any time in recent memory since they let you recognize the genuine business people from the phony ones.

Furthermore, regardless of whether you're battling to turn into a business person yourself or you are merely hoping to unite with a characteristic head, consistently search out these highlights both in yourself and in others since they will guarantee the durable and

superb initiative that expanded the likelihood to make progress
you long for.

CHAPTER FIVE

HOW TO FIND THE WINNING PRODUCT

You have distinguished your market and niche. You have found out about the market and niche, have done some statistical surveying on the premiums and issues individuals have right now you have picked.

Presently the time has come to

1. Find out who the most significant players as far as products are right now;

2. Check out what they offer;

3. Choose among the contribution the product or administration you like and generally feel good with and

4. Optimize this for your prosperity!

Finding the principal players is very simple as it is sufficient to type in your fundamental keyword phrase into Google and see what natural outcomes spring up. Thus, if we picked as a model the market niche of skiing and have chosen to begin with the sub-niche and part of "head protectors for skiing," this is actually what you would type into Google to discover the main online deals point for ski caps.

When all is said in done, talking about products, you have to make an understood distinction between physical products (as the protective caps in the above model) and data products. Regularly online marketers incline toward offering data products mostly. This has a couple of reasons:

1. You don't need to keep any stock;

2. You don't need to fret over coordinations nor expenses of sending the products to individuals;

3. People can get their buy quickly, by just downloading (in a large portion of the cases) what they had requested;

4. It is quick and convenient: it may take you even US$15k to make a data product, yet once it is done, ready for action, there is fundamentally no more cost included - so it turns out to be profoundly gainful to you and your business.

A few niches may, however, demand physical products to advertise; you may have your creation, which is a physical product. Gain from the best in your niche to perceive how they oversee it and become much more useful than they are.

Be it a physical or a data product that you picked, make a point to

1. Find the enormous players in your niche;

2. opt-in to their rundown;

3. Read and check all they have;

4. Make a rundown of the considerable number of things you like and what doesn't speak to you;

5. Buy from them if conceivable or if nothing else consider doing as such;

6. Do a little market test before settling on one specific product or administration and a nitty-gritty marketing plan and technique to run.

Creating an Irresistible Product That Sells Like Crazy

Product creation is one of the most significant advances online that you have to ace to manufacture an active web business. The purpose behind this is to pick up the influence that you have to succeed; you need your products.

Right now might want to impart to your procedures to make products that will sell quite well.

1) Offer serious estimating

Particularly today, with the downturn and high oil costs, individuals are less ready to go through as a lot of cash as in the past. Thus it is significant that your costs offer worth. I recommend that you test various values to see which changes over the best. Here and there, a particular price will change over very well far superior to another, and you have to discover which one it is.

2) Add extra rewards

Regularly you will get individuals who will shift back and forth. You have to get them to make a move. You can do this by offering significant rewards. A strategy that numerous fruitful marketers use is they offer bonuses that appear to be more significant than the first product. Regularly individuals who are not yet chosen will follow up on the idea as the time touchy rewards will be a decent motivating force to buy it.

3) Offer your rival's extraordinary selling suggestion as a little something extra

In a severe market, it tends to be exceptionally hard to succeed. If you are battling to sell units of your product, I recommend that you include your rival's novel selling suggestion as a little something extra. Your purchaser will get a great deal of significant worth for cash, and this will swing things into your kindness.

Ways to Find Winning Products Every Time

What to offer, what to offer, what to sell. That is probably the most significant inquiry you'll be posing to yourself when fabricating your online store. How do a few hides away up, causing six and seven figures while others have a significant, fat zero? It comes down to having winning products. What's more, luckily, you should simply discover one to become wildly successful. So right now, going to answer a typical outsourcing FAQ: "How might I locate a triumphant product?" I separate the eight most straightforward approaches to discover such (and the specific thing that helped me locate my triumphant product)—time to get those dollar bills you all.

Most online stores have blockbuster records. This is incredible for clients who need to see the best products an online store can offer. Yet, for online retailers, smash hit singles are a cracking goldmine.

What's more, new business people don't misuse them enough.

Most express that the drawback to outsourcing is that everybody is selling indistinguishable products from you. In any case, I like to take a gander at it with a glass half full methodology: if everybody's selling similar stuff, you can undoubtedly sell it as well. Furthermore, if you comprehend what their smash hits are, at that point, you can sell a triumphant product. To discover the product that causes you to hit the bonanza, all you have to do is a tad of serious research.

Here are a couple of instances of websites with open success records.

1. Amazon Best Sellers

Along these lines, I will be a Captain Obvious and start with the conspicuous decision first.

Amazon has blockbuster records for truly every classification. That, however, they're refreshed each. Single. Hour.

You will discover some brand name products on success records like Lego and FujiFilm above. Nonetheless, you can likewise find some unbranded products that are additionally effectively accessible.

2. Wish's Winning Products

Wish is another case of an online retailer who plugs their top of the line products. Investigate the feline towels on the base right corner. More than 50,000 individuals have paid those towels off Wish's website, so they're certainly a triumphant product.

The cool thing about this feline towel is that you can quickly tell just from taking a gander at it that it's a spur of the moment purchase product. The more significant part of the triumphant products on Wish are obliged to pull in the spur of the moment purchase. So they usually would excel in visual stages like Facebook and Instagram.

So when glancing through smash hit records, keep your eyes open for spur of the moment purchase products. A few trademarks for spur of the moment purchase products incorporate things like:

Beautiful (or outwardly stands apart while looking over)

Evokes a passionate response ("I need this" or "This is lovable" or "I love this")

Diverse plan or style from anything you've at any point seen

3. Addition Your Competitor Here

The more significant part of your rivals has success records. Look at them. Regardless of whether you can't locate their precise product, by considering their product assortments, search for designs inside top of the line products.

In case you're in design, online retailer Suzy Shier has a patterns class. Inside the patterns class, you'll discover smash hits. In any case, similarly as intriguing that they likewise separate their apparel into style patterns. This can help give you a thought of what sorts of designs inside the style niche are mainstream at present. Under models, you see classifications like athleisure, creature prints, and plaid. In this way, you can search for design inside those sorts of ratings, so you're selling the most recent patterns.

Ardene is another retailer that has a patterns area. Sufficiently smart, when you look at their blockbusters, the primary thing that shows up is a plaid hoodie, which affirms that this pattern is ablaze at this moment. So in case, you're hoping to sell ladies' design, having a couple of plaid things can assist you with getting a few deals.

The more you glance through contender websites, the more you'll discover examples and associations among top brands. You can consolidate these examples as you construct your product assortment.

4. eBay Watch Count

Discover the product you should sell utilizing Watch Count, which permits you to perceive what's famous on eBay. You can either discover winning products on hyper-focused on catchphrases like 'ionic hairbrush' to see the photographs and style that is most well known at present.

Or on the other hand, you can expand your catchphrases so you can locate the hits in your niche. So rather than an ionic hairbrush, you'd simply search hairbrush. Or, on the other hand, rather than blossom stockings, you'd simply search tights.

The best things to outsource are the ones recorded with the most watchers. Remember that while doing a restricted search like an ionic hairbrush, the number of watchers will be lower since you're explicit and that the ionic hairbrush is still uncontrollably mainstream, notwithstanding a smaller amount than the tights.

Likewise, you'll notice that with the two arrangements of pictures that there are always numerous products that appeared to see. Making your photographs along these lines can also assist clients with seeing the whole determination before clicking onto your product page (and it can help tempt them more since there are more alternatives for them to see).

5. Screen High-Performing Ads

We live in a universe of scrollers. We look through articles, newsfeeds, and product pages. Be that as it may, have you at any point halted to figure what could occur if you didn't look past a perpetual flood of posts?

My reality changed because, at some point, I quit looking to take a gander at a Facebook advertisement.

Yet, in some way or another, the promotion commitment on this triumphant product was not normal for anything I'd at any point seen before, demonstrating that it was probably the best thing to outsource. High as can be. Many remarks. Companion labeling like you wouldn't accept—a vast number of preferences.

Everybody needed this product.

It was practically difficult to accept that these remarks were genuine. In any case, they were.

I chose to search for a comparable product with Oberlo. It was a significant, brilliant cover, so I attempted various catchphrases like "seashore cover" and "reflection cover." After a touch of searching, I found the specific, same product.

6. Unicorn Smasher

Are you searching for an Amazon product research instrument? Unicorn Smasher encourages you to locate the top of the line

Amazon products for nothing. With this convenient Chrome expansion, you can discover the costs, smash hit rank, surveys, appraisals, and assessed deals in a solitary look. What's more, this information appears for every Amazon product insofar as you're on the .com area.

How about we investigate the information while searching for kitchen products. You can decide to sort any of the Chrome augmentations by any of its headers. Here I chose to see dependent on assessed income, yet you can likewise see by value, rank, surveys, appraisals, and whether it's satisfied by Amazon.

A convenient stunt for dropshippers to locate the best things to outsource is to see dependent on the number of venders. If there are various dealers for a single product, the product can be found on AliExpress. For instance, if iRobot Roomba just has one merchant and you see that iRobot is additionally the brand name, you likely won't have the option to sell the product since it's marked. Nonetheless, numerous merchants show that the product probably isn't marked, and anybody can sell it as well.

7. Utilizing Oberlo to Find the Product

Inside Oberlo, you can gain admittance to information for different AliExpress products. You can discover which products have had deals and which haven't. Be that as it may, you can likewise see how later those deals are. Is it safe to say that they were in the previous 30 days or the last half-year?

How about we peruse the watchword neckband. While perusing accessory, we can discover request volume by clicking "Request check" in the dropdown adjacent to "Sort by."

At the base, you'll see product measurements. You'll need to take a gander at all of these subtleties to assist you with settling on a choice. The 4.7-star rating is extraordinary. I usually prefer to remain above 4.5 stars. However, remember that if there are more than 100 audits, anything over a 4 star is an excellent product to browse.

Imports disclose to you what number of others are selling winning products like this one. With regard to site visits, I like to contrast it and request from the most recent 30 days. At the point when you isolate orders from the previous 30 days against total online visits (likewise from the last 30 days), take a gander at the percentage you get. If it's above half, you likely have a triumphant product on your hands. Anything lower than that and your advertisement evaluating may wind up costing you to an extreme.

With regards to Orders, verify whether the requests in the previous 30 days are high. If they're taller than the last a half year, you likely got it before the pattern exploded. You don't have to dishonor an excellent product given it either. This heart accessory, despite everything, got 2500+ deals in the previous 30 days that is still madly high. Regardless of whether the pattern is kicking the bucket, you can even now profit by it if deals in the previous 30 days are in the hundreds or higher.

8. Step by step instructions to Use Google Trends to Find Winning Products

Google Trends is a famous free instrument you can use to see whether a product is developing or declining in fame. Peruse this to discover an inside and out breakdown about how to utilize Google Trends to find winning products. Be that as it may, meanwhile, we should separate some fundamental thoughts on the most proficient method to discover the product utilizing this device.

Utilizing Google Trends, enter the product type. For instance, a popular AliExpress product is a rose in a glass that you can sell as wedding focal points, a Valentine's Day blessing, or a piece for the home stylistic theme. I include "rose in glass" to see the search volume prominence and presto.

How to discover winning products to sell on Shopify?

Tips no 1:

Ensure that your product page has in any event 400 words on it. Something to remember when you're making your website Google inviting is that Google is a robot, a machine. It comprehends the best is numbers and content.

At the point when Google sees you have heaps of elegantly composed content on your product page, shows to them you care about, giving your client an extraordinary experience. Eventually, Google has one objective, and that is to take care of its clients' issues. So when you're putting heaps of words on your page, it shows to them that is what you're attempting to utilize bunches of distinct applicable terms.

Tips no 2:

Shop assess

We're taking a gander at here is a website called shop assess. We're taking a gander at the hot products segment. We simply take one product. For instance, we take a Wi-Fi IP camera named the child screen. It is an approach to screen your resting infant from your genuine cell phone. So this is an excellent product that we may sell.

You can see that it's indeed expanded. What we will do is we will make sense of how to focus on this awful kid and send ethics to this product that will be intrigued enough to purchase this product. So what we will do is we will head into audience bits of knowledge.

Audience bits of knowledge resembles a cheat sheet for Facebook Ads. Again Facebook Ads has more than two billion month to month dynamic clients. So your purchasers are on Facebook regardless of what product you sell. There are 55% ladies, 45% men.

Presently if individuals who are keen on child screens, 90% percent are ladies, just 10% are men. We can likewise observe significantly further cheat codes by seeing what different pages of individuals who are keen on infant screens.

We can go out and target individuals out there who are ladies. We saw that 90% of individuals who are keen on child screens are ladies. Not a great deal of men are going out there and purchasing child screens. So we will target just ladies.

Etsy

Etsy is an online commercial center only like Amazon, eBay, with outsider vendors. It's an immense wellspring of deals and traffic with more than 35 million dynamic purchasers on the stage. I like it for novices. It's strangely modest to list things. They're only 20 pennies for an entire month posting with a small deals charge.

This article is tied in with directing people to a Shopify store, not an Etsy store. You can do what I did when propelled my first useful online store at the young age of 16. I would show some popular products from outsider commercial centers and develop a nearness on there. You would guide those clients to your store.

Tips no 3:

Presently we will hop into a hot website. We will type in everybody does it directly here into a help called SEM surge. If we press search semrush will let us know is the place precisely their traffic is originating from. If you are keen on various things, it will be distinctive every time for you. So we will come into the SEM surge. We will type in the space of a website we know an online business store; that we know is detonating in prominence at present.

The most underutilized paid to promote stage right currently is Instagram. Particularly if you are utilizing video advertisements on the scene, and they are performing better than Facebook. As you look through an Instagram feed, you notice the ads in it.

CHAPTER SIX

WHICH MARKETING CHANNELS TO USE

A marketing channel is the individuals, associations, and exercises essential to move the responsibility for from the purpose of production to the point of utilization. It is how products find a workable pace client, the shopper, and is otherwise called an appropriation channel.

Kinds of Marketing Channels

There are fundamentally four kinds of marketing channels:

1. Direct selling;

2. Selling through go-betweens;

3. Dual dissemination;

4. Reverse channels.

Direct Selling

Direct selling is the marketing and sale of products straightforwardly to shoppers from a fixed retail store. Hawking is the most seasoned type of direct selling. Present-day direct selling incorporates deals made through the gathering plan, one-on-one shows, and personal contact courses of action just as web deals. The immediate personal introduction, exhibit, and offer of products and administrations to buyers, for the most part, in their homes or at their occupations.

Purchasers profit by direct selling given the comfort and administration benefits it provides, including personal exhibition and clarification of products, home conveyance, and liberal fulfillment ensures. Rather than diversifying, the expense for a person to begin a free immediate selling business is commonly low, with almost no necessary stock or money responsibilities to start.

Direct selling is not quite the same as direct marketing in that it is about individual deals operators coming to and managing customers while direct marketing is about business associations looking for a relationship with their clients without experiencing a specialist/expert or retail outlet.

Direct selling frequently, however not generally, utilizes staggered marketing (a salesperson is paid for selling and for deals made by individuals they select or support) as opposed to single-level marketing (salesperson is paid uniquely for the business they make themselves).

Selling Through Intermediaries

A marketing channel where middle people, for example, wholesalers and retailers, are used to making a product accessible to the client is called a roundabout channel. The most aberrant pathway you can utilize (Producer/maker – > specialist – > distributer – > retailer – > customer) is used when there are numerous little makers and various small retailers, and an operator is utilized to help arrange an enormous stock of the product.

Double Distribution

Double conveyance depicts a wide assortment of marketing courses of action by which the producer or wholesalers utilizes more than one channel all the while to arrive at the end client. They may sell legitimately to the end clients just as offer to different organizations for resale. Utilizing at least two channels to draw in a similar objective market can, in some cases, lead to channel strife.

A case of double dissemination is business group diversifying, where the franchisors, permit the operation of a portion of its units to franchisees while at the same time owning and operating a few units themselves.

Switch Channels

If you've found out about the other three channels, you would have seen that they make them thing in like manner — the stream. Every one streams from maker to middle person (if there is one) to purchaser.

Innovation, nonetheless, has made another stream conceivable. This one goes in the turn around bearing and may go — from buyer to delegate to the recipient. Consider bringing in cash from the resale of a product or reusing.

There is another qualification between turn around channels and the more conventional ones — the presentation of a recipient. In turning around the stream, you won't discover a maker. You'll just find a User or a Beneficiary.

Six Marketing Channels You Can Prioritize in 2020

1. Pay-Per-Click Marketing

To the extent marketing channels go, pay-per-click (PPC) publicizing is as yet an incredible juggernaut, particularly with the differing alternatives now accessible to brands. There is a high expectation to consume information for every stage, so if you can bear to enlist an organization to deal with your battles for you, we prescribe that.

There are two overwhelming powers in the PPC world nowadays: Google Ads and Facebook/Instagram Ads. Google search promotions will assist you with associating with clients who are searching for products or administrations like yours.

In the interim, Google's showcase advertisements and Facebook's paid social promotions will permit you to make the request and acquaint your administrations with clients who may not be looking or even realize you exist.

You can become familiar with how to take advantage of Google Ads here and Facebook Ads here.

2. Online networking

Online networking is a significant player in the marketing scene at this moment. Clients are effectively searching out brands they like or are keen on, and expanding quantities of clients are taking to online networking to research or settle on purchasing choices.

Internet-based life additionally offers relevant network building openings that you indeed won't find anyplace else. Regardless of whether you're merely sharing in the background content on your page or making a gathering, including your business, you ought to use internet-based life for everything it has.

3. Email Marketing

Email marketing is the best technique for direct reaction marketing there is. Clients have selected into got notification from you, so they're all the more ready to open those messages to find out about the most recent products, deals, and how to profit by them. Email marketing can be perplexing, so we've canvassed it inside and out here.

4. Your Website

A few businesses don't think about their website as a marketing channel, yet as a general rule, it might be the most significant one. This is the place clients will come when they're keen on becoming familiar with your business, and if they can't discover answers to their inquiries rapidly, they won't stay sufficiently long to see. Your site should offer a decent early introduction, and it ought to speak to your business, image, products, and administrations in the manner in which you need it.

5. Content Marketing and SEO

Content marketing is somewhat similar to an investment account. Over the long haul, you get intensifying enthusiasm, making it considerably increasingly important. The posts can offer SEO benefits for an exceptionally prolonged period to come as individuals keep on searching them out, and the entirety of your substance can give significant relationship building and lead age capacities. Content marketing shows authority and expertise, all while helping you arrive at clients at various phases of the channel and hitting the same number of catchphrases as you can.

6. Informal Marketing

Informal marketing has consistently been one of the best marketing channels, and that will proceed on an on-going premise. You'll get over it if a salesperson discloses to you that you need that watch, however when your companion calls attention to the amount they love wearing it consistently on account of all the bright highlights, you'll take more notification.

There are two essential strategies to empower verbal marketing. Referral projects and rousing on the web surveys for various stages of web-based, including Google, LinkedIn, and Yelp.

CHAPTER SEVEN

HOW MUCH MONEY IT TAKES TO GET STARTED

Affiliate Marketing (AM) is a business, and similarly, as with some other activity, you have to put away some cash toward the start. Individuals continue asking how a lot of money is expected to begin in AM and whether it's even conceivable with a little spending plan. So let me investigate this point, to enable you to comprehend the stuff to turn into an affiliate marketer regarding financing.

As a matter of first importance, we have to sort one thing out – to sell anything by any stretch of the imagination, you need the guests (traffic), and there are two potential ways to deal with getting it – PAID and FREE (natural). The straightforward rationale behind these two methodologies decides how much $ you will need to begin. If you choose to work with PAID traffic, your costs will be higher, obviously.

This is clear and straightforward. Be that as it may, to honestly choose what approach would be better for you, we have to jump into this somewhat deeper. The two methodologies have their upsides and downsides, so let me attempt to think about them.

Stars of Paid Traffic:

– You can begin getting guests promptly, everything necessary is to make a record at some traffic source, finance your career, make a crusade, and dispatch it. You may need to stand by some an opportunity to get your campaigns affirmed. However, that is typically only several hours.

– You choose how much traffic you will purchase. If you have the financial limit for this, solitary anything is possible. This is the highest favorable position of the "paid" approach – when you have a crusade that works, you can open the conduits and begin making 1000s of $$$ per day. Improving efforts isn't simple, yet it truly can work this way. Super affiliates who run a massive amount of volume per day, usually are working with paid traffic.

– You choose what traffic you will purchase and who you get it from. Suppose you have an incredible product. However, it just acknowledges guests from Austria, they must peruse on a Samsung SmartPhone, and they should be associated through the Orange portable bearer? This isn't an issue with paid traffic; you can pick precisely what sort of traffic you need to purchase.

– You needn't bother with any site to purchase traffic. It's not as simple as it was previously, yet you can at present bring in cash by sending guests straightforwardly to the product pages, without keeping up any site of your own.

Masters of Free (Organic) Traffic:

– Well, it's free: This is the highest favorable position of this methodology. You will, in any case, need to make some minor ventures and invest a ton of your energy in it. However, the traffic itself is free. Produce content that individuals might want, and the guests will come to you in the end.

– Free natural traffic will, in general, be increasingly steady, it won't bite the dust starting with one day then onto the next.

Except if you get prohibited by google, for instance, so center on whitehat techniques for traffic building.

– Organic traffic is generally of high, discover something that your guests are keen on, and they will change over. You can likewise offer this traffic to some traffic networks or individual purchasers.

– Since you need a website to get natural traffic, you are constructing a benefit that can transform into an automated revenue source. When a site is positioned, everything necessary is to refresh it now and again, and it can continue bringing in cash for quite a long time. My longest running site was begun in 2003, and it is as yet bringing in money, 13 years in a row! Building locales dependent on natural traffic can likewise be a piece of your leave procedure; you would have something to sell.

Let me start with PAID traffic again:

– A higher spending plan is required. Since you have to purchase all the traffic, you need the financial limit for it. Without a doubt, the base I would suggest would be $1000. If you don't have this sort of cash, paid traffic isn't for you, not yet. You have to assemble the spending limit somewhere else first, perhaps even with natural traffic. Traffic isn't the main cost: you will likewise require a server, domain(s), following arrangement, spy tool ... I will summarize it somewhat later on.

– You will free cash from the outset, and this is entirely inescapable. Every one who, at any point, began with paid traffic was losing money from the start. If you figure you will be unique, you are incorrect. PERIOD! This is something you have to acknowledge, in any case, don't begin with paid traffic.

– You should manage some degree of misrepresentation – traffic networks sell bots, affiliate networks clean leads ... these are irritations you need to become accustomed to. We as a whole need to manage that; no one is resistant to this, so it's not something just you'd need to battle with. Simply required to take note of that.

– You can lose a great deal of cash! Reconsider before settling on any choice, watch your battles intently, and utilize all means imaginable to restrain your drops.

– There are no ensures that you will make it. Not every person has the correct mindset or aptitudes to make it with paid traffic. Try not to feel that since you contribute $1000, you are ensured to begin making benefits. Numerous individuals come up short at this. However, on the other hand, it's equivalent to a business.

– Running paid traffic is magnificent when all clicks fine and dandy, yet it very well may be super unpleasant when it's most certainly not. When testing new products, sources ... that is no joke "not bringing in cash" you are losing it. This is again something you need to become accustomed to.

Free Traffic Has Cons Too:

– You have to run content destinations to assemble natural traffic by any means. Regardless of whether you decide to concentrate on SEO (search engine optimization), Viral locales, or Social media, you will consistently need to manufacture substance to pull in the guests.

– You have to put a great deal of time into your locales; somebody needs to compose/produce the substance. You can likewise employ somebody to do it for you, yet this will drive your expenses up a ton. You additionally need to refresh your locales to safeguard your search engine rankings for a more extended period.

– It takes any longer to fabricate natural traffic contrasted with utilizing paid promotions. As a rule, you have to create content for quite a long time without getting a lot of guests. It's anything but difficult to surrender and quit delivering content when nobody is taking a gander at it.

– When building SEO traffic, you are necessarily Google's bitch. What google gives, google can take. Since they claim such a massive % of the market, if they boycott you, your site is done.

– Organic traffic is a blend of GEOs (nations), traffic types (portable, tablet, work area), and so forth ... this makes it somewhat harder to adapt every hit. You can't generally make uncommon ADs for each language that your guests talk, and visits from individual nations will be simply squandering your Bandwidth bill since they originate from countries that no one need's to promote/sell in.

I could go on with the PROS and CONS, yet I would state the most significant has been secured, and I'm sure you, as of now, comprehend the principle contrasts. If I summarized it in one sentence, it would be something like this: Working with PAID traffic requires a way higher spending plan, and you can consume a ton of $ with it. However, the potential benefits are more top as well, and you can begin immediately. Natural traffic can return progressively stable benefits, yet for the most part, in the lower range and get ready to manufacture content for a considerable length of time before observing any profits.

So How Much Money Do You Need To Start With Either Of Them?

Let me attempt to summarize the inescapable expenses related to beginning in AM, both with paid and natural (free) traffic.

PAID Traffic First:

– You need some facilitating to put greeting pages (Lps) on, and you can attempt without Lps as well. However, you will begin utilizing presentation pages in the end, at any rate. When starting, you can pick a modest VPS or Cloud arrangement from organizations like beyondhosting.com, vultr.com, or digitalocean.com ... I hope to spend anyplace between $20 and $50 per month, in light of what plan you pick.

There is a considerable amount of hosts so pick anything you desire, yet remember a specific something – with paid traffic; speed is a significant factor, you need every click that you purchased, to hit your points of arrival. Try not to go for shared facilitating like bluehost.com, hostgator.com, and so on ... these are modest, yet they are not reasonable for paid traffic battles.

If you utilize static (Html just) Lps, you can likewise use a CDN, rackspace.com cloud petitions, for instance. These are charged per GB moved. LPs usually are extremely "light" pages so that it will be practically free. I'm paying under $5 per month, and I'm serving 100s of thousands of hits per day. It will rely upon the KB size of your LPs.

– You additionally need TRACKING; this is an absolute necessity. With paid traffic, it's significant to know precisely what sort of traffic changed over to purchase a more considerable amount of that. What's more, this is tracker's main event; they will show you precisely what guest made a change – what site/arrangement they originate from, what nation, what gadget ...

There are many trackers out there. However, some of them are viewed as the best ones. We had a survey on STM Forum in the relatively recent past, and these five turned out as champs: Voluum, Thrive Tracker, FunnelFlux, Adsbridge, and CPV Lab.

Every one of them is charged on a per month premise, except CPV Lab, which is a one time charge. Some are self-facilitated, which implies you need to utilize your server or CPV for this: CPV Lab and Funnel Flux. The remainder of them is facilitated and Thrive both a facilitated and a self-facilitated adaptation.

Voluum begins at $99 per month for 1.000.000 occasions. 10.000.000 occasions plan is $399.

Flourish begins at $99 per month for oneself facilitated variant and $299 for the facilitated one.

FunnelFlux is a level $99 per month, per permit. The offer just a self-facilitated adaptation for the present, so you need your server as well.

CPV Lab is a onetime charge of $297, which incorporates one year of help and updates. Extra help is discretionary and costs $147 per year. This needs a server again, too, as it's a self-facilitated tracker.

Asbridge offers a free essential arrangement for up to 50.000 visits per month. This is a low cutoff, so it's just useful for the initial hardly any days, the following arrangement comes at $25 for 100.000 visits. 1.000.000 visits plan is $75 per month.

Every one of the trackers has a few advantages and disadvantages, so it's difficult to prescribe one, however, let me attempt it in any case. FunnelFlux gets my vote if you need a self-facilitated tracker, it has a lot of decent choices. Voluum is most likely the best-facilitated tracker, yet it gets costly with high volume. That is the place Thrive takes over as their high volume plans are increasingly moderate. Asbridge is a well-known decision among amateurs, on account of the free essential arrangement, yet with higher volume, the costs grow up to a similar level similarly as with rivalry.

– The next thing you MUST have is a VPN (Virtual Private Network) programming. The most famously known is HideMyAss.Com. What this delicate does is concealing your whole area and supplanting your IP address with one of their private ones. Along these lines, you can surf the net as though you were associated with any nation on the planet.

This is valuable when you need to check what your opposition is advancing in any given GEO of the world. Since basically, all traffic networks use GEO focusing on, you just observe ADs targeted at your nation, except if you counterfeit it with a VPN.

– if you can bear the cost of it, I would prescribe to get a spy tool as well. I utilize the Adplexity group of apparatuses; they have separate devices for versatile, local, grown-up, and work areas. Having a spy tool is certainly not an absolute must. However, it unquestionably helps a TON.

These apparatuses "surf" the web and gather Intel pretty much a wide range of contenders' battles, so you can without much of a stretch break down them in one spot. Along these lines, you know precisely what is advanced where ... right from standard, through the LP to the genuine product.

Outline For Paid Traffic:

Unquestionably the base is VPS ($20-$50 per month) or a CDN ($5 per month), tracker ($25 – $99 per month), VPN ($5-$15 per month) in addition to in any event $20-$30 per day for traffic. If you can manage the cost of it, including $150 per month for a spy tool. This implies, given the tracker and facilitating you pick, you need at any rate $635 for the first month. If you choose a VPS, the expense goes up to $655-$670. Picking an increasingly costly tracker will kick the costs up by another $75, so that would generally mean $750. Include a government agent device, and you are at $900.

To stand a reasonable possibility at succeeding, you need assets to cover at any rate three months. Indeed, even thou you will free from the start, some portion of the cash will return as far as income created (not benefit), so you needn't bother with a numerous of 3 to cover the initial three months. In any case, it would be a smart thought to get ready in any event $1500 – $2000, if you are not kidding about paid traffic AM.

Looking At Starting With Organic Traffic

As I previously referenced, not every person has the monetary allowance for working with paid traffic straight away. Numerous affiliates start with natural traffic, and once they develop their financial limit, they move to paid traffic. This is a generally excellent procedure as well. Also, it's lovely to have a side pay set up while walking into paid traffic – it assists with dealing with the pressure.

– The most significant factor here is TIME. Start now. It will take a long time to get a few positions in google and different SEs (search engines) to get saw via web-based networking media to fabricate content that can draw in guests. Try not to pause and start NOW. Try not to stress if you don't have a perfect arrangement; you can clean things as you go. You can resolve the little glitches later on, yet you unquestionably can't return to the past.

– You should construct a site or a network of locales. Check my more established post about structure, a system of small niche locales to get some motivation. You need a few CMS (content administration framework) to run a site. You have two choices here once more, either pick a costly one (or exceptionally coded) or pick a free one.

I firmly prescribe, to begin with, the free arrangements, the most well known are WordPress and Joomla. I like WordPress more, yet a few people incline toward the other one, so the decision is yours. These CMS frameworks are mainstream to the point that you can do nearly anything with them, even e-looks, for instance. Enthusiasts of the stage delivered a considerable amount of alleged "modules" that you can introduce and construct propelled destinations with.

These frameworks both utilize a TEMPLATE framework; formats are one of a kind structures/designs that you can download either for nothing or get them. The costs for entirely propelled arrangements start at around $20; there is a considerable amount of great ones at $40-$50. Look at TemplateMonster.Com. For instance, there is a fuckload of them to pick a structure.

– Domain or spaces – Pick something identified with the subject of your site(s), yet don't go through a month searching for the perfect area name. The significance of a space name is no place as large as it used to be. What's more, wtf is a "google"? They caused it to up, and now everybody comprehends what it speaks to, you can attempt the equivalent. You can pick up spaces for a couple of pennies with the assistance of Godaddy.Com coupons, for instance.

– You have to have the site(s) someplace. The necessities on facilitating speed are not all that exacting likewise with paid traffic, so even a mutual arrangement could carry out the responsibility. There are also some free has accessible, yet I'm not a fanatic of anything free – you get what you pay for. Get a modest VPS or a cloud arrangement, digitalocean.com or vultr.com ought to carry out the responsibility fine and dandy. However, any facilitating with not too bad audits will be sufficient to have a little site.

Start with a modest arrangement, and if you figure out how to develop, you can generally overhaul. The beneficial thing is, except if you intend to assemble free grown-up locales, you needn't bother with 10.000s of visits to make better than average income. Attempt to pick a subject that you are acceptable at and fabricate content dependent on your insight. Accept this blog, for instance, I'm acceptable at I's job, so I expound on it. For the individuals who might want to comprehend the stuff to assemble a site this way, I made a segment where I will present the month-on-month progress, look at it here.

– You ought to likewise manufacture an email list/pamphlet; there are many answers for this. You can utilize free modules for this once more, yet individuals, as a rule, arrive at better outcomes with paid instruments. There is a great deal of them: Aweber, Getresponse, Mailchimp … these beginning at $15 - $20 per month and increment as your rundown develops.

There is a massive amount of different things that you could put resources into – like substance makers, coders, courses to show you how to do one or the other ... however, in all actuality, to START, you simply need an area, CMS framework, and a server + a considerable amount of your time.

Outline For Free (Organic) Traffic

How about we summarize the costs expected to begin "distributing" – Domain ($1-$10 per year), Hosting ($5-$20 per month), CMS (free), Template ($0-$50), Email Collection ($0-$15 per month). We are taking a gander at an underlying expense of under $10 if we figure out how to locate a modest area and utilize free modules at every possible opportunity.

If we choose to purchase a superior facilitating, propelled format, and a paid email list arrangement, the cost will go up to about $90 for the underlying mechanism (in addition to first month expenses) and afterward $35 per month. I don't know I think about whatever other business where you could begin THIS CHEAP!

I'd prefer to save your consideration for a couple of more seconds and reveal to you one more thing: if you are hoping to gain 1000's of $$$ per day, building locales for natural traffic is presumably not your last goal. Some regions make that sort of cash, and we, as a whole, know the anecdotes about websites or online administrations that sold for millions. However, the likelihood of this transpiring is VERY little.

Without a doubt, it can occur, yet it will take long stretches of challenging work and exceptional thought. The more typical path is, to begin with, natural traffic, develop the financial limit, and afterward move to paid traffic to raise the income.

Making enormous aggregates of cash is simpler with paid traffic. It's not straightforward using any means; however, if you figure out how to decipher the code, it's just a matter of a couple of months to begin making 100's of $$$ in a day by day benefits. I know a lot of individuals who make $10.000 – $15.000 benefit per month with paid traffic, and those are not the large mutts. Super affiliates make $1000s in profit per day, and some are sitting on the top who reach $10.000s or even six figures in benefits in a single day.

I am a major aficionado of a half and half methodology as it were. Having a couple of automated revenue natural traffic locales is the thing that keeps my psyche in harmony when my paid battles suck and lose cash. When the paid crusades assume control over, the significance of these destinations diminishes; it is only an additional salary that is pleasant to have. Be that as it may, since each paid crusade kicks the bucket sooner or later, the cycle begins once again and over.

Assemble destinations for dependability and ideally, to have something to sell when the need emerges. Remove a portion of the cash and put it into paid traffic and check whether you can make it there. Take the best from the two universes. You can likewise check this more seasoned article of mine to peruse progressively about the natural VS paid methodology.

The amount of Money Do You Need To Start Affiliate Marketing.

While it is conceivable, to begin with, affiliate marketing at for all intents and purposes no expense, if you need to prevail in the business and bring in some cash, you ought to be set up to go through some money first. Consider it an essential business venture. Here are the run of the mill costs you'll be taking a gander at if you need to set up your own business as an affiliate marketer.

Affiliate marketing costs

I expect that, since you understand this, you, as of now, have a PC that is associated with the web. So the following things you have to get your affiliate marketing business ready for action are:

An area name

You'll require a website. Furthermore, for that, you need a space name. You can enlist an area name with Namecheap for as meager as $4 per year.

Facilitating

You'll require someplace to have your new website on the web. Facilitating can be bought for as meager as $6-7 per month. Look at HostGator or pick an area and promoting bundle with Namecheap.

That is it. You're all set. Simply add substance and affiliate connects to your website, and you're presently an affiliate marketer.

Is it's as simple as that? You could stop there and not spend another dollar. Be that as it may, I recommend you continue perusing.

Discretionary Extras

I state discretionary, yet in case you're extremely genuine about your affiliate marketing business, these are an easy decision. A space name and website facilitating might be everything to getting a website. However, there's a whole other world to affiliate marketing than just having a website. Putting resources into a portion of the beneath will make your life simpler, and significantly improve your odds of having a fruitful affiliate marketing business.

Website design enhancement and Keyword Tools

Compelling catchphrase research is critical. You'll require this for your SEO (and PPC) endeavors. There are free watchword research instruments. However, some are justified even despite the cash you have to pay for them, for example, SEMRush, from $69.95 per month, which additionally offers a lot of investigation reports, and that's only the tip of the iceberg.

PPC

Done astutely, Google's paid promoting framework can give you an extraordinary profit for your venture. You set the sum you are eager to pay for each click your promotion gets. However, you'll likewise be contending with different sponsors who are offering on your catchphrases as well. So it tends to be very simple to become excited and spend too far in the red. So don't endeavor PPC except if you realize what you are doing first, else you'll be tossing cash down the channel.

Hope to pay on ordinary between 20-50p per click for known to medium serious niches, to 50p or more of severe slots. Plan an every day spending plan of around £10, although it's prudent to set aside a financial limit of about £100 ($150) with which you can test and decide if you are getting a decent profit for your speculation.

Email Marketing

Email marketing is a vital marketing instrument, empowering you to rapidly and effectively arrive at enormous quantities of potential clients. AWeber is the best. Contingent upon what number of endorsers you need, you'll be paying from $19 per month. However, you can attempt it free for 30 days first.

Pictures

If you need your website or blog and its substance to have an expert, quality look, you'll have to put resources into some stock photography because, because of copyright laws, you can't merely utilize any picture you need that you discovered on the web. Locales like Dreamstime empower you to purchase credits that can be used to pay for downloads. Loans for up to 11 pictures are accessible for under $10.

Redistributing

You can't hope to know it all about affiliate marketing, and all things considered, you can't expect to do everything yourself. So instead of attempting to do everything, eventually, you should get some assistance by re-appropriating some work. Enter the specialist. You can pay somebody who has what it takes and information that is missing to do anything from improving your website plan to make a change over substance for it.

Look at Elance and Upwork for consultants gaining practical experience in the aptitudes that you're inadequate. I hope to pay in any event $15 per hour/employment to significantly more, contingent upon the individual specialist and their experience.

Complimentary gifts You Can Use to Start Affiliate Marketing.

Fortunately, there are a lot of free apparatuses online that you can use to further your potential benefit. So take advantage of them.

Google Analytics

Each affiliate marketer needs Google Analytics. It's the best free examination administration accessible, and without it, you should be maintaining your affiliate marketing business visually impaired.

Google AdWords Keyword Planner

Albeit free, the Google AdWords Keyword Planner requires you to have an AdWords record to utilize it, which can be a problem in case you're not hoping to do any PPC. Be that as it may, it is, for the most part, viewed as the best, and will furnish you with some great details to go with your catchphrases, for example, rivalry level, average CPC and that's only the tip of the iceberg. Less problem, and still free, is Keyword Tool.io.

Preparing

Try not to squander your cash on books, guides, and costly affiliate marketing preparing. There is an abundance of data to be found uninhibitedly on the web and a lot of free preparing projects, for example, our Affiliate Training Course. Be that as it may, don't invest such a lot of energy attempting to get the hang of all that you can that you neglect ever to begin. Once in a while, the best learning strategy is to hop directly in and do it simply.

What are the fundamental costs when you are merely beginning an affiliate marketing

If you were to simply pay for the essential expenses of setting up a website, you could hope to spend under $10 per month. That is under $120 per year. Tiny right?

Be that as it may, your lucrative potential indeed relies upon whether you have the correct instruments.

So when you give some genuine thought to the immense contrast all – or even only a portion of those additional items above will put forth to your affiliate marketing attempts and the achievement you harvest from it, you'll understand that the other venture is well justified, despite all the trouble.

Ensure you have some income to begin, and just use the cash you can bear to lose. Since recollect, affiliate marketing, similar to any business, isn't an ensured approach to wealth!

CHAPTER EIGHT

PRACTICAL EXAMPLE

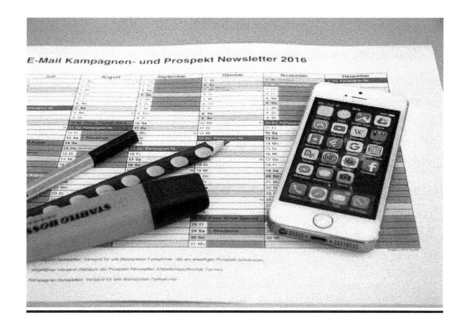

The most agent affiliate marketing models? Amazon and the locales 'consistently convey' and 'gear watch.'

Locales related to the Amazon affiliate program flourish, less for the commission earned yet for the assortment, security, and esteem of Jeff Bezos' internet business. Perhaps the best case of affiliate marketing procedures is Everyday Carry, a fascinating site of surveys of endurance articles.

In Everyday Carry, it is conceivable to discover investigations of Swiss Army Knives, watches, electric lamps, contraptions, knapsacks, note pads, and different products, which are vital in the baggage of the courageous open. Every one of their connections leads to Amazon products, where the buy is made. The equivalent occurs in Gear Patrol, a site that covers a more noteworthy number of products and market niches.

Rigging Patrol is another of Amazon's best instances of affiliate websites. It is characterized as an everyday men's magazine, gaining practical experience in movement, knowledge, nourishment, and innovation. Notwithstanding getting a great many daily visits, this site has a massive network of faithful adherents, who are diverted to Amazon through affiliate joins. It is away from a successful win relationship!

Uswitch And The 'Cash Saving Expert' Site

Cash Saving Expert was established by Martin Lewis, is situated in the UK, and flaunts one of the most moving affiliate marketing cases. The reason for this site is to show you how to set aside cash and teach you on principle money related instruments.

The topic of Money Saving Expert doesn't help utilize the affiliate frameworks of Amazon, eBay, or other necessary projects. In any case, this site is exceptionally productive gratitude to the affiliate connections of uSwitch, TotallyMoney, Tradedoubler, or Affiliate Window, among others. No ifs, ands or buts, one of those instances of affiliate marketing to mimic.

The Home Depot And The 'Buyer Search' Site

Buyer Search is your product suggestion and examination site. It was made in 1999 with an inquisitive crucial: take out the business distortion and deceptive nature of brands on the Internet.

By personally inspecting each new product, Consumer Search can suggest the most elite from every class and market niche. Because of the autonomy of its experts, the general population depends on the straightforwardness of its assessments.

Shopper Search income originates from connections to affiliates of The Home Depot, an incredible U.S. retailer of DIY and family unit products. While Consumer Search wins a commission for every deal, The Home Depot builds guest traffic and accomplishes ground-breaking backlinks.

ebay And The 'Wonder Cycles' Site

Wonder Cycles is the aftereffect of an astounding mix of BigCommerce and the eBay index. This online shop spends significant time in products and extras for cyclists, just as bikes and related hardware. As indicated by its makers, the strategic Glory Cycles is "to utilize the web to associate our clients with precisely what they are.

Wonder Cycles has been an extraordinary accomplishment since its dispatch in 2001, which isn't just because of the excellent administration of its originators. eBay and its supply of products have likewise contributed. Both have helped each other to make progress, which is one of the mainstays of affiliate marketing.

What Are The Best Affiliate Programs For Ecommerce?

As indicated by Business Insider, pay from the utilization of affiliate programs has developed by 10% per year since 2015, and this dynamic is relied upon to proceed until 2021. This marketing procedure is compelling for both online businesses and their partners.

Notwithstanding Amazon Associates and its notable affiliate program, numerous internet business organizations have comparative procedures. They stick out:

- Etsy Affiliates: Despite its low bonus of 4%, Etsy has one of the most intriguing affiliate programs, with a wide assortment of products that draw in a broad audience.

- eBay Affiliates: With exceptionally high commissions, somewhere in the range of 40% and 80%, eBay's affiliate program rivals Amazon's, offering different answers to adapt outsider websites and applications.

- The Zalando Partner Program: Zalando's affiliate payments are 8%. However, it has a wide choice of attire, frill, and shoes online to give. Like eBay, Amazon, or Etsy, Zalando has a client network and a perceived brand, which brings included worth.

- AliExpress Affiliate: with a variable commission of up to half, AliExpress rivals the past ones, and regardless of its short direction (it was propelled in 2010), its affiliate program is a reference in online business.

These and different instances of affiliate marketing are motivating. In any case, new businesses and moderate size organizations ought not to imagine that this marketing methodology is out of their span. Despite their size, division, or product, every single online retailer will prevail with regards to propelling their affiliate program.

Affiliate Marketing – Practical Examples Helps To Grow Brands

Prepared to get your image out there and tap into sections of your audience that you experience experienced issues coming to previously? If your answer is correct, at that point, affiliate marketing is actually what you should be paying regard for.

The reason is apparent. You associate with affiliates who will advance your image as an end-result of remuneration dependent on performance. As a trader, you possibly pay when the member can create brings about the type of lead age or deals. It couldn't be less complicated.

Then again, making sense of where to begin can be a test.

There are numerous roads that affiliates can use to advance your image. The way you decide to take is entirely needy upon your objectives and what your proposed advertising is going to best react to. Given this, we've assembled a couple of instances of affiliate marketing techniques with the goal that you can more readily survey, which will make the best fit for your image and your objectives.

Know Your Niche

You will have more noteworthy accomplishments with affiliate marketing if you put a little idea into who will be seeing your image. Without a doubt, some affiliate marketers are uncontrollably effective, advancing the scope of products and administrations. With the correct group, this can work.

In any case, the objective is to put your image is perspective on purchasers who are going to click and convert. For some brands, this implies concentrating on your niche advertising. The site howtocleananything.com is a curious case of niche-based affiliate marketing.

This site offers exhortation filled substance on the best way to clean everything. Honestly, from your Birkenstock ties to your gut button, they have it secured. While the guidance ranges from clinical consideration to family tips and everything in the middle of, it's wholly brought together under a typical topic. Each post contains and an affiliate connection, and guess what?

It bodes well when matched with the substance delivered to go with it.

This is an extraordinary case of how matching with the correct affiliate for your objective market can approach substantial gains in changes and your ROI.

Assemble Reviews... Lots of Them!

It doesn't make a difference what your image is, or how you're marketing it, audits matter. From a buyer point of view, they regularly affect picking your picture or your competitor's. More individuals trust surveys that they find online over those from a confided in companion or relative.

Primary concern? What buyers read about your product or administration online issue. One approach to utilize affiliate marketing is to pick affiliates that utilization an audit stage as the base of their site. One of our preferred models is NerdWallet.

Intended to administer down to earth counsel on everything monetary, NerdWallet offers surveys on a wide range of products and administrations identified with the budgetary business.

What truly affects with survey-based affiliates is decency. Search for branches that produce top quality, edible substance. You need a certified vibe from your members when they're looking into your image.

It's an extraordinary thought to manufacture a relationship with your affiliates before starting work together. Think about the contribution of your product or administration to the affiliate for gratis for them to utilize and get to know before they start advancing your product. A brand that has personal experiences is going to put on a show of being sincere to your target group.

Affiliates That Offer Real-World Value

There are two things that individuals are hoping to escape the substance they see on the web. They either need to be engaged; they need the material to include a massive incentive in their life or both. If you are adjusting yourself to an affiliate, which depends on content creation, ensure that what they are delivering meets the criteria for progress. Probably the best substance for affiliate marketing offers a whole world, down to earth appeal that will keep the audience returning for additional. We should take a gander at MoneySavingExpert, for instance.

At the point when you land here, the primary thing you notice is that the site is stuffed with content. To start with, it's all quality substance that is exceptionally applicable to the intended interest group. Also, there's something irregular about this site. It gets no cash from publicists. All income originates from affiliate joins.

Stop and consider that for a moment. Affiliate joins are performance-based. That implies this site possibly brings in cash when those connections produce activity. Do you figure they would continue utilizing this model if it wasn't working for them?

We're speculating the response to that question is no, so they should make a significant activity for their affiliate vendors.

Coupon Sites, Deals and Promotions

Another method for extending your image's scope through affiliate marketing is by having a nearness on destinations that are set up to offer coupons, arrangements, and advancements on accomplice brands explicitly. While this sort of affiliate relationship unexpectedly works apiece, however, with the correct procedure, it very well may be similarly viable. For instance, Nomad Coffee Club uses this well by joining forces with bloggers doing giveaways and product audits alongside particular limits.

Instead of utilizing substance and impact to push your image, you depend on the purchaser's affection for a deal. Any individual who looks around online realizes that finding the best arrangement is a piece of good times. Coupon locales assist them with an excursion by interfacing them with the best method on your product or administration.

You support a coupon or advancement. The site posts it, alongside those of different brands that they are working with. The way to making this work is understanding that your SEO technique should be upgraded to create results for you on their page. A large number of the best arrangement destinations will help with this procedure.

Pause, Did We Forget to Mention Video? To what extent has it taken you to peruse this article as yet? 5 minutes possibly? Something astounding has occurred in that measure of time.

Around 1,500 hours of YouTube content has been transferred. Consistently, there are 300 hours of video assigned for review. Presently, consider what it could mean for your image if you had a nearness on a portion of that video content. The potential is gigantic.

Affiliates with a YouTube nearness can advance your image legitimately, or through a pennant on their video. Exactly how effective can YouTube affiliate marketing be? Simply see this person.

Ou may know him as the friendly face behind Ryan's Toy Review, or you may know him as the $11 million affiliate master. The reason for this affiliate marketing procedure is that a YouTube influencer/superstar advances your product or administration in their video, right now audits. The drawback is that it very well may be increasingly hard to follow traffic with this kind of relationship, except if a connection is incorporated with the substance.

The upside is that the video is immense. It's the favored sort of substance for most web clients, particularly those that are getting to content from their cell phones. This implies your image gets put before a more prominent, increasingly drew in audience, which involves more transformations and benefits in your pocket.

That is a Start, But What Else?

Along these lines, there were some extraordinary instances of various styles if affiliate marketing. It takes more than guides to begin, and you additionally need some useful exhortation. Here are five hints to remember, regardless of what kind of affiliate marketing you decide for your image.

1. A little research implies cash in your pocket. Before you begin, you have to have a thought of what your rivals are doing and what they're paying to get it going. To draw in the best affiliates, your rates should be severe.

2. Speaking of rates, it's satisfactory to have a couple of stunts at your disposal. Consider having a level rate that you offer to all affiliates, including every single new agreement. At that point, have a second remuneration level for your best-performing affiliate accomplices.

3. Start on the correct foot. Openness is of the utmost importance. If you can't impart promptly and effectively with your affiliates, at that point, it's presumably not going to be the best working relationship for you. You need to have the option to share product subtleties, deal data, rules, and even conceptualize how your image could be best advanced.

4. Have a lot of rules set up. Choose how much freedom your affiliates can take with your image. It is correct to say that you are okay with them offering a rebate that you didn't affirm or utilizing your product such that it wasn't expected? Put forward all the guidelines before you begin.

5. Have a financial limit at the top of the priority list, yet be versatile. If you've arrived at where you've met or surpassed your affiliate marketing spending plan, see what it's accomplished for you regarding ROI. In case you're creating deals and a decent benefit, there's no motivation to adhere to the specific numbers you've written down.

CHAPTER NINE

EARNING WITH AFFILIATE MARKETING

Could You Make Money With Affiliate Marketing?

Would you be able to bring in cash with affiliate marketing? The short answer is true; affiliate projects can procure additional money and even full-time pay from home. The long answer is somewhat more confounded. Like any home pay adventure, achievement comes less from what you decide to do to bring in cash, yet whether you do what should be done effectively and reliably.

The Reality of Affiliate Marketing

The issue with affiliate marketing, in the same way as other self-start venture alternatives, are the supposed masters and make accessible money programs that propose affiliate marketing should be possible quickly and with little exertion. Chances are you've perused cases of affiliate marketing programs that state you can make countless dollars a month doing nothing. Or on the other hand, they recommend you can set up your affiliate site, and afterward overlook it, but to check your bank stores.

The truth in affiliate marketing is that it resembles most other work-at-home endeavors; there are rare sorts of incredibly wealthy people, a significant number who are sufficient enough to meet their objectives, and a ton who aren't making anything.

The inquiry isn't generally whether affiliate marketing is a practical salary choice (it is); however, whether you can make affiliate marketing work for you. No one but you can conclude that, however, to enable you to complete, you can check our past post on the advantages and disadvantages of Affiliate Marketing.

To what extent did It Take Other Affiliate Marketers before They Started Making Money?

While the facts confirm that "it depends," I will expect that you're savvy enough to realize that. It relies upon your niche, how long you put in per week, how genuine you are tied in with succeeding, and how quick (or moderate) of a student you are. Hell, even karma assumes a job.

Be that as it may, you know the entirety of this. You simply need a general answer. Would you be able to begin bringing in cash this week? This month? This year? With affiliate marketing, to what extent does it take?

Here's the exact reply answer, and you probably won't care for it. Affiliate marketing takes around a year to begin seeing achievement. In any event, a visible and reliable achievement that is the thing that most expert Affiliate Marketers said.

I can hear you now... "A YEAR?! That is to say, I need to invested energy, cash, and exertion for a YEAR before I see any achievement?"

Practically, in any case, I accept with shockingly better arranging, vision, objective, and challenging work, you can begin procuring cold cash in 6 Months!

Presently, this doesn't mean you won't bring in cash when you simply start; this solitary implies that your income will be capricious, sparse, and conflicting.

The amount Can You Earn from Affiliate Marketing?

Two inquiries we regularly get posed:

"What amount is it conceivable to win from affiliate marketing?"

"If I quit my place of employment, to what extent will it take me to acquire X/day?"

The two answers rely upon your fitness, yet I understand there are an unquenchable want reliable figures. In this way, here's my interpretation of the issue...

There are five gaining sections right now.

Affiliate Apprentice – Losing cash.

Low-Level Affiliate – Anywhere from 0N - N5,000

Halfway Affiliate – Anywhere from N5,000/day up to N50,000/day.

Significant Level Affiliate – Anything above N50,000/day.

One of the different laws of Affiliate Marketing is: "Income is vanity and benefit is Sanity."

As it were, if a person is making an income of N100,000 per day and a benefit of N5,000 and someone else wins N50,000 in revenue; however, a profit of N10,000. The subsequent person is in an ideal situation when contrasted with the primary affiliate marketer.

Adjusting Expectations to Earning Potential

My response to the inquiry, "If I quit my place of employment, to what extent will it take me to gain X/day?" is regularly a quick "Perpetually," and here's the reason.

Numerous affiliates neglect to adjust their procuring desires to work that is really equipped for conveying the ideal salary.

Here's a breakdown of where each kind of affiliate is probably going to contribute his time:

Low-Level Affiliates: Focuses on pockets of benefit around the web. He overlooks economies of scale for high edge battles on littler traffic sources that will, in general, be incredibly unstable. Models incorporate dating destinations, little scope Facebook Ads, Juicy Ad purchases.

Middle Affiliates: Focuses on high volume traffic sources with littler edges than the Beginner, however more volume. They are indecently grouped around the dating niche (and all the more as of late grown-up dating). Intense rivalry on massive traffic sources lessens the size of the pie for all—keen movers right now versatile marketing and pop traffic.

Significant Level Affiliates: Focuses on mass-advertise media purchases and enormously versatile traffic sources. Regularly exchanges comfort (self-serve traffic hotspots) for direct investments with better edges and the entirety of the pie. More serious hazards included, progressively capital required.

How Speedily Can One Make Money With Affiliate Marketing?

Individuals new to this entire web marketing business come in not just hoping to bring in cash online as though it was an undeniable right to web clients, yet they additionally need to make it quick!

In any case, how quick would you be able to bring in cash with affiliate marketing?

This is an inquiry I get day by day either on the Wealthy Affiliate stage, where I tutor my understudies or through the inbox.

While I do comprehend the inquiry and the significance behind it, it's tough to offer a straight and proper response to it.

If you simply need to bring in cash quick with affiliate marketing, at that point, I am unfortunately this business isn't for you.

I don't know about some other business (on the web or disconnected) that can bring in cash as quickly as some would anticipate that it should be (if you are aware of something if it's not too much trouble, let me know in the remark area underneath).

Additionally, I don't get your meaning by quick?

Do you mean a day, a week, or a month?

There are various degrees of "quick" here, and keeping in mind that I do trust it's conceivable to begin bringing in cash rather rapidly, you're in all probability must do in any event 6 to a year of work before you start seeing some outcome worth gloating about.

Presently, when I offer that response to whoever asks, generally, I don't recover an answer, yet in some cases, I do get the infrequent "Why?".

I wouldn't fret noting this. I am here to assist individuals with beginning with affiliate marketing, so if they need to realize to what extent it will take them and why it would take such a long time, I am glad to reply.

Here's the reason it will take you a couple of months up to an entire year before you begin seeing a few outcomes.

The 'Affiliate Marketing" Learning Curve

If you are a prepared affiliate marketer with experience in building beneficial niche destinations, (above all else you wouldn't ask) yet, also, you do get an opportunity of bringing in cash in the initial barely any weeks or somewhere in the vicinity.

The explanation for this is there is an expectation to absorb information that you necessarily need to get over on your approach to making full-time wealth with affiliate marketing.

Simply think about the advantages of affiliate marketing for a second:

1. Free time

2. Be your chief

3. You find a good pace while you rest

4. and so forward.

You think these advantages are going to simply fall on your lap since you chose to google "how to bring in cash with affiliate marketing?".

Indeed, even with all the assets on the planet to show you (and I will give you my best preparing underneath), you, despite everything, are going to need to gain proficiency with the procedure – and it is anything but a process you can adapt rapidly.

There are a ton of things that you have to know before you begin bringing in any cash and that that incorporates figuring out how to develop a website, understanding watchword research and how it applies to affiliate marketing, composing content, fixing your substance, discover niche affiliate projects to join, etc.

Simply that would take you, in any event, a month to truly nail it down "like a master," and that is just if you are placing in at any rate 6 to 8 hours of work each day.

Presently I am sure that a great deal of you don't have that sort of additional time on your hands that you can simply commit to watching video aides and pursuing affiliate programs.

The point being is that regardless of whether you do things directly as it so happens, which is hard yet possible with the correct preparation, you are taking a gander in any event 2 to 3 months to begin seeing some salary and learning all the ropes.

You Need To Build The Traffic First

One thing individuals who need to bring in cash quick with affiliate marketing disregard is the way that you need an audience to offer to.

Building an audience sufficiently large to bring in cash from and developing it to believe you likewise require significant investment.

Presently once more, you can do this in a month, or you can do this in a year; everything relies upon a lot of factors; however, in any case, it will set aside an effort to get an ace.

There are affiliate marketing niches that will, in general, bring in cash quicker than others; however, you indeed must be fortunate to discover something you need to advance, that pays well, and there's practically no opposition in.

How Quickly Can You Start Making Money With Affiliate Marketing?

You can begin from today, yes, today.

As the old Chinese saying goes, the best time to plant a tree was 20 years prior; the subsequent best time is today.

If you are prepared to acknowledge the way that you won't make "quick cash" with affiliate marketing, at that point the open door is directly here before you to begin learning and working to ideally in a couple of months have the option to make steady pay with your new side-hustle.

Presently I cannot guarantee you that you will be effective. However, I can assure you – an even better assurance that if you read the rest of this post, you will be destined for success in bringing some respectable cash in the coming a very long time with affiliate marketing.

To what extent will It Take to Make Money with Affiliate Marketing?

Utilizing the above strategies, mainly if you follow the Wealthy Affiliate guide, you will undoubtedly have seen some achievement in as little as 2 to 3 months, with a full-opportunity pay coming in anyplace between month 7 and 12.

You may believe it's far to go the time yet will pass in any case.

You can spend it either looking into data bouncing from one blog entry to the next, or you can begin from today and know precisely where you will be in a couple of months.

"What amount is it conceivable to acquire from affiliate marketing?" "If I quit my place of employment, to what extent will it take me to win X/day?"

The two answers rely upon your fitness. However, I understand there's an unquenchable yearning for reliable figures. Along these lines, here's my interpretation of the issue...

There are five procuring sections right now.

1. Affiliate Apprentice – Losing cash.

2. Low-Level Affiliate – Anywhere from $0/day up to $300/day.

3. Intermediate Affiliate – Anywhere from $300/day up to $3,000/day.

4. High-Level Affiliate – Anything above $3,000/day.

5. The 'Pack of Dicks' Affiliate – He who considers anything short of $10,000/day to be 'treating it terribly.'

We were exposed at the top of the priority list that we're discussing benefit here, not income.

Technically, a person procuring $300,000/month in income could be more awful off than the person making a consistent $100/day with no outgoings. He would need to be visually impaired, imbecilic, hard of hearing, alcoholic, and idiotic to keep gulping such a thin edge. Yet, it features one of the different laws of affiliate marketing:

Income is vanity, and the benefit is mental stability.

A remarkable trait of our industry is how the powerful can fall medium-term, regularly in great design.

You can go from acquiring $3,000/day to grass all in about a mid-day break, what's more, the other way around.

An Intermediate affiliate may drop a level after losing his best battle. At the same time, the Affiliate Apprentice can turn Top Doggy Baller medium-term if he lurches into an unsaturated niche and makes it pay (a day by day event in 2009, uncommon in 2013).

The Bag of Dicks Affiliate may keep on prospering, or lack of concern may chomp him in the arse. However, he'll generally be a sack of dicks as long as he makes a decision about others for how cheerful they ought to be with their pay.

$300/Day versus $300/Today

Numerous affiliates can't tell their day by day salary from their present pay.

The unstable idea of the business makes it a thoughtless dream to compute your yearly compensation on the rear of one day's benefits.

If this is your first day of affiliate marketing and you gain $1000, don't expect that you'll bank $365,000 in the following year.

Your present profit, comparable to compensation, is $2.73/day.

Rehash your prosperity tomorrow, at that point the following day, etc. into the not so distant when you be able to begin tossing out unconventional multipliers on a salary that isn't yet yours.

What Are Established Affiliates Earning?

In the setup affiliate network, I would state that the majority of us operate in the Intermediate procuring class.

Note that by 'set up,' I'm discussing affiliates working all day in the CPA space.

Just as of late, a survey was hung on the STM Forum (I prescribe you join) asking, "What amount do you acquire in a year?"

That is a ton of moolah in anyone's money.

If you take the middle of this little example ($81,000 to $120,000), it means between $221/day and $328/day in benefit. I would put this at the very beginning of the Intermediate section, mostly because the salary must be continued throughout a year.

What's more, this section is the place most settled affiliates remain.

Note: Not all affiliate discussions are made equivalent. If you somehow happened to take a middle example from The Warrior Forum, I'd wager my crap that the average profit would scarcely cover the run of the mill London gas bill.

The bounce from winning $300/day to acquiring $3,000/day and continuing it is the thing that isolates a fruitful, built up CPA affiliate from the absolute best in the business.

It's significant, the best in the business are not generally the most joyful with their salaries.

Adjusting Expectations to Earning Potential

My response to the inquiry, "If I quit my place of employment, to what extent will it take me to win X/day?" is regularly a quick "Always," and here's the reason.

Numerous affiliates neglect to adjust their acquiring desires to work that is equipped for conveying the ideal salary.

Here's a breakdown of where each sort of affiliate is probably going to contribute his time:

Low-Level Affiliates: Focuses on pockets of benefit around the web. He disregards economies of scale for high edge crusades on littler traffic sources that will, in general, be incredibly unstable. Models incorporate POF dating efforts, little scope Facebook Ads, Juicy Ad purchases.

Middle of the road Affiliates: Focuses on high volume traffic sources with littler edges than the Beginner, yet more volume. Disgustingly grouped around the dating niche (and all the more as of late grown-up dating). Intense rivalry on enormous traffic sources lessens the size of the pie for all—brilliant movers right now portable marketing and pop traffic.

Elevated Level Affiliates: Focuses on mass market media purchases and colossally adaptable traffic sources. Frequently exchanges accommodation (self-serve traffic hotspots) for direct purchases with better edges and the entirety of the pie. More serious hazards included, progressively capital required.

Understudy Affiliates – Focuses, perpetually, on the entirety of the above mentioned, to his burden.

Sack of Dicks Affiliate – Focuses on Fox News.

Things being what they are, what would you like to be? What are you glad to be?

If your desires are to such an extent that you are pleased with an extra $100/day, at that point screw anyone who instructs you to toss down $10,000 on an expensive media purchase, POF is a splendid low-level traffic source (with a couple of Intermediate individual cases which depend on economies of extension), and you need never change your jacket.

If you are content with the middle of the road winning section, at that point in like manner, you can stand to maintain a strategic distance from direct purchases and hazardous speculations; however, you will most likely need to progress past the okay pockets of benefit supported by beginners.

Notwithstanding, if you are the sort of affiliate who's going to feel like he lets loose missing until he's gaining $5,000/day, at that point, take a rude awakening.

Is it accurate to say that you are submitting your time and vitality to the kinds of battles that are measurably and strategically prone to open up the acquiring potential that speaks to what you need?

There's no reason for cutting out small scale niches on POF if your heart thumps for a million-dollar pay.

It's an essential procedure.

What are you going to chip away at that can convey a salary that you're content with?

Fuck, that is an instruction forever, not merely affiliate marketing.

We CPA affiliates will go in general float towards High-Level pay targets, most likely because we are youthful, voracious, offensive, unshowered mountain trolls with a hunger forever's extravagances.

Furthermore, that is fine. However, there's a trick.

Everyone has an acquiring edge that speaks to a state of unavoidable losses—furthermore, many neglect to remember it.

Your life circumstance may direct that $200/day is the apex of money related inspiration. You can drive yourself to achieve this objective, yet any further and the motivation starts to slip. That is a state of consistent losses. Consider it your usual range of familiarity. Any work to progress past this point accompanies the extra weight of pushing you out of that safe place, and thus delaying sets in, alongside the double devastating feelings of trepidation of disappointment and achievement.

Numerous affiliates battle to take their businesses to the following level because the idea of the game is to such an extent that you can be a 'Halfway' banking one of the top 1% of pay rates in the populace.

Why drive it further?

There's a valid justification why we must be forceful, greedier, and pushier than most. Affiliate marketing isn't a lifelong stepping stool in any conventional sense.

We are just ever as effective as our last crusades.

We can't advance through the positions. There aren't any. There are no fallbacks, no safe arrivals, and no space for a performance marketer to live off past wonders.

CONCLUSION

Thank You

Affiliate marketing isn't hard, yet it requires information, arranging, and reliable exertion to make any critical pay. Your general odds of bringing in cash with an affiliate program are most likely no preferable and no more terrible over some other kind of web-based business. Your financial progress relies upon how well you execute your affiliate business plan.

While there isn't a great deal of cost in firing up as an affiliate marketer, there are a couple of things that you have to do if you genuinely need to bring in cash marketing others' products. One of the essential requirements for any effective affiliate program is to have your very own site. While it is conceivable to buy promotion space on locales and to publicize through Google Adwords, this is a momentary technique setting up an essential website that has a specific center that will have a significant effect on the accomplishment of your program. Remember that your site doesn't need to be confounded with a ton of blaze media, liveliness, or other extravagant fancy odds and ends. If you plan on concentrating on affiliate marketing systems that focus on the home purchaser, you are in an ideal situation with a first site that will stack rapidly on a dial-up association. Dial-up is still amazingly famous in various areas.

Online payments are an incredible method to get your affiliate payments and monitor your profit effectively. From this holy messenger, you might need to investigate opening a record with one of the more famous online administrations that send and get reserves. E.g., PayPal. Another significant perspective is deciding exactly what your contact data will be, in regards to correspondence with your affiliate program. This would incorporate an email Address and physical postage information. The email address ought to be one you have put aside explicitly for your marketing business.

Picking the best products for your specific circumstance have to do with what you know and the amount you think about it. For instance, a person that has worked in media communications for several years will most likely see a lot about communication, related administrations, and innovation that are utilized inside that industry. Another angle about setting up with the correct products to elevate has to do with where you see a niche to fill in. Finding a populace or business division that gives off an impression of being, to a great extent, overlooked in the marketing procedure can give the motivation you have to make a fruitful affiliate marketing program.

Try not to permit yourself to get debilitated just because everything isn't apparent as you start this piece of the procedure. Rehearsing some persistence and allowing yourself to locate the correct products to advance as a component of the program will just serve to make you progressively devoted to the accomplishment of the program. At last, you will discover the products that will prompt an extremely useful affiliate marketing plan and give you an attractive income stream, yet additionally a great deal of personal fulfillment.

Lightning Source UK Ltd.
Milton Keynes UK
UKHW020638200121
377380UK00011B/955

9 781914 306325